Lean Supply Chain Management Essentials

A Framework for Materials Managers

Lean Supply Chain Management Essentials

A Framework for Materials Managers

Bill Kerber and Brian J. Dreckshage

CRC Press
Taylor & Francis Group
Boca Raton   London   New York

CRC Press is an imprint of the
Taylor & Francis Group, an **informa** business

A PRODUCTIVITY PRESS BOOK

CRC Press
Taylor & Francis Group
6000 Broken Sound Parkway NW, Suite 300
Boca Raton, FL 33487-2742

Library of Congress Cataloging-in-Publication Data

Kerber, Bill.
 Lean supply chain management essentials : a framework for materials managers / Bill Kerber and Brian J. Dreckshage.
  p. cm.
 Includes bibliographical references and index.
 ISBN 978-1-4398-4082-5

1. Materials management. 2. Production control. 3. Business logistics. 4. Lean manufacturing. I. Dreckshage, Brian J. II. Title.
TS161.K455 2011   658.7--dc22

Visit the Taylor & Francis Web site at
http://www.taylorandfrancis.com

and the CRC Press Web site at
http://www.crcpress.com

To my wife, Joan—the one and only true love of my life.

Bill

To three people who have helped me over the years:

My wonderful wife, Suzanne, who has enriched my life, Art Lundgren, who started me on my Lean journey, and to my good friend, Bill Kerber, who got me involved with supply chain management and who always made me laugh.

Brian

Contents

Introduction

The idea for this book came over dinner in St. Louis one night. Brian lives in St. Louis, and Bill was working for a client there. We have known each other since we were young men, when we both worked for a productivity consulting firm and were assigned to several projects together. We had vaguely kept in touch over the years, so the St. Louis project was a welcome chance to catch up on things. On that night, Bill was doing a typical diatribe on how the supply chain needed to be approached much differently when adopting Lean, and Brian was bemoaning the dearth of helpful examples of key parts of Lean and clear explanations of the same. We decided that we should put some words where our mouths were, and agreed that we should write a book for supply chain professionals. And that was that, nothing further happened … until Bill was diagnosed with esophageal cancer in February 2009. Having not much else to do, the idea of writing the book resurfaced, this time with the added attraction of filling in the days between treatments. So, after a tough year of treatment and recovery, here we are at last, getting something done in spite of all odds—the largest odds of which were, of course, our own laziness.

So why a book about Lean supply chain management? Although there are many great books on Lean, we have found that these books are either short on details or focus too much on specific tool-based or engineering aspects of Lean, such as operator balance charts and standard work or rapid changeover. Further, several recent books have focused on the philosophical and people aspects of Lean, so this aspect also seems well covered. However, it seems that outside of pull systems, little attention has been paid to how Lean addresses the traditional issues surrounding supply chain management, such as priority and capacity planning and control. We have written a book targeted to the supply chain professional that focuses on the materials management aspects of Lean, such as leveling work into the value stream and the concept of every part every interval (EPEI). Additionally, we hope to fill in a lot of the missing details with clear explanations regarding why you are doing what you are doing (with Lean components) and how these fit together as a system.

Why is it important to discuss Lean in the supply chain? There are a large number of people who feel that the traditional materials planning environment, typically embodied by an enterprise resource planning (ERP) system, is a good support system for a company that wants to adopt Lean practices. We don't think that this is the case, so we felt it necessary to point out why, and then to elaborate on an alternate approach to the supply chain issues that must be managed in all companies. This alternate approach supports Lean thinking and uses many of the common tools of Lean. As will be stated several times within the chapters, much of Lean is counterintuitive and goes against conventional wisdom. It is important to have an understanding of the thought behind Lean as well as the tools, since neither will be especially effective without the other.

Lean thinking evolved after the Second World War, mainly out of necessity. The Toyota Motor Corporation needed to rebuild its company. Unfortunately, it had to do so with very little in the way of natural resources, supply base, or most importantly, money. From this environment grew a philosophy that can be summed up in a few short words: produce without wasting any resource.

In 1950, Eiji Toyoda returned from a tour of U.S. automakers and gave an assignment to Taiichi Ohno: improve the Toyota manufacturing process so that it equals the productivity of Ford. It is estimated that Ford was approximately ten times more productive than Toyota at that point, so this was a rather daunting assignment. Ohno studied three production systems: Ford, to learn about flow; General Motors, to learn about producing variety; and supermarkets, to learn about pull. He also closely followed the teachings of Edwards Deming on quality. He then returned to Toyota and began to experiment with his findings, looking to find the best ways to produce products without wasting resources.

Looking back, it appears that a grand blueprint was being followed, and historical documents and presentation tools such as the House of Toyota lend weight to this viewpoint. In fact, this was not the case. The creation of the Toyota Production System was a result of the scientific method in application. As problems arose, experiments were conducted to see the best way of solving the problem. The best way was then adopted and disseminated as part of the overall solution.

Toyota has unquestionably displayed a tenacious consistency over 70 years in building competitiveness and in honing the fundamental capabilities that underlie that competitiveness. That consistency, however, has masked a stunning array of happenstance, confrontation, confusion, wrong turns, and occasional crisis. The ability to nurture a capacity for perseverant organizational learning amid that chaos is arguably Toyota's most essential core competence.

—**Koichi Shimokawa and Takahiro Fujimoto,** *The Birth of Lean*

Can we now use a "blueprint" to achieve Lean success in our own companies? Not really. While we now better understand the thinking and tools that have been successful in adopting Lean, the fact remains that each company and each situation is still unique. So it is still necessary to approach Lean in the scientific way, with a methodology and mindset that allows for experimentation, failure, and continuous learning. Because of the uniqueness of each situation, what we have tried to do is to take the principles learned from the fifty-plus-year journey of Toyota, the basis of Lean, and extend the thoughts and spirit of the learning into other environments, such as high-mix situations. What we want to do in this book is provide a basis for beginning to apply Lean thinking and techniques into your own supply chain.

MYTH WHAT TPS IS NOT	REALITY WHAT TPS IS
A tangible recipe for success	A consistent way of thinking
A management project or program	A total management philosophy
A set of tools for implementation	Focus on total customer satisfaction
A system for production floor only	An environment of teamwork and improvement
Implementable in a short- or mid-term period	A never-ending search for a better way
	Quality built in process
	Organized, disciplined workplace
	Evolutionary

Source: Glenn Uminger, *Toyota Motor Manufacturing North America.*

Lean Basics

We will begin by defining the roles, objectives, and responsibilities of supply chain management, first from a traditional framework, covering the basics of supply chain management, then describing the Lean basics, exploring the conflicts between Lean and the traditional framework.

> **Supply chain:** The global network used to deliver products and services from raw material to end customers through an engineered flow of information, physical distribution and cash.
>
> —*APICS Dictionary*, **12th edition**

Supply chain management (SCM) is the planning and management of all activities involved in sourcing and procurement, conversion (make), and logistics management activities. The steps generally included in the discipline are: (1) plan, (2) source, (3) make, (4) deliver, and (5) return.

Another definition is provided by the *APICS Dictionary* when it defines SCM as the "design, planning, execution, control, and monitoring of supply chain activities with the objective of creating net value, building a competitive infrastructure, leveraging worldwide logistics, synchronizing supply with demand, and measuring performance globally."

Materials Management

The APICS Dictionary defines materials management as "the grouping of management functions supporting the complete cycle of materials flow, from the purchase and internals control of production materials to the planning and control of work in process, to the warehousing, shipping and distribution of the finished product."

Essentially, materials management is a portion of supply chain management, generally confined to the four walls of a company, and perhaps including the first level of suppliers to that company. We are going to cover this set of materials management and supply chain functions from a Lean perspective in this book.

The roles and responsibilities of supply chain managers are to manage the materials flow, often from forecasting to distribution. The objectives are: deliver the expected level of customer service (customers' perspective), and minimize costs through the supply chain.

So, from the dictionary definitions, the roles and responsibilities are clear and generally don't change in Lean, but the objectives of supply chain managers *do* change in the Lean world. Minimizing costs does not necessarily equal eliminating waste, which is the objective in Lean. We have often been taught that maximizing the use of company assets is also an objective, but as we will discuss, that often leads to bad decisions.

Other common objectives for supply chain managers include:

- Optimize usage of assets.
- Minimize assets.
- Control inventory levels.
- Reduce supply base.
- Head outsourcing effort to reduce cost.

Traditional Planning and Control Framework

To help with the supply chain management effort, an entire system of support has evolved over time. This framework (Figure 1.1) begins with long-term planning, typically covering the horizon from six months to as long as three to five years into the future, embodied by executive sales and operations planning (here broken down into business planning, sales planning, and operations planning; in our opinion these three processes are better managed as a single process called executive sales and operations planning) and forecasting. From there, the process proceeds into increasing levels of detail, and is generally organized into pairs of processes, one for planning and one for execution, or one for priority planning and one for capacity checking.

This is a closed-loop planning and control system, meaning that each process is checked for feasibility before proceeding to the next step. In practice, the checking does not often happen in many companies. From here on forward, we shall refer to this environment of planning and control as ERP, in deference to the software that guides the practice for many companies.

Enterprise Resource Planning (ERP)

ERP is a business model framework for planning all of the resources of a business—starting with strategic planning and linking through to execution. Process disciplines are integral to successful ERP predictability, and management systems can provide accountability. ERP systems are the information technology tools or software for which some of these process links can become automated, with information shared across functional areas and business transactions efficiently processed.

—*APICS OMBOK*, 1st edition

This framework works well in a make-to-stock environment, which is where it was mainly formed. It is less than ideal within these environments: engineer-to-

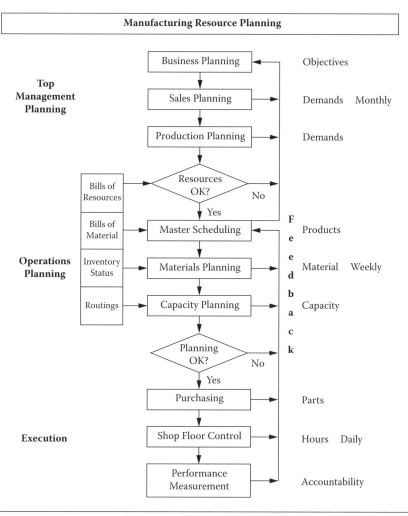

Figure 1.1 The traditional planning and control hierarchy.

order, make-to-order, and process industries. Because so many of the processes in the framework have an inventory control focus, the planning system is less effective where inventory is less important to customer service.

When we discuss how well this framework performs in these various environments, this requires a "blinders off" type of discussion. When we say it works well, we mean that generally the logic functions well. ERP and embedded material requirements planning (MRP) are generally straightforward and logical, and the ability to run thousands of transactions through automated MRP has been a genuine boon to the planning and inventory control community. However, forecasts drive many of the logic assumptions, and as we all know, forecasts are usually wrong. As we move away from make-to-stock environments into make-to-order environments, this inaccuracy causes more and more waste until it becomes untenable.

Being less than ideal refers to the fact that the logic starts to "thin," meaning that in many cases the logic is focused on only one desired result, such as obtaining a certain inventory level. In many environments, inventory control takes second or third place to balancing demand and capacity or providing short lead time to customers. Because the ERP system has made certain assumptions about what is important to manage through the programs provided, the planning functions of ERP become less and less helpful as you move away from a make-to-stock environment. Planning in a "to order" environment usually requires managing a customer order backlog, with perhaps an inventory of intermediate or subassemblies, since many customers will not endure an entire bill of material lead time.

Problems with ERP in Make-to-Order Environments

Forecasting drives a lot of the planning in this traditional framework. What would you say, with certainty, about any forecast? It will be wrong. As we all know, this has a direct impact on how we service the customers; to do a better job, we often have to hold more inventory (waste) than we would like to hold, sometimes lots more. In make-to-stock environments, where the items have relatively consistent demand, the inventory level can mask this forecast error. In make-to-order environments, however, where the parts are often more plentiful and the demand is more erratic, it may take significantly more inventory to mask the forecast error. This level of waste becomes a target of Lean. Unfortunately, as we move away from having inventory targets drive the logic of balancing supply and demand, the ERP system has less and less to offer in terms of decision support.

A completely different alternative to balancing supply and demand is to balance demand and capacity. In many environments, adding or subtracting capacity is difficult, especially in the short term, so keeping capacity constant and flexing either inventory or backlog is an important capability of the scheduling system. Unfortunately, most scheduling logic commonly available assumes capacity to be infinite. The software is geared to balance supply and demand, not demand and capacity. This means that the algorithms for scheduling these environments are usually not very helpful for the scheduler. To be sure, if you are competent, controlling capacity via the traditional master production scheduling process is certainly viable, but how many companies still struggle with this simple concept? Finite scheduling only complicated this even more, drove up software costs, and, more often than not, failed to work. Shop floor control, an important element in the ERP model, is essentially nonexistent for most companies. In most ERP systems, shop floor control consists of a list of work orders/items to be worked on, with a finish date. There is no logical combination of similar items, nor any other attempt to be "efficient." So, essentially, most shop floor control is a list of items to be completed, with a due date. That is simply a plan, and there is very little control going on.

What Is at Issue?

The ERP system works, but is it still viable? If set up and used correctly (more of the exception than rule) in the right circumstances, it is usable. We also must recognize that ERP systems now consist of many more functions that have little or nothing to do with material planning, such as fixed assets, general ledger, banking, human resources management, and a host of other functions, and that because of this ERP will be with us for a long, long time. For our purposes, then, we would like to just focus on the portions of the ERP system that are involved with pure supply chain functions. We think, despite all of the efforts to the contrary by the ERP vendors, that the ERP planning and control environment and the Lean environment are not really compatible from a tool set standpoint, or even a thinking standpoint. Lean, or the Toyota Production System, has been in the United States since the 1980s but generally has not reached its potential. What has been missing? Probably many things, but among them has been putting Lean in the context of a complete operating system. In the course of this book we will present Lean as a complete materials management system. The question we wish to pursue is "Are there alternatives to ERP planning?" We think so.

Lean, as the Toyota Production System, has been around a while and, like many systems, poorly implemented and understood. We see companies doing a lot of Lean things—5S systems and even Kanbans—but they still use ERP to plan and run their operations. Clearly, in our opinion, these companies are not Lean, nor will they ever be by using ERP planning to run the company. The purpose of this book is to show you how to convert your current ERP focus to one that is truly Lean. This will not require you to abandon ERP, but to turn off/ignore the things that simply don't work well and replace them with simple Lean tools.

In the rest of this chapter, we will provide an introduction to Lean, provide some simple definitions of Lean, and then try to put Lean into perspective from a philosophy and tools viewpoint.

What is Lean? Lean is a philosophy that seeks to:

- Focus on flowing value to the customer
- Eliminate waste from all processes
- Right-size the resources (machines, material, people, time, etc.)
- Provide the tools for people to continually improve their work

Lean manufacturing: A philosophy of production that emphasizes the minimization of the amount of all the resources (including time) used in the various activities of the enterprise. It involves identifying and eliminating non-value-adding activities in design, production, supply chain management, and dealing with the customers.

—APICS Dictionary, 12th edition

Lean production: A business system for organizing and managing product development, operations, suppliers, and customer relations that requires less human effort, less space, less capital, less material, and less time to make products with fewer defects to precise customer desires, compared with the previous system of mass production.

—Lean Lexicon, 4th edition, compiled by Lean Enterprise Institute

In addition to defining Lean, let's make sure that we are all on the same page when defining *philosophy*:

- The rational investigation of the truths and principles of being, knowledge, or conduct
- A system of principles for guidance in practical affairs

—Dictionary.com

It is important to note up front that Lean involves the entire company, not just the manufacturing part. While the above definition of Lean from the *APICS Dictionary* is focused on Lean manufacturing, the word *Lean* has expanded to include administrative functions as well.

Why is Lean being so widely adopted? Companies go Lean to:

- Increase velocity
- Decrease working capital
- Increase cash flow
- Increase inventory turns
- Gain market share
- Increase profitability
- Meet customer demand

Suppose your board of directors has just handed down the above list of objectives for your company. If you were CEO, how would you go about achieving these objectives? Who would get which objective? Typically, different departments (materials management, manufacturing, customer service, for example) would get different objectives. Or a set of special teams would be created, one for each of the goals. Either way, these are traditionally conflicting measurements, so as each area goes off to achieve their goal, they will invariably create problems for several of the other areas. For instance, the team that has to improve customer service will want increased inventories, which is in direct opposition to the "lower inventories" team's objectives. Once the two groups lock horns, one or the other will lose, or they will both make no progress at all. You can ask, "What do you think will happen as the teams try to achieve the isolated improvements called for?" The answer is probably nothing of any impact, as all of the teams will work at odds. Dividing by job function doesn't work very well. What are the alternatives? We think Lean is one of them.

Five Lean Principles

Lean begins with the customer.

- Specify what creates *value* from the customer's perspective.
- Identify all steps across the whole *value stream*.
- Make those actions that create value *flow*.

- Only make what is *pulled* by the customer just in time.
- Strive for *perfection* by continually removing successive layers of waste.

—**Womack and Jones,** *Lean Thinking*

Specify What Creates Value from the Customer's Perspective

This is usually approached with the question "What will the customer pay for?" Lean must begin with a determination of what value the company provides. One of the most popular conceptions in Lean is that all employees must learn to see with the eyes of the customer.

Identify All Steps across the Whole Value Stream

A value stream is all of the activities, both value-added and non-value-added, to go from raw material to finished product. We could add from order to cash and from product concept to product launch to this to be more inclusive. A process called value stream mapping is used to accomplish this step. For more on value stream mapping, see the APICS Lean Enterprise Survey Class, or the Learning to See Class from the Lean Enterprise Institute.

Make Those Actions That Create Value Flow

One-piece flow is the ultimate objective, with first-in–first-out (FIFO) flow next, then finally pull: no push of product or activity. The implication here is that the non-value-added activities will be eliminated, which is one of the focuses of Lean: the elimination of waste.

Only Make What Is Pulled by the Customer Just in Time

This drives us to more of a make-to-order environment, which from a supply chain perspective is different than the solution present in the Toyota Production System. Part of the focus of this book is to deeply explore this step, and to provide understanding of what this step really means, define the various factors that effect how well this approach will work in the various environments of production, and suggest alternate solutions based on the environment.

Strive for Perfection by Continually Removing Successive Layers of Waste

This is the continuous improvement approach that is often talked about when discussing Lean. Note that implementing continuous improvement techniques without the first four principles will probably bring disappointing results. It cannot be overemphasized that Lean is a complete system of operation, not a quest for "low-hanging fruit."

A *value stream* is made up of the parts from a product family, defined as a set of parts that go through roughly the same processes. It should be stated that a company often consists of many value streams. A value stream is usually defined as the activities within the four walls of a single company (raw material defined as the parts used by the company as the starting point of manufacturing, and finished goods being defined as the items that the company sells or ships). The value stream goes from receiving to shipping. Or at least this is the level where you should start a Lean effort. One of the goals of supply chain management is to link up value streams from various companies and make the material flow throughout the supply chain. Our definition here has expanded the LEI definition to include two support streams: the engineering effort (concept to product launch) and the administrative one (orders to cash). These are typically covered in the information flow section of a value stream map, but the definition of a value stream needs to include them.

Value-added activities are any activities that customers are willing to pay for. In some industries, this includes some activities that would be non-value-added in other industries. A prime example is inspection, which is sometimes paid for by the customers (such as in the aerospace industry). Non-value-added activities (waste) include everything else. Non-value-added activities use resources but add no value. However, not all non-value-added activities can be eliminated. We will call these non-value-added but necessary activities. The easiest way to determine whether an activity is non-value-added but necessary is to ask: If this activity is eliminated, will the result be more or less waste?

Part of the key to Lean is to begin to look at operations and activities with the eyes of the customer. It may seem obvious that we would only want to do value-added activities, but this is a much more difficult task when viewed from a customers' perspective. Many things must be done that fit the non-value-added but necessary category.

To pick up on our previous example of these two types of non-value-added, let's talk about inspection. Many people consider inspection waste, even if the customer is paying for the activity. But consider the following scenario: you are going to start a low-cost airline, and because you have figured out that inspection is waste, the people who look at the plane to make sure the wings are bolted on tightly won't be working for your airline. Who wants to be the first to sign up? Until we create a technology where bolts stay tight forever, this is non-value-added but necessary.

How do we determine if an activity is waste or non-value-added but necessary? We ask a simple question: If we eliminated this activity, would the result be more or less waste than currently? We know that inspection is not value-added in most cases, but if we stopped doing it, would there be less waste because we don't have inspectors, or more because the customers now occasionally receive a bad product?

Types of Activities

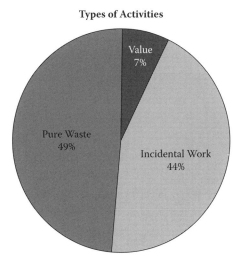

Figure 1.2 Pie chart depicting the classification of activities within a company from a Lean perspective. Notice how small the value-added slice of the pie is.

The reaction of most people when they see Figure 1.2 is to say that the value-added slice is too small. However, when you create a value stream map, it is not unusual to see the process time being less than 1% of the total lead time through the value stream, in which case the value slice in the chart is too large. Remember, part of Lean is learning to look at things differently.

Lean Focuses on Three Major Areas of Waste

- **Muda:** Waste. Any activity that doesn't add value. Value is usually defined as anything the customer will pay for.
- **Mura:** Unevenness, or variability. Variability is seen both in the demand for production and in the processes themselves.
- **Muri:** Overburdening employees or processes.

The focus of many Lean efforts has been to eliminate muda. Unfortunately, lots of the muda is created by mura. We will explore this in depth in Chapter 3. Supply chain managers are in a unique position to address the waste of mura.

House of Toyota Framework

Figure 1.3 shows the full scope of Lean. Note that in the center of the house are the people, an aspect of Lean that is often overlooked. The House of Toyota is one possible framework to understand the entire scope of Lean. To help explain the Toyota Production System to employees and suppliers, the House of Toyota graphic was created by Taiichi Ohno and Eiji Toyoda. They chose the house shape because it was a familiar one—and also conveyed stability.

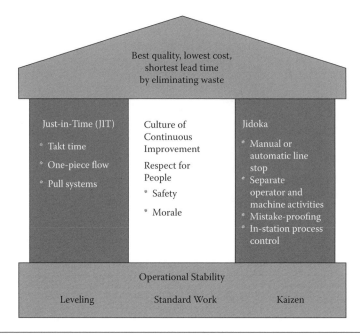

Figure 1.3   Picture of the House of Toyota, which shows the major elements of Lean. We will use this framework to explain the various pieces of Lean in this chapter.

House of Toyota: Operational Stability

- Leveling demand (heijunka). *Heijunka* is defined as the distribution of production volume and mix evenly over time. This will represent the single point schedule in the value stream, in this case at the finished good level.

   Load leveling: Spreading orders out in time or rescheduling operations so that the amount of work to be done in subsequent time periods tends to be distributed evenly and is achievable. Although both material and labor are ideally level loaded, specific businesses and industries may do one or the other exclusively [for example, service industries].

   —APICS Dictionary, 12th edition

   We will later expand the leveling discussion to include environments where complete mix leveling is not practical.
- Standard work defines the content, sequence, and timing of work. The goal is to have the least waste in the processes. We need to agree on a definition for *standard work*: *defining the content, sequence, and timing of work to achieve an optimum process for manufacturing product.* Standard work is a key element that is often ignored during Lean implementations. Standard work has been compared to the printed feet in an Arthur Murray dance class.

   Henry Ford said: "To standardize a method is to choose out of the many methods the best one, and use it. Standardization means nothing unless it means standardizing upward. Today's standardization, instead of being a barricade against improvement, is the necessary foundation on which tomorrow's improvement will be based. If you think of 'standardization' as the best that you know today, but which is to be improved tomorrow—you get somewhere. But if you think of standards as confining, then progress stops." With this thought in mind, it is obvious that standard work is one of the cornerstones of continuous improvement.

Kaizen: Continuous improvement of an entire value stream or an individual process to create more value with less waste. There are two levels of kaizen: 1. System or flow kaizen focusing on the overall value stream. This is kaizen for management. 2. Process kaizen focusing on individual processes. This is kaizen for work teams and team leaders.

—*Lean Lexicon*, **4th edition**

House of Toyota: Just in Time

Just-in-time (JIT) production: A system of production that makes and delivers just what is needed, just when it is needed, and just in the amount needed. JIT and jidoka are the two pillars of the Toyota Production System. JIT relies on heijunka as a foundation and is comprised of three operating elements: the pull system, takt time, and continuous flow.

—*Lean Lexicon*, **4th edition**

- Takt time refers to the pace at which the customer is buying products. Takt time is one of the keys to determining how much labor and machine resources are required in the value stream.
- One-piece flow is the production method that has the least amount of waste, so this is the method that is the goal of Lean.
- If one-piece flow cannot be achieved, then pull is used. At its simplest, pull can be thought of as simply replacing what has just been used. It is a way to have the value stream produce what the customer has just purchased, meaning that the value stream begins to operate in a make-to-order fashion.

Pull (system): 1) In production, the production of items only as demanded for use or to replace those taken for use. 2) In material control, the withdrawal of inventory as demanded by the using operations. Material is not issued until a signal comes from the user.

—*APICS Dictionary*, **12th edition**

Pull production: A method of production control in which downstream activities signal their needs to upstream activities. Pull production strives to eliminate overproduction and is one of the three major components of a complete just-in-time production system.

—*Lean Lexicon*, **4th edition**

We will describe pull production in some depth in Chapters 4 to 6.

House of Toyota: Jidoka

Jidoka is a composite term meaning manual or automatic line stop. Many jidoka stories revolve around the ability of the operators to stop the line any time a problem is encountered. Jidoka includes many other elements, though, most of which can be summed up in the thought of passing no bad parts to the next operation. The term *jidoka* as used in the Toyota Production System can be defined as automation with a human touch. One way to think of this concept is to approach a process as though it were going to be performed by a machine, meaning that the workplace design must facilitate movements to be very precise and the tool placement to be very precise, and then do the job with a human instead. The concept of stopping the production line when a defect occurs is a difficult one for most U.S. manufacturers, and thus needs emphasis as Lean is adopted. The idea is that problems should be solved as soon as they appear, rather than reviewed later. An interesting side benefit of stopping the line as problems occur is that there is great urgency to solve the problem so that the line can begin producing product again. This tends to keep the entire company's focus on the production area.

The elements of Jidoka include:

- Separate operator and machine activities
- Mistake-proofing
- In-station process control

Jidoka includes self-stop as well as mistake-proofing, single-minute exchange of die (SMED), visual controls, 6 Sigma/SPC (Statistical Process Control), separating human and machine work, 5S, etc. Defined broadly, it's all about the physical improvement of the manufacturing process/value stream; contrast it with JIT, which is about flow and pull and scheduling activities—in some sense system activities associated with the physical process but not the process itself (from Chris Gray).

Jidoka means that a machine safely stops when the normal processing is completed. It also means that should a quality or equipment problem arise, the machine detects the problem on its own and stops, preventing defective products from being produced. As a result, only products satisfying the quality standards will be passed on to the next processes on the production line. "Since a machine automatically stops when processing is completed or when a problem arises and is communicated via the 'andon (problem display board),' operators can confidently continue performing work at another machine, as well as easily identify the problem cause and prevent its recurrence. This means that each operator can be in charge of many machines, resulting in higher productivity, while the continuous improvements lead to greater processing capacity" (from the Toyota website).

House of Toyota: Goals

These three goals ultimately contribute to competitiveness and the ability to satisfy the customer:

- Improve quality
  - One-piece flow improves quality on its own. One-piece flow improves quality because the next process uses the piece shortly after it has been produced at the previous process. This means if a defect occurs, there will not be very many pieces produced with the defect, since the defect should be found quickly after it has been made. In batch-oriented production, any quality problem potentially could be replicated throughout the entire batch before it is found at a downstream process.
  - Focus on product quality through jidoka. Being able to stop the process to fix any problems is a powerful technique to inject urgency into the problem-solving process. Further, using mistake-proofing and in-station control techniques will help bring focus to making the part correctly the first time.
- Reduce cost. The least amount of waste in a system will result in the lowest total costs. Again, it is important to understand that Lean is not focused on cost reduction.
- Reduce lead time. Flow and pull produce shorter lead times than push systems. Because of the emphasis on one-piece flow, first-in–first-out flow, and pull systems, it is very typical for the queues in between processes to shrink significantly during the Lean implementation. Because of this, the lead time to the customer will typically be shorter. Further, as the value stream gains both speed and flexibility, the ability to produce to the customer order is improved.

House of Toyota: Improvement and Respect

People are at the center of Lean. The tools that we have discussed so far are all present to help people be more effective at their jobs.

- Culture of continuous improvement
- Respect for people
  - Morale results from employees having a voice and driving improvement. One of the primary things that management must do is to create a culture of learning and scientific experiment. It needs to become okay to try new things, with the understanding that every thing that is tried will not work the way it was planned. This goes hand in hand with respect for people. It is important to recognize that most companies take great effort to make sure that they hire the best people possible for each job. Once they are hired, however, we tend to place a very hierarchical command and control organization over them, limiting their effectiveness and creativity. Liker makes the following points in the Toyota Way about the importance of people: "(Lean) focuses on supporting and encouraging people to continually improve the processes they work on." He has devoted two

of his fourteen principles of Lean to people development: "Principle 9: Grow leaders who thoroughly understand the work, live the philosophy and teach it to others. Principle 10: Develop exceptional people and teams who follow your company's philosophy." Everyone wants to play for a winner, and conversely, it is no fun to play for a company that is struggling to stay afloat. With Lean, employees not only get to watch improved results, but they get to participate in the improvements.

- Safety. Improvement is never made at the risk of poor safety. The point on safety goes back to the people-focused culture that must be developed for Lean to be most effective. While we don't think that any company is intentionally ignoring safety issues, the emphasis on safety first is an important one. Both of these points are good discussion opportunities for quiet times around the water cooler. How is the morale at your company? Why do you think it is that way? What can be done to improve it?
- Community involvement. A company must be more than a place for shareholders to make money. It needs to be part of a community, from the aspects of both providing meaningful employment to the citizens of the community and being a good corporate citizen. The company and its employees must actively participate in the activities of the community.

Lean: Additional Considerations

Lean isn't just for manufacturing. The support and office areas also have wastes that can be addressed, and the techniques for attacking this waste are not much different than the ones for manufacturing.

Lean companies manage by primarily visual means. The visual factory takes the place of many of the elements of shop floor control, with an emphasis of seeing the situation on the factory floor instead of on reports. The visual factory means that problems can be seen by all involved, such as when a FIFO lane is full and production must stop; it is easily seen by the people feeding the FIFO lane, by the people using the parts, and by the supervision of the area. Measurements are meant to help everyone in the value stream help make improvements, so everyone needs to be able to see what the measurements are saying.

Order and organization are very important. Order and organization are often embodied in the 5Ss:

- Sorting: Refers to sorting of all the tools, materials, etc., in a work area and keeping only essential items.
- Simplifying: Focuses on the need for an orderly workplace.
- Cleaning: Sweeping, systematic cleaning, and shining.
- Standardizing: Developing standard work practices.
- Sustaining: Maintaining and reviewing standards.

It is also important to know that many traditional measurements will be in conflict with Lean objectives:

- Efficiency of employees
- Standard hours
- Standard cost system

The first two of theses measurements encourage overproduction—the more is better approach. The standard cost system will often show that the Lean effort is making things worse (to remove inventory you need to make less product than is being sold, so there is a tendency to "underabsorb" the overhead, making costs look worse).

A Toyota Leader's View of the Toyota Production System

The Toyota Production System is an operations management system to achieve goals of the highest quality, lowest cost, and shortest lead time via engaging people toward goals. It consists of many management approaches, technical tools, and philosophies and basic ways to think Lean (Figure 1.4).

This is a much more complicated view of the Toyota Production System, the basis of Lean thinking, but it also goes one level deeper to show the philosophy and tools behind the system. We will try to cover almost all of these elements during the course of this book.

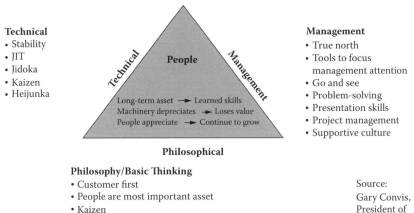

A Toyota Leader's View of the Toyota Production System

Toyota Production System=Operations Management System to achieve goals of highest quality, lowest cost, shortest lead time via engaging people toward goals.

Technical
- Stability
- JIT
- Jidoka
- Kaizen
- Heijunka

People

Long-term asset ➝ Learned skills
Machinery depreciates ➝ Loses value
People appreciate ➝ Continue to grow

Management
- True north
- Tools to focus management attention
- Go and see
- Problem-solving
- Presentation skills
- Project management
- Supportive culture

Philosophical

Philosophy/Basic Thinking
- Customer first
- People are most important asset
- Kaizen
- Go and see   Focus on floor
   - Give feedback to team members and earn respect
- Efficiency thinking
   - True (vs. apparent) condition
   - Total (vs. individual) team involvement

Source: Gary Convis, President of TMMK

Figure 1.4 Diagram of a leader's perspective of the Toyota Production System by Gary Convis. It represents a different view than the House of Toyota, emphasizing more of Lean thinking. (From "The Toyota Way," by Jeffrey K. Liker, © 2004. Reproduced with permission from McGraw-Hill Companies.)

Technical

- Stability: This means eliminating mura wherever possible.
- JIT: Just in time is one of the pillars of the House of Toyota, consisting of takt time, one-piece flow, and pull systems.
- Jidoka is the other pillar of the House of Toyota, consisting of manual or automatic line stop, separating operator and machine activities, mistake-proofing, and in-station process control.
- *Kaizen* is a Japanese word meaning improvement. Kaizen is a daily activity, the purpose of which goes beyond simple productivity improvement. It is also a process that, when done correctly, humanizes the workplace, eliminates overly hard work (muri), and teaches people how to perform experiments on their work using the scientific method and how to learn to spot and eliminate waste in business processes.
- *Heijunka* is defined as the distribution of production volume and mix evenly over time.

Management

- *True north* is the internal compass that guides you successfully through life. It represents who you are as a human being at your deepest level. It is your orienting point—your fixed point in a spinning world—that helps you stay on track as a leader (Bill George, www.truenorthleaders.com).
- Tools to focus management attention. These tools would include the use of A3s, for Kaizen activities.
- Go and see is also known as going to the gemba (actual place where work occurs), and is a significant difference for managers beginning a Lean journey. In Lean, it is considered vital for leaders to understand the work being performed in great detail, so that if something goes wrong, it can be seen. Standard work plays a vital role in this process.
- Problem solving is a key talent for leaders in Lean. Understanding how to do root cause analysis (five whys), apply the scientific method (plan, do, check, act), and apply the various tools available, such as scatter diagrams, Pareto charts, fishbone diagrams, etc., are important skills for Lean leaders.
- Presentation skills: Being able to concisely present a problem and a countermeasure is a valued skill, and is important to convincing teams that a certain path will be the best one. In an environment where consensus is highly valued, being persuasive helps leaders lead.
- Project management: Since one of the main roles of all managers in Lean is to help solve problems, it is inevitable that at times all leaders end up managing a larger project of improvement.

- Supportive culture: One of the most important thoughts in the Toyota philosophy is that the culture must support the people doing the work.

Philosophy/Basic Thinking

- Customer first: As stated before, seeing the situation through the eyes of the customer is a basic starting point for Lean. This carries through not only in identifying waste, but also in such areas as design and administration, which support the customer experience of the company.
- People are the most important asset. This is not just words, but is truly the basis for the way a Lean company does business. Kaizen is based on respect for people's ability to think and improve their work. To make this happen, the support system and the leaders must be focused on helping the employees. People, as opposed to machines, will appreciate over time, given the correct treatment and environment in which to grow.
- Kaizen: Improvement occasionally occurs in a large burst, but more commonly it happens slowly, one small gain at a time. The compound effect of all of the small changes that can be achieved by a full workforce completely engaged in improvement activities is usually significant.
- Go and see: We have already discussed that the most important step in solving any problem is to go and see the situation personally. Indeed, it is considered a prerequisite for participating on an improvement activity.
- Give feedback to team members and earn respect. *Hansei* is a word meaning reflection. In Lean, it is meant for people and teams to face the true facts of any situation, recognize weaknesses, and address them. It is considered an insult to people's potential to not point out their weaknesses and help them improve.
- Efficiency thinking: True (vs. apparent) condition. True efficiency means producing the number of parts that can be sold while utilizing the minimum number of operators and equipment possible. True efficiency is the result of "genryo management" and results in true cost reduction. Apparent efficiency would be reflected in a standard cost system, where the part proves to be cheaper as more are made, regardless of whether the parts are sold or not. This leads to overproduction, one of the eight deadly wastes.
- *Genryo* means "limited resources" and refers to the time after WWII when Toyota was nearly bankrupt and had to learn to manage with almost no resources, either material, equipment, labor, or money.

Planning and Control Hierarchy

Figure 1.5 should be familiar to most supply chain managers; it is the traditional framework for planning and controlling priority and capacity in what we are going to

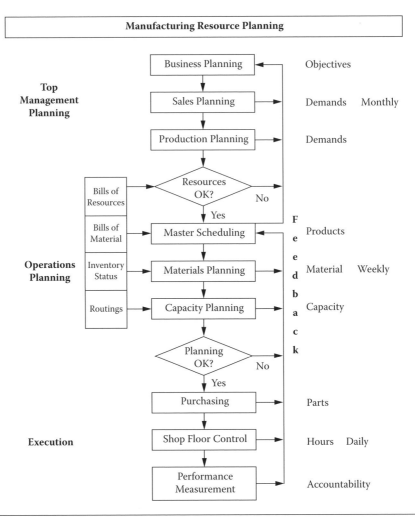

Figure 1.5   This graphic has long been accepted as the way to control production within a manufacturing facility. It serves as the basis for most enterprise resource planning systems.

from here on call the ERP model. This, to us, represents a unique way of approaching the task of managing materials. We will use this as the basis of comparison to a Lean planning and control hierarchy, shown in Figure 1.6.

Lean Planning and Control Chart

Figure 1.6 is the alternative version of a planning and control system, unique to a Lean environment.

Starting at the top, Lean wants to first create product families that can then become value streams. A product family is a set of parts that go through roughly the same processes.

Value stream mapping is done for each product family, and determines how the value stream will operate, as well as providing a list of kaizen improvement activities that will need to be worked on to achieve the future state.

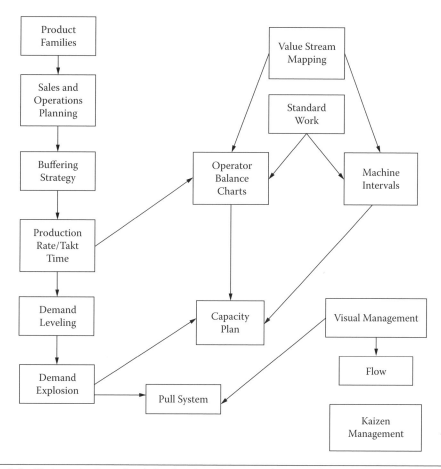

Figure 1.6 The Lean planning and control system shown here covers the same tasks as the ERP framework, except that it uses Lean tools and techniques.

Sales and operations planning is the same as it is traditionally, with the same objectives and processes.

Buffering strategy determines how work into the value stream will be leveled, one of the seven principles of a Lean value stream.

The production rate: Takt time comes from the production rate determined in the sales and operations plan. This rate becomes the heartbeat of the value stream and determines how fast product should be produced.

Demand leveling is the execution of the buffering strategy, and is often called heijunka. This demand leveling occurs at the pacemaker operation, which is the operation where flow to the customer begins.

The heijunka plan creates demand for all of the other processes in the value stream and can be obtained by a simple gross explosion of the heijunka plan through the bill of materials.

Standard work refers to defining the content, sequence, and timing of work to achieve an optimum process for manufacturing product. Standard work has been compared to the dance steps in an Arthur Murray dance class.

The operator balance chart determines how many people are required to perform the work required at the takt rate, and is the first part of the capacity plan.

Machine intervals determine how large the lot size needs to be to perform the run-time, and setup times required to produce at the takt time. This is the second input to the capacity plan.

The capacity plan contains the work time, effective work time, number of people, machine shifts, and intervals for the machines and the takt time.

The pull system is planned using the demand explosion from the heijunka schedule, then executes replenishment based on part usage.

Kaizen management is the philosophy of continuous improvement in action through project management and on-the-floor activity.

Here are a few of the areas where the Lean planning and control hierarchy differs significantly from the traditional one:

- Leveling production
- Pull systems
- Flow
- Interval to determine lot size

The four areas listed here are the main areas where we will discuss significant differences between the Lean approach and the traditional approach shown in the ERP framework. We will spend a few minutes on these in the next few pages, then deal with each one in more depth in subsequent chapters.

Leveling Production

Leveling production is one of the main ways to address mura, one of the three main classifications of waste.

- The key concept is to make the same products in the same quantities in the same timeframes on a repetitive basis.
- Once in a while, say monthly or quarterly, the mix of production is reviewed and adjusted to meet the actual demand.

Eliminating the variation of different products and varying quantities in production reduces lots of other wastes. This doesn't mean that all products are built in the exact same quantity, but that each product has a production quantity that doesn't vary from build cycle to build cycle.

In most companies we still see the mura of trying to "make the numbers" at the end of reporting periods. (Which are themselves completely arbitrary batches of time.) This causes sales to write too many orders toward the end of the period and production managers to go too fast in trying to fill them, leaving undone the routine tasks necessary to sustain long-term performance. This wave of orders—causing equipment and employees to work too hard as the finish line approaches—creates the "overburden" of muri. This in turn leads to downtime, mistakes, and backflows—the muda of waiting, correction, and conveyance. *The inevitable result is that mura creates muri that undercuts previous efforts to eliminate muda.* In short, mura and muri are now the root causes of muda in many organizations. Even worse they put muda back that managers and operations teams have already eliminated once.

—*James Womack Newsletter*, **July 6, 2006**

Does it look like this for your company? How will you ever break this destructive cycle?

The other point to make here is that there has been a primary focus on muda in the Lean efforts so far. As stated in the quote above, we need to address the other two types of waste to gain long-term improvements. Supply chain managers are in a unique position to address mura.

Pull Systems

- Pull systems have a significant effect on standard MRP logic.
- The MRP logic that says if a product is in stock it doesn't need to be made is no longer valid.
- The new logic says that when a part is used, you make it and put it back in stock.
- "No netting" is the way to think about this.

It is very difficult to simulate the pull system logic using the logic of MRP. This is because MRP is planning to either a zero inventory or a safety stock level, while the pull system is simply trying to replace what has been used. If we ignore the inventory, then we can make the two logics match up. But if we do that, why have an MRP with netting logic at all? It should also be noted that MRP is a forward-looking system, creating supply based on anticipated usage, while the pull system is a reactive system, creating supply based on what has already been used. The stability of the demand is critical to both.

A simple gross explosion of the heijunka schedule using the bill of material is all that is needed for the planning aspect in the Lean value stream.

Flow

The more flow you can design into the value stream, the shorter the lead time will be and the less waste there will be. Flow, not pull, is the main objective of Lean production. Flow takes the form of either one-piece flow or first-in–first-out (FIFO) flow. Keeping the material moving is one of the primary objectives when designing the value stream. Flow in either form will have less waste than a pull system, because flow will only contain items that have been sold and scheduled, while the pull system will need to have some of all the parts that can possibly be needed, so flow will have less waste than pull. Creating flow eliminates levels in the bill of materials (BOM). As we eliminate the need to stock parts, we can eliminate the BOM levels necessary to keep track of this inventory.

Interval as Lot Size

The interval can be thought of as the equivalent of the period order quantity lot size, but it is much more integral to the Lean planning process than lot sizing in a traditional system.

- Lot sizing in Lean is done as a function of capacity.
- The more available capacity, the smaller the lot sizes can be.
- Interval drives set up reduction activity as well as scrap and rework reduction activity.

Every part every interval is often a difficult concept to grasp, but it is a powerful and important concept in Lean. The basic idea is to fit the runtime and the setup time into a specific timeframe, with the basis of the idea being that the volume that is required in any time period is fixed (based on the sales and operations planning [S&OP] production rate) and that the variable to how much work will be done is the number of setups that will be done.

In this chapter we have set the groundwork for the rest of the book, which will describe the Lean planning and control system, as well as contrast this system with the ERP model for planning and controlling production materials. We began by defining supply chain management in both a traditional (ERP) environment and a Lean environment. We then did a brief overview of Lean, including some principles from Lean thinking from Womack and Jones, and a review of the House of Toyota framework to cover the basic tools of Lean. We then showed a new planning and control flowchart using only Lean tools, which we contend will be a better support system for managing materials in a Lean environment. We closed with a brief elaboration on a few of the largest differences between the new Lean planning and control flowchart and the traditional ERP model.

In the next chapter we will begin describing the Lean supply chain management planning and control approach, starting with managing independent demand. We will describe the role of executive sales and operations planning in setting supply chain strategy, and then discuss forecasting characteristics and methods. We will finish the chapter with an alternative to forecasting: close relationship with customers.

2

EXECUTIVE S&OP, FORECASTING, AND CUSTOMER RELATIONSHIPS

Chapter 2 will cover three very important topics that have to do with demand planning. These topics are executive sales and operations planning, forecasting, and customer relationships.

Executive Sales and Operations Planning

Executive S&OP: That part of Sales & Operation Planning that balances demand and supply at the aggregate volume level, aligns units and dollars, and helps to establish relevant policy and strategy at both the volume and mix levels.

—Thomas F. Wallace and Robert A. Stahl, Sales and Operations Planning: The How to Handbook, 3rd edition

A process to develop tactical plans that provide management the ability to strategically direct its businesses to achieve competitive advantage on a continuous basis by integrating customer-focused marketing plans for new and existing products with the management of the supply chain.

—APICS Dictionary, 12th edition

The fact that sales and operations planning (S&OP) is both tactical and strategic indicates the importance of this process in the overall scheme of managing a manufacturing company. The distinction between traditional sales and operations planning and executive sales and operations planning is that many people have extended sales and operations planning into the mix space (balancing demand and supply at the part level), while executive sales and operations planning deals strictly with the aggregate volume of planning. Why executive? It can be very difficult to get an executive to be interested at the part level detail, so limiting the process to decisions made at a strategic level keeps them engaged.

Role of Executive S&OP in Lean

- The executive S&OP process stays the same as in the traditional environment.
- Executive S&OP sets the production rate for the value stream.
- This in turn sets takt time.

What we want to emphasize here is that executive S&OP and Lean are not in conflict, and there is no need to change an effective executive S&OP process because Lean principles are being adopted. In the simplest view of the connection between the two, one of the primary tasks of executive S&OP is to review aggregate demand and set an appropriate production rate for a product family. This production rate can be taken into the Lean environment and used to calculate the takt time for the value stream. Later on we will address the fact that the executive S&OP family may not contain the same definition of a product family as the Lean value stream.

Lean and executive S&OP do different things. Lean needs help in filling in the long-term planning horizon. It can do this with executive sales and operations planning. The following bullet points are meant to compare the two processes and show that they really do not overlap very much at all and, if used correctly, they are very complementary. There is always a need in all companies to do long-term planning, and this is the strong point of executive sales and operations planning.

Lean Manufacturing

- A basic approach to manufacturing that emphasizes/focuses on flow
- Has a focus on eliminating waste from processes
- Strong on execution
- Planning and control processes usually cover a short future horizon
- Drives improvements to the operating environment
- Flow and pull work best with stable and linear demand

Executive S&OP

- Tools for forward decision making
- Strong on planning
- Long future horizon
- Balances supply and demand across the supply chain
- Can be used in many different environments

Because of the complementary elements, Lean and executive sales and operations planning work best when they work together.

What Is Executive S&OP?

Sales and operations planning is an executive decision-making process designed to balance demand and supply (at the volume level). It is also the forum for setting relevant strategy and policy for production. Finally, it integrates financial and operating plans (it updates/validates the annual business plan). It serves as top management's handle on the business.

Why an executive decision-making process? Because the implications of changing production rates or inventory levels are far reaching and need perspective from a high level. Changing production rates means changing both the material plan and the capacity plan. From a supply chain point of view, the change in the material plan is most important, since it will be important to make sure that supply partners are capable of the change and are prepared for it. Changing the capacity plan may involve capital expense, and at the very least may involve adding or subtracting labor, which is always a serious matter. Finally, a financial view of the potential impact of these changes needs to be considered, and the executive S&OP process includes financial information to help make the proper decisions.

Executive S&OP Focus

It is important to differentiate between sales and marketing, even though they are often lumped together. Sales departments are involved with specific customers and are focused on obtaining orders for product. Sales departments operate at the mix level. Marketing is involved with the classic four Ps: product, price, place, and promotion. Marketing spends a lot of time at the volume level. Executive sales and operations planning is a marketing-oriented activity. Master production scheduling is a sales-oriented activity.

The purpose of Figure 2.1 is to properly position the executive S&OP process from both a timeframe and a detail viewpoint. Because the executive S&OP process deals at the family level (volume only, not specific part numbers), the timeframe for decisions is longer than if specific part numbers were involved. The point is that the executive S&OP process is not a scheduling process, but is instead a planning process. As

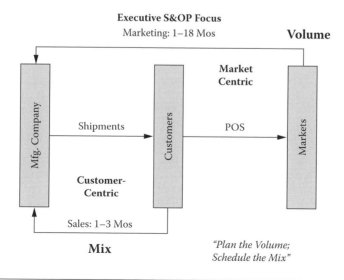

Figure 2.1 The positioning of executive S&OP. The main point is that executive S&OP is a tool for long-term planning that operates at the volume (product family) level.

we discussed, marketing is a process associated with promoting for sale goods or services. The classic components of marketing are the selection and development of the *product*, the determination of *price*, the selection and design of distribution channels (*place*), and all aspects of generating or enhancing demand for the product, including advertising (*promotion*).

In most businesses, the sales funnel does not provide enough future visibility to facilitate decision making at the strategic level, such as how much future capacity will be needed, or how much material will be needed from the various suppliers in the supply chain. The thought we wish to plant in your mind at this point, to be followed up on later, is that an extrinsic forecast method, such as a leading indicator, is more appropriate for this purpose, as opposed to sales history.

Executive S&OP Process

Figure 2.2 shows the classic five-step process to manage an executive S&OP cycle. Typically, each step is attended by a different set of people, with some overlap between participants in the steps. Top executives typically only need to attend the step 5 meeting, which should be between one-half and one hour in length.

This is the classic five-step process, typically performed monthly:

Step 1—Data gathering: This activity involves updating the files with the data from the month just ended and generating the new information for sales and marketing people to use in developing the new forecast. Recent production data are also gathered for use in the supply planning meeting.

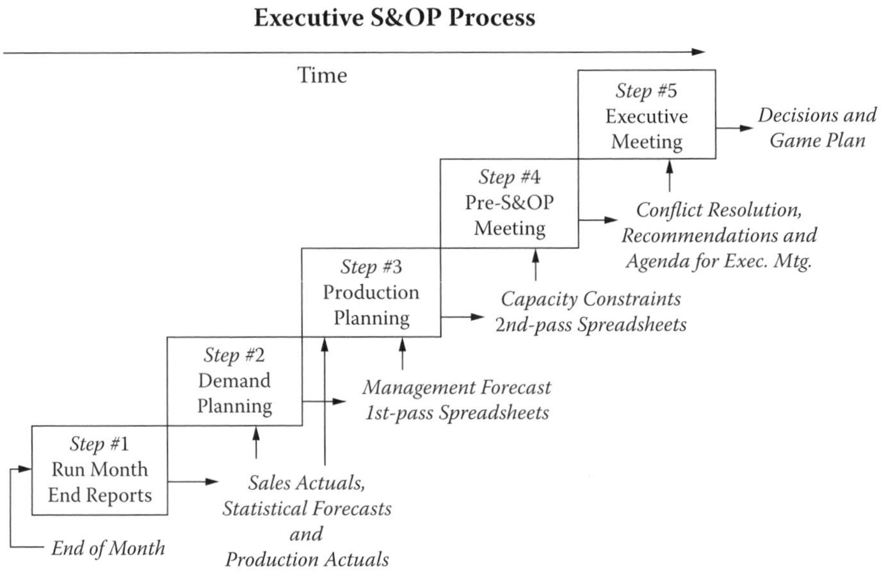

Executive S&OP Process

Figure 2.2   The five-step process of executive sales and operations planning.

Step 2—Demand planning: The people in sales and marketing review the latest data, discuss any other known intelligence, and determine the product family forecast into the future.

Step 3—Supply planning: The people in operations review the latest data, including the new forecast, previous production levels, and the latest inventory levels, and set new production levels for each product family. These levels are checked for feasibility using rough-cut planning.

Step 4—Pre-S&OP meeting: At this meeting the demand team and the supply team try to resolve any conflicts, such as capacity problems or inventory level issues. Any issue that cannot be resolved within the policies, strategies, and existing business plan become an item for the executive meeting.

Step 5—Executive meeting: At this meeting the top executives of the company review the recommendations of the pre-S&OP meeting and modify or approve them, resolve any conflicts that could not be resolved in the pre-S&OP meeting, and update the business plan if necessary.

Implementing the S&OP plan entails using one or more production strategies. When we talk about production strategy, we are specifically addressing the question of how demand will be met with production. In general terms, there are three production strategies:

- Level: Most often associated with make to stock. To achieve a level production, a buffer against variable demand must be used. Level can also be associated with make-to-order value streams by use of a variable customer order backlog.
- Chase: Most often make to order. Also could be called variable capacity.
- Hybrid: Used in both environments.

This discussion comes down to pursuing a production strategy of making to shipment, making to supermarket, or a mix of both. A brief recap: Level means that the same volume of the product family will be produced in each time period, so that the capacity requirement will be the same across the time horizon. Chase means that the value stream will produce the same amount as the demand for the period, which means that the capacity will need to change as the demand level changes. Hybrid is a combination of the two, meaning that sometimes the value stream will produce to a level capacity, and sometimes the production rate will be changed to more closely match the demand. This strategy is often employed in seasonal businesses, with a few production adjustments made as the seasons pass.

Executive S&OP has three distinct data formats that match up to these three strategies. We will simply refer to these as displays for simplicity sake.

We have traditionally dealt with three displays:

- Make to stock (often level)
- Make to order (often chase)
- Finish to order (hybrid)

The three displays have different data elements on them; for instance, the make-to-stock display has inventory while the make-to-order has customer order backlog. The finish to order has both, since both are being managed.

These three different displays are necessary because we're dealing with three different variables. Obviously, the make-to-stock display is dealing with an inventory of finished goods that we allow to grow or shrink according to demand. In the make-to-order environment we are either adjusting capacity to match demand or managing a customer order backlog, which we also allow to grow or shrink according to the demand level. The finish-to-order display must accommodate both an inventory of semifinished parts as well as a backlog of the finished item, which is then made to order. We also have three buffers available to us to help meet independent demand: inventory, or finished goods, customer order backlog, and capacity. These can all be treated as variables to meet the variability of the independent demand.

Product Families

For the next few paragraphs we will address the role of product families in executive sales and operations planning and in Lean manufacturing. While the product family is very important to both of them, we're going to try and impress upon our readers that a part does not necessarily have to be in the same family in both Lean and executive S&OP.

- Executive S&OP families should be market driven.
- Lean families should be manufacturing (process) driven.
- They are different because they serve different purposes.

It is only when the resources are aligned with the market that the product families for executive S&OP and Lean can be the same.

S&OP families: In executive S&OP, families are aggregate groups of products that are similar in the way that customers or markets view their use. Executive S&OP families are used to develop a reasoned and reasonable forecast based on market trends, grounded in intrinsic and extrinsic leading indicators. A grouping of end items whose similarities allow the markets to be best anticipated, and enable resources to be planned.

Lean families: In Lean manufacturing, the term *families* is used to mean the grouping of products that are manufactured by the same resources. This is often called a value stream. The idea is to create a synchronous flow in manufacturing that allows products to be produced at a uniform and linear market-driven rate—known as takt time.

These two product families obviously serve very different purposes, and therefore it should come as no surprise when they have very different make-ups. For the family in executives sales and operations planning, it is important to get a group of items that can be anticipated by an external market, as opposed to a group of items that can only be forecast based on their individual histories. This is because sales and operations planning is largely an exercise in anticipating future markets and deciding how the manufacturing and production facilities will meet those markets.

In the Lean manufacturing world the main purpose of the product family is to help facilitate the creation of flow in the value stream. Because of this, it is desirable to have a family of products that travel through roughly the same processes in the manufacturing facility.

Aligning Families and Resources

Figure 2.3 shows how a set of simplifying assumptions is used to link the product family production plan to the resources used to produce the product family. The 60 and 40% figures would be captured in a bill of resource and used in the rough-cut planning process, or as a driver to determine the volume for each value stream for takt time calculation.

Resource planning is a simple way to take basic assumptions about volume and mix distribution and project them down into resource usage.

> **Resource planning:** Capacity planning conducted at the Business Plan Level. The process of establishing, measuring, and adjusting limits or levels of long-range capacity.
>
> *—APICS Dictionary*, **12th edition**

The resource plan is the result of multiplying the production rate for a product family times the simplifying assumptions in the bill of resources, and adding together all of the requirements to obtain the needed capacity for each resource. At this point, we are dealing with volume-only projections, not any mix issues. This tends to make the assumptions a bit simpler than when you are dealing with mix, if only because the data set is smaller.

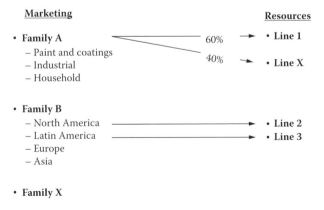

Aligning Families and Resources

Figure 2.3 Shows how simple assumptions can translate the production volume for a product family into the requirements for a resource.

For example:

- Fifty percent of the total wagon forecast is plastic wagons.
- If the forecast is one thousand for next month, five hundred units should be forecast for the plastics value stream for plastic wagons.
- A similar process would occur for all families in the plastic value stream.

We could go a step further and have a factor in hours for each wagon, say 1.2 hours of work per wagon (based on the standard work), which would mean that this forecast results in 600 hours of work for the month.

This is an example of how a simplifying assumption combines with the production plan to create the requirement for a particular resource. We would then have a set of factors (or simply takt time and standard work, as will be shown later) that determine how much work is required to produce five hundred wagons in the value stream, which would then provide a capacity plan for machines and labor.

Takt Time and Executive S&OP

The current Lean definition has takt time as effective working time divided by demand rate. Effective working time is the amount of total time minus paid breaks and lunch. In most circumstances, we would be better off making it effective working time divided by production rate (from S&OP plan).

Takt time is an important concept in Lean. Takt time is used to set the rate of sales for the value stream. The word *takt* can be interpreted to mean "beat." The question that we need to think about in conjunction with executive S&OP is whether the traditional use of takt time will serve for all of the possible production strategies supported. The traditional definition of takt time is effective available work time divided by demand. This suggests a chase strategy, in that demand and production will be the same. So planning and measuring production based on the demand rate (again, the same as the production rate in a chase strategy) is what we are doing with the traditional definition of takt time. Obviously, for value streams where a chase strategy is employed, this will be fine, but for those with a leveling strategy this will not work well. But what about Toyota, where this originated? Doesn't it level production? It is true that Toyota employs a leveling strategy in its value streams, but in a situation that is almost unique, it also has a chase strategy in these same value streams, in that the production and demand are made to match over each interval. So the definition of takt time is not an issue for Toyota. We will discuss this more in Chapter 3.

The point that we are making here is that the only environment (or production strategy) where this definition (takt time equals effective working time divided by demand) really makes sense is if the value stream is employing a chase strategy; i.e., sales and production are designed to be the same in the interval. For many environments, however, this strategy is not the least wasteful one, for instance, where a seasonal business pursues a level or a hybrid strategy, and therefore has many intervals where the production and the sales rate will not be equal. Note that one of the purposes of takt time and the definition based on demand is to bring focus on the needs of the customer as opposed to the needs of production. In other words, is it more important to produce as much product as possible and fully absorb overhead? This discussion must occur in the executive S&OP process for our modified definition to be completely effective. But assuming that we have our eyes firmly on the customer as we form our strategy, then we will contend that our modified definition of takt time will perform better for all environments.

What Does Takt Time Do?

- Sets the "beat" in the form of pitch for production
- Determines how many people will be needed for the line
- Provides "the bar" for operator balance charts for line balancing

For all of these, takt would be better represented by the production rate from S&OP. It makes little sense to plan and measure to the demand rate if that is not what the production strategy calls for in terms of production rate.

Pitch is the preferred method of measuring to see if a value stream is producing at the takt rate. If we are going to measure if the value stream is producing at the correct rate, it would be better to measure at the agreed upon production rate in all cases, as opposed to the sales rate, which will be meaningful to the factory floor only in the case of a chase strategy. An easy to understand example is the following: If inventory is higher than desired, the only way it will reduce is to produce less product than is being sold. If takt rate and the value stream are configured and staffed to produce to the demand rate, inventory will stay constant. Only by configuring and staffing to the executive S&OP production rate can we change inventory (or backlog) levels.

Forecasting

We will now move into the process of trying to predict future sales, which is where the executive S&OP begins.

> **Forecasting:** The business function that attempts to predict sales and use of products so they can be purchased or manufactured in appropriate quantities in advance.

> *—APICS Dictionary*, **12th edition**

Our desire in the short term is to eliminate the item level forecast by reducing lead times so that they are shorter than the customer will accept for delivery. For long-term planning, we need a forecast with the correct level of detail to support the executive S&OP process.

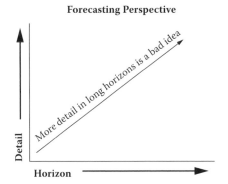

Using item level forecasts to make long-term decisions is asking
for trouble.

Figure 2.4   This graphic should remind you of the chaos curve, where there is more uncertainty the farther into the future you go.

Forecasting Perspective

Detail involves going from business level to family level to part number level (Figure 2.4). Detailed forecasts may be fine for short-term horizons, but they are typically very inaccurate in long-term horizons. We want to come back to the discussion of forecasting mix vs. volume. The point here is that long-term forecasts, which should be used to drive the executive S&OP process, do not need item level detail, and therefore should be driven by a different forecasting process than the one that will drive the heijunka or master production schedule.

Forecasting Basics

- Forecasts are typically more accurate in the short term.
- Forecasts are typically more accurate for groups of items.
- Forecasting is a process.

Any forecast that you create needs to keep these basic truths in mind. Trying to fight against these is not usually a good idea, for instance, trying to forecast by item number three years in advance. The first two of these points should be well understood by most supply chain managers, and are logical and almost self-evident.

The third point should spur some thought, as there has been a trend for forecasting to become more the domain of the computer than of the human. The thought is that if the correct algorithm can be found, then the forecast will take care of itself and all will be well. This is just not the case, as conditions continually change in the market, products go through natural life cycle changes, and competitors and customers have new directions and initiatives. All of these dictate that the forecast needs to be a process that has input from a number of sources and weighs the various factors before deciding what the future demand may be. Again, this is a process, not a formula or a "press the button" answer.

	Forecast	Time Frame
Business plan	Market direction	2 to 10 years
Sales and operations	Product lines and families	1 to 3 years
Master production schedule	End item and option	Months

Figure 2.5 This chart shows that there should be different forecasts for different purposes and timeframes in any operations control system.

Demand Patterns

Dependent vs. Independent Demand

- Only independent demand needs to be forecast.
- Dependent demand should never be forecast.

Independent demand vs. dependent demand is an important concept that is generally understood and heeded within a plant or facility, but is generally ignored across the supply chain. Dependent demand is demand that can be calculated based on existing schedules rather than forecast. For the most part, the supply chain experiences only dependent demand between companies. And yet almost all companies forecast the demand that they expect from their customers, and only a few receive a projection of demand from their customers. We will spend more time discussing this later in this chapter.

What Should Be Forecast?

Figure 2.5 shows that there are three distinct uses for forecasting, with different purposes and different time horizons. This suggests that there should be multiple forecast processes in most companies. The alternative is to have one forecast process that starts with the business plan forecast and disaggregates as more detail is needed. The common way to do this now seems to be to start with the item level forecast and then aggregate it to obtain summary level forecasts. This method gives no market visibility and accumulates all of the item level mistakes up to a strategic decision-making level.

General Methods of Forecasting

- Qualitative—Based on intuitive or judgmental evaluation.
- Quantitative—Based on computational projection of a numeric relationship.
- Intrinsic—Based on historical patterns of the data itself from company data.
- Extrinsic—Based on external patterns from information outside the company.

These four characteristics of forecasting are very useful in categorizing forecasting approaches. A quantitative and intrinsic forecasting method is the most common in use today, but it is also being used in many cases where a qualitative and extrinsic forecast would serve the need better, such as to support the executive S&OP process.

This is another important set of concepts. Again, to generalize, most forecasts in use today are quantitative and intrinsic. This means that they are forecasting the future based on the results of the past. In some cases this will work well, but in many others it is not the correct approach. In particular, when dealing with families and strategic decisions, a more appropriate approach would be an extrinsic, qualitative method that takes into account all of the various factors that may affect future demand.

Qualitative Techniques

- Based on intuition and informed opinion
- Tend to be subjective
- Used for business planning and forecasting for new products
- Used for medium-term to long-term forecasting

The fact that these forecasts are subjective has caused them to be discounted vs. more "scientific," computer-algorithm-based forecasts. However, these forward-looking forecasts can improve over time with practice and attention.

The difficulty with qualitative approaches is that they require quite a bit of effort for the people involved in creating the forecast. The people involved must understand customers, markets, products, and their uses, as well as the vision for the future of the company. This combination is typically found in your more experienced people who usually have lots to do just to keep up with their "normal jobs." So obtaining their time to participate in a forecasting exercise can be difficult. But since this is one of the primary inputs to a strategic decision-making process, the importance should warrant the time investment.

Quantitative Techniques

- Based on historical data usually available in the company
- Assume future will repeat the past

Even though many forecasting systems now have multiple algorithms that they use to create forecasts, and many use focus forecasting techniques, all of them still rely on the past to project the future. Not all markets and products are that stable.

Most forecasts are based on quantitative techniques, and operate at the item level, even when that level of detail is not required. This method is prevalent, even though it is usually not appropriate, because it can largely be done by a computer with little intervention from people. It is thus much less work to generate a quantitative forecast than it is to generate a qualitative forecast. Unfortunately, since most of forecasting, especially for long-term purposes, must be about anticipating the markets, the qualitative forecast is the correct one for long-term planning.

Extrinsic Techniques

- Based on external indicators
- Useful in forecasting total company demand or demand for families of products
- Can be based on "leading indicators"

Leading indicator: A specific business activity index that indicates future trends. For example, housing starts is a leading indicator for the industry that supplies builders' hardware.

—APICS Dictionary, **12th edition**

These leading indicators can be anything, from housing starts to birth rates to gross national product to unemployment rates. While difficult to identify, finding a leading indicator for a product family is very valuable, as the future can be predicated based on information that isn't speculative. An example would be in the lawn mower business, where housing starts were a reliable indicator with a high degree of correlation, and an offset of five to six months. In other words, if housing starts increased this month, we could expect an upturn in mower sales in five to six months.

Pyramid Forecasting

The model in Figure 2.6 is most appropriate for the discussions that we have been having, as it differentiates the various levels of detail that can be forecast, and shows that forecasts can be rolled up or forced down. The model that we have been advocating so far would involve forecasting at the top levels of the pyramid (total company, business unit, and product family), and forcing the agreed upon forecast through the lower levels of detail. In its most advanced state, a user can enter a forecast at any

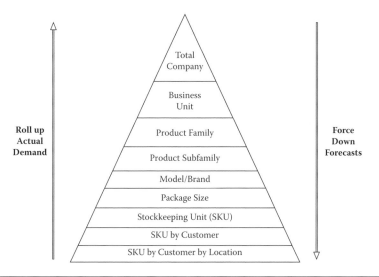

Figure 2.6 Picture of what is known as pyramid forecasting. You can enter any level of the pyramid with manual data and force it up and down to the other levels.

level of the pyramid and aggregate data up or explode down through all of the layers of the pyramid.

Forecasting as a Process

Figure 2.7 shows a schematic of the inputs and outputs of forecasting, with the decision-making process in between them. The history element can be managed by an intrinsic forecast. The other inputs have nothing to do with historic data, and therefore have to be handled in an extrinsic manner, calling for extrinsic (such as leading indicators) and qualitative techniques. What this suggests is that most of the inputs to a good forecast have nothing to do with historical data, but are instead focused on looking into the future, concerned with what the customers, competitors, and markets may do as opposed to what they have already done.

Below are a few examples of market drivers (leading indicators):

- Birth rate
- Consumer confidence index
- Housing starts
- NASCAR TV ratings
- Price of gasoline

These are just a few examples of what should be viewed as practically a limitless range of possibilities for finding leading indicators. Any potential forecast driver should be tested for correlation using statistical techniques, readily available commercially. Many indexes are available from professional societies or the government, and some unexpected relationships are sometimes found between these indexes and sales history. Once a correlation has been found, then the index can be used to drive the

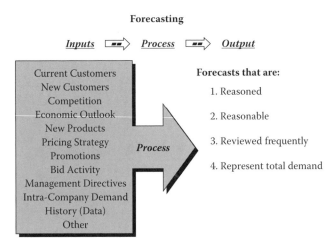

Figure 2.7   Shows that forecasting involves much more than simply taking historic data and extrapolating it into future projections. The process referred to is how to weigh all of the various inputs from different sources and create the one forecast that all can agree to. (From www.tfwallace.com.)

forecast, either based on the indexes' forecast or based on the indexes' actual data and a forward offset, as in the case of housing starts and lawn mower sales cited earlier.

Ways to a Better Forecast

- Better algorithms: Alluring, but mostly an empty promise.
- Work more closely with customers: More work, but great rewards. For example, an initiative called collaborative planning, forecasting, and replenishment (CPFR) was developed in the late 1990s, but very few companies have had the courage to openly collaborate with their customers. Misplaced fear, leading to distrust, has been the primary reason why this initiative has failed. With hundreds of thousands of dollars, or even millions, on the line, one would think that simply talking to one's customers would be better than trying to guess what they are going to do, but as the old saying goes, "None of us are as dumb as all of us," so we keep doing the same things, and foolishly expecting different outcomes.
- Make the forecast less important: Shorten response times in all areas. This is one of the primary benefits of implementing Lean.
- Narrow the scope: Try to forecast only the predictable items.

Improving the forecast is an important objective for many companies. Listed are four possibilities for making the forecast better. Only the first one works within the existing framework of a statistical forecast. There are times when a different formula will provide a better forecast, such as when a seasonal product is being forecast without use of a seasonal factor. But with the sophistication of software packages for forecasting available today, these opportunities are becoming rarer. This suggests that many companies would be better off pursuing the other options. The most promising is to forge closer relationships with customers, obtain demand data directly from their planning processes, and eliminate the forecast altogether. We will talk more about this a bit later. The third option is to take advantage of the improvements that Lean will make in the response times across the company, from a production lead time perspective as well as from the time it takes to process data and information in the support areas. One of the things that Lean does well is shorten response time and lead times, meaning the forecast doesn't have to project as far into the future. Remember, the forecast will be more accurate in shorter timeframes.

The last point refers back to certain items not being suitable for statistical forecast methods, and alternates should be found for these items. Limiting the forecast to items that have a normal demand distribution will improve the accuracy of the forecast.

An Alternative to Forecasting: Supplier Partnerships

This follows up on the idea that most demand in a supply chain should be treated as dependent demand and therefore not forecast. This level of cooperation between supplier and customer is far less common than it should be.

- Supplier is viewed as an upstream work center to the plant.
- Suppliers share information.
- Cost reductions are equally shared.
- Suppliers must:
  - Have reliable quality
  - Have reliable delivery

The idea here is that the best alternative to improving the forecast is to actually eliminate the forecast and simply use the planning information of the customer as the projection. This should be more accurate than an independent forecast ever could be, and it will have the advantage of helping spur discussions of future plans between the two parties. This requires an atmosphere where the two parties are truly partners, however, not just two companies doing business together. We will discuss this in some depth in Chapter 10.

Developing Suppliers as Partners

Mutual trust and shared risk and reward are underlying principles of being able to build a partnership relationship with your suppliers. We offer a few principles for beginning to have your customers and suppliers as partners:

- Clean your own house first.
- Challenge them.
- Teach them.
- Learn to take advantage of their technology advancements.

These are just a few ways to help develop true partners in the supply chain. An important base for this that is not listed here is mutual trust, which is necessary for most of the other activities to occur. It is also important to understand that being a partner doesn't imply being "soft." Partners can, and probably should, be very demanding of each other. For more on this, reference Jeff Liker, *The Toyota Way*.

Partners vs. Vendors

If you believe in companies being as strong as their supply chains, then you need to be doing everything you can to get rid of vendors and instead develop partners.

- Partners share.
- Partners suffer together and flourish together.
- Partners help each other.
- Do you have partners or vendors?

Vendors are companies that you buy things from. Partners are companies that you work with for mutual benefit. Remember that one of the main objectives of forming partnerships with customers and suppliers is to eliminate forecasts on dependent demand items in the supply chain.

In this chapter we have dealt with long-term planning issues, reviewing executive sales and operations planning, forecasting, and customer-supplier partnerships. Our conclusions can be summarized by saying that the executive sales and operations planning process is most suitable for long-term strategic planning in a Lean environment, as long as it is recognized that the product families that both rely on should, in most cases, be different. As far as forecasting goes, we would conclude that most forecasting done by companies today is at the wrong level of detail and does not fit well with the general principles of forecasting. And as far as partnering with other links in the supply chain, this is still much rarer than it should be, especially when we recognize that most links in a supply chain contain only dependent demand.

In Chapter 3 we will address the vital activity of taking variable independent demand and creating a Lean production schedule that meets the strategy of the value stream and gives the customer the desired level of service.

3
Leveling and Heijunka

In this chapter we will address one of the elements of the base of the House of Toyota: leveling. We will start with the ideal situation, as created within the Toyota Production System, characterized by high-volume, low-mix production with long horizons of frozen customer orders that enables a heijunka schedule, then explore environments where heijunka is not possible, such as high product mix, and make or engineer to order.

Leveling Value Streams

> In general, when you try to apply the Toyota Production System [TPS], the first thing you have to do is to even out or level the production. Leveling the production schedule may require some front-loading of shipments [to dealers] or postponing of shipments and you may have to ask some customers to wait for a short period of time. Once the production level is more or less the same or constant for a month, you will be able to apply pull systems and balance the assembly line. But if production levels—the output—varies from day to day, there is no sense in trying to apply those other [pull] systems, because you simply cannot establish standardized work under such circumstances.
>
> —Fugio Cho, Toyota president, in Jeffrey K. Liker, *The Toyota Way*

This quote is a very important one to understand to set up the rest of the chapter. It points out that the Toyota Production System is not a make-to-order system, and that to make the Lean approach work, it is more important to level the work than it is to make to customer order. The rest of the chapter explores the implications of this quote, starting with how Toyota goes about this leveling, then discussing other options that may be better suited for other environments.

It is important to understand that even though we have equated Lean with removing waste, this is just one element of Lean. As we have stated from the beginning, Lean is meant to be a complete system and philosophy for running a company. For many companies, though, Lean is still just the set of TPS tools that assist in the identification and then steady elimination of waste (muda), which improves quality, reduces lead time, and reduces costs. And while this is not a bad set of results, muda is only one of three wastes that should be addressed. Viewing only the muda aspect, the tools of Lean, such as kaizen, poka-yoke, the five whys, and the 5Ss, become focused on waste elimination, providing a series of "point solutions." In this way Lean can be seen as taking a very similar approach to other improvement methodologies. For these companies Lean is not a system but a tool kit to solve specific problems in production.

The alternative approach to Lean manufacturing, which is promoted by Toyota, is one in which the focus is upon implementing flow of work (eliminating mura) through the system and not upon waste reduction per se. The tools to implement flow include heijunka (production leveling), takt, standard work and operator balance charts to create one-piece flow, first-in–first-out (FIFO) flow, and pull production (by means of kanban). As we showed in the House of Toyota diagram of Lean, these tools are all part of the big picture. The system picture also, of course, includes the other tools of Lean listed in the waste focus approach, but does so in a total system context, using the tools to solve problems that arise from trying to create flow and pull through the supply chain.

The difference between these two approaches should be obvious. The second approach encourages a system-wide view of the value stream, encouraging solutions that will improve the performance of the entire value stream. The first approach encourages a narrow focus, with the hope that the entire value stream will benefit from local improvements. It has been shown that the implementation of smooth flow exposes operating problems that have always existed, and thus implementing flow causes waste reduction opportunities to naturally occur. This also exposes problems that the tool-based approach never uncovers. Some Toyota staff have expressed surprise at the tool-based approach, as their view is that many of the tools are patches made necessary where flow could not be fully implemented, and are thus not aims in themselves. We are advocating the second, systematic approach in this book.

> **Buffer stock:** Goods held, usually at the downstream end of a facility or process, to protect the customer from starvation in the event of an abrupt increase in short-term demand that exceeds short-term production capacity. The terms buffer and safety stock often are used interchangeably, which creates confusion. There is an important difference between the two, which can be summarized as: Buffer stock protects your customer from you (the producer) in the event of an abrupt demand change; safety stock protects you from incapability in your upstream processes and your suppliers.
>
> —*Lean Lexicon*, **compiled by Lean Enterprise Institute, 4th edition**

The purpose of a buffer in this chapter is to enable production to be as level as possible. Instead of considering only inventory as a buffer, we are also going to include customer order backlog and capacity as possible buffers, allowing us to address many different production environments and to present several different possibilities for how to take variable customer demand and produce a level schedule. We are also going to make a distinction between leveling mix and leveling only volume or work content. The most desired environment is to level mix, which also levels work content. This means that both the capacity plan and the material plan will be repetitive over each timeframe (interval). This is the definition of heijunka, the most desirable production schedule.

Mix and Volume Variability Definitions

- Mix variability is a measure of how often the models and their variants actually are sold.
- Volume variability is measured by simply determining whether the total amount of work required in the factory by the customer orders varies significantly from period to period.

We should make an up-front distinction between selling a level mix and producing to a level mix. Toyota produces to a level mix but clearly does not sell a level mix to the public. What actually happens is that it produces to a level set of orders from the dealers, who have an inventory that absorbs the difference between what is sold and what has been produced in any period. The activity at the plant is to take the dealers' orders and parse them up into equal segments, so that each model and option shows up in the schedule at the same rate as it has been ordered; for instance, half of the units ordered have DVD players, so every other unit in the schedule will have a DVD.

Volume variability is only concerned with whether the sales can be covered by the capacity within the plant on an average basis. In other words, if we average selling 5,000 pounds of product each week, how far away from the 5,000 pounds are the actual sales during any week? Standard deviation and mean absolute deviation are two examples of how to measure this variation.

Buffer with Finished Goods Inventory (a la TPS): Make to Stock

It is necessary to understand a bit about the Toyota environment to make sense of what is written about how the company does this. It should be pointed out that Toyota owns no finished goods inventory, so by strict definition Toyota is not a make-to-stock company, but a make-to-order one. We don't believe that this fact invalidates placing them as a manufacturer that produces to a finished goods inventory, since the destination of the finished cars is often an inventory on a dealer's lot. From a supply chain viewpoint, ownership of the inventory is not as important as its presence and purpose.

Stock Amount

In a make-to-stock strategy in Lean, where inventory is being used as a buffer, there is no correct level of inventory, and therefore there is no inventory target. To reiterate, we are more concerned with creating a level production schedule than we are of having a certain inventory amount on hand in the short term. This is immediately in conflict with the traditional enterprise resource planning (ERP) view of inventory, which is that finished goods inventories should be managed to a specific target. However, if a constant inventory target is held, then production must vary to match demand, and we will not be able to level the production schedule. So we must come to grips with an

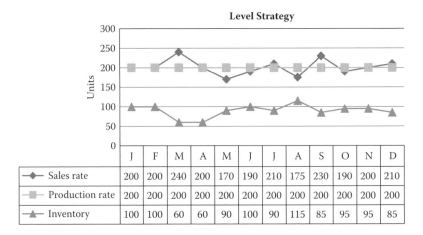

	J	F	M	A	M	J	J	A	S	O	N	D
Sales rate	200	200	240	200	170	190	210	175	230	190	200	210
Production rate	200	200	200	200	200	200	200	200	200	200	200	200
Inventory	100	100	60	60	90	100	90	115	85	95	95	85

Figure 3.1   A leveling strategy using inventory as the buffer against variable demand, keeping capacity (production) constant.

environment where inventory will vary inversely with demand, since we will be holding production constant and varying inventory (Figure 3.1).

Inventory is the most common method used to buffer value streams. The usual approach for many companies when they approach managing finished goods as they implement Lean is to implement a kanban system for the finished goods products. This would mean that all items are in the finished goods inventory and would be shipped on demand, at which point the value stream would receive a signal to simply try to replace what was shipped. What this does in reality, however, is to simply pass the demand variation of the marketplace into the pacemaker process of the value stream. The key concept of using inventory as a buffer should be to provide level work for the value stream. The result of this is that having inventory should not be the goal; it is instead the result of the production strategy. What this means is that the presence of inventory allows the value stream to produce a constant amount of work even when the demand from the customer is erratic. Because the demand will vary and the production rate will not, the inventory will vary in the opposite direction from demand; i.e., when demand is high, inventory will go down, and vice versa.

Bill of Materials Shape Helps Dictate Strategy

The bill of materials (BOM) "shape" is sometimes called the component structure shape. The shape is determined by the number of parts used at each level of the bill of material—the more parts that are used, the wider the shape is at that level. Bills are always drawn with the end items at the top and the dependent demand parts at the bottom. In discreet industries, the bill of material has a basic A shape. Outside of the discrete industries, other bill shapes exist. For example, a pharmaceutical company or a refinery has a V-shaped bill—a few items are processed into many items (Table 3.1).

We will start by looking at the A-shaped BOM. In the shape in Figure 3.2, a few end items are made from many parts, materials, and components. In this circumstance,

Table 3.1 Various Bill of Material Shapes and the Types of Industries Where You Are Likely to Find That Shape

SHAPE	END ITEMS	COMPONENTS	EXAMPLE
A	Few	Many	Auto makers, construction
V	Many	Few	Meat processing, refining
X	Many	Many	Computers, electronics
T	Many	Few	Stationery, jewelry

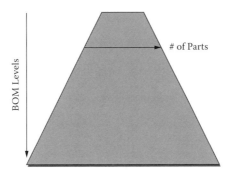

Figure 3.2 In this shape a few end items are made from many parts, materials, and components. An example would be an equipment manufacturer, such as automobiles, lawn mowers, capital equipment, etc. This shape lends itself to making to stock.

the demand for lower-level components will tend to be dependent on both the volume and mix variability for end items. Because the demand for the lower-level components will tend to be very mix sensitive with this type of shape, Toyota has chosen to completely level the mix within the factory, and allow the finished goods to absorb variation in both mix and volume.

This strategy calls for the possibility of all finished items to be in the finished goods inventory. They may not necessarily be in finished goods at any one time, but because of the way the strategy works, any one of the possibilities for finished goods combinations may end up in inventory. In practice, the ones that sell less than the dealer forecast are the ones that will end up in inventory.

Can you state why this shape suggests make to stock? Answer: The most logical place to carry inventory is the spot in the BOM that has the least part numbers and the most flexibility, in this case the end item.

How Lean Fits In: Make to Stock

This slide in Figure 3.3 places the strategy into the context of Lean. The supermarket is placed at the narrowest point in the BOM shape, namely, at the finished goods level. The production of product can then be based on a pull from the supermarket (with some allowances for leveling). The customer only has to wait for the product to be shipped, so lead time to the market is kept to a minimum. The lead time through the value stream to replenish the supermarket helps to determine the inventory level, so speed counts in this strategy.

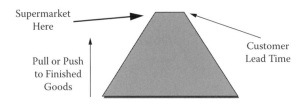

Figure 3.3 shows how the strategies of Lean fit into the BOM shape where a few finished items are made from many components and raw materials.

Heijunka is defined as the distribution of production volume and mix evenly over time. This will represent the single point schedule in the value stream, in this case at the finished goods level.

Using the word *push* (Figure 3.3) here is intentional and should spur some discussion. Toyota does not, by strict definition, push product into the value stream. Everything produced in the plants are made to an order. However, it is not really a demand pull through the supply chain, since the order from the dealer is based on forecast of future demand, not on actual demand. It would be our contention that in the face of imperfect markets, i.e., the customers buy different quantities and mixes in each interval, there will need to be at least some items pushed to obtain a level schedule.

Leveling Production Mix vs. Sales Mix: Heijunka Scheduling

- Forecast = 100 A, 50 B, and 50 C this month.
- At twenty days in the month, this is ten per day.
- Production sequence = A B A C A B A C A B A C, etc.
- The actual sales may not equal the forecast.
- A finished goods inventory handles this.

This is an example of how mix is leveled. At Toyota, this is based on the car orders placed by the dealers. In other environments, it may represent the forecast amount for each option. The key is that production makes the average amount of all products, without regard to the actual sales to the general public as they are realized. Next month, if the sales mix has changed, then the sequence will be reset to reflect this change. In practice, there are lots of combinations of models and options that would make the schedule much more complex, but this is how it would work for all of the options available.

Heijunka and paced withdrawal (we will discuss more about paced withdrawal in Chapter 5) are often implemented on the factory floor via a Heijunka box, a post-office-box-like setup divided into pitch periods (Figure 3.4).

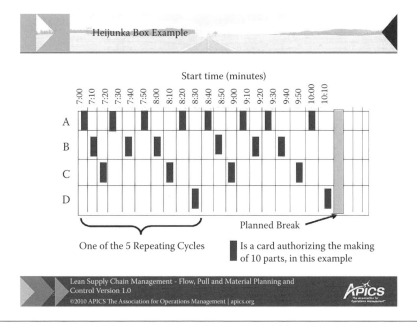

Figure 3.4 An example of a heijunka box.

Takt time is one minute. In 440 minutes we are going to produce 440 pieces. Forty percent of them are Part A, 30% of them are Part B, 20% Part C, and 10% Part D. Each of the parts fit into a container holding ten pieces, so it has been decided to make pitch ten minutes. The heijunka box has thus been divided into ten-minute segments, with each holding a card for one container of parts. Based on the volumes of each part, we can use 10 as a common denominator, meaning that in ten pitch periods we will make at least one kanban of each part (see every part every interval in Chapter 7.) Four of these pitch periods will contain Part A, three will contain Part B, two will contain Part C, and one will contain Part D. We have spaced them out to make a pattern of ABC–AB–ABC–AD. This pattern will reoccur throughout the shift, as well at throughout the planning period, until the mix is adjusted in an executive sales and operations planning cycle.

Leveling Mix

- Pull systems work better when mix is leveled.
- Shared resources can be synchronized based on the production pattern. A shared resource is a process that produces parts for more than one value stream.
- Capacity requirements for the value stream will fit the average requirements during each interval.
- FIFO lanes are kept to a minimum regarding the need to balance operations for a mix.

There are many advantages to completely leveling the mix in a value stream. Most of these revolve around the fact that most long-term planning involves some sort of averages for the product required in the value stream, from the amount of equipment needed to the manpower employed to the size of supermarkets. Because leveling the mix means producing the average, the decisions made in the long-term planning will generally work as designed. In other words, short-term variations will be eliminated, and therefore the short-term schedule will match the long-term schedule.

Leveling Mix in a High-Product-Mix Environment

- High inventory investment.
- Potentially high obsolete inventory.
- Potential poor customer service (reliant on forecast accuracy). The forecast will most likely be inaccurate, due to the high mix variability.

If a company does decide to level the mix in a high-mix-variability value stream, there will probably be some poor results. This list is by no means exhaustive, but these are still serious considerations for management.

So why is it so difficult to forecast in a high-mix environment? We think there are many reasons, among them: there are often many part numbers, meaning the sheer volume of parts makes it difficult to spend enough time to produce a valid forecast based on the process described in Chapter 2; demand is usually erratic at the part level, which makes using any formulas based on history very unreliable; there are often many different customers, so it is difficult to establish close relationships with enough customers to help with forecasting; and often the parts have little or no history of demand, so again, formulas based on historic demand won't work very well. There are, of course, many other reasons why forecasting may be unreliable in a high-mix environment, but we think these should be enough to encourage companies to pursue other avenues.

So if we cannot level mix in all environments, do we simply accept a schedule produced as normal, or is there something else that should be considered? Our answer is that you should still at least level for volume only. Let's call this leveling work content, because that will be the intent of this strategy. Because we cannot level mix, which levels both the material plan and the capacity plan, we will settle for leveling the capacity plan and compensating for the mix issues with some extra buffers for materials. The reason for this is that in some value streams the high mix of products does not allow for leveling of the entire mix of products without a significant amount of waste, so the strategy must somehow level work into the value stream without the waste accompanying a full supermarket of slow-moving items. This can usually be done by keeping a supermarket of only high-volume, frequently ordered items, and treating the rest of the items as make to order. Because they are in the sales mix most often, they are the most likely items to keep in inventory. The reason is not what you may initially think. What will happen is that in periods where demand is higher than capacity, we will produce all of the make-to-order items first, then see how much capacity is left to replenish the make-to-stock items. For any make-to-stock items that don't fit into the capacity available, they will simply have less inventory on hand at the end of the interval. When demand is less than capacity, we will add replenishment of the items that were skipped previously. The high-volume items have several advantages as a buffer: they are less likely to become obsolete, and because they are frequently ordered, it is easier to adjust the inventory level on them. This allows us to make the following points about leveling for work content only:

- The buffer for the value stream may (or needs to, or should) contain only high-volume items.
- We need to have separate strategies for high-volume and low-volume items when creating the schedule.
- Interval should be based on a time slice of volume and the number of items sold during the time slice.

Interval: The period of time in which every product of the value stream is produced to match the customer demand rate.

Because not all of the items will be produced in each interval, the interval in this strategy needs to be revised to be the required items to build in a period, based on what is actually sold in the period, not all of the products in the family. We will call this the make-to-order interval, as opposed to the every part every interval, which is used in a mix-leveled environment. We will talk more about the make-to-order interval in Chapter 7.

This strategy requires the separation of the supermarket items from the rest, with the following rules usually in place: load the schedule with the make–to-order items first, and then fill the remaining capacity with the supermarket items (Figure 3.5).

By definition, the parts will have no inventory, so we will produce them using a chase make-to-order strategy. This leaves only so much room to produce the make-to-stock parts, shown in Figure 3.6.

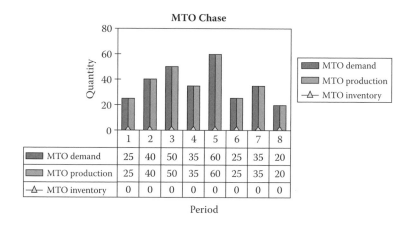

	1	2	3	4	5	6	7	8
MTO demand	25	40	50	35	60	25	35	20
MTO production	25	40	50	35	60	25	35	20
MTO inventory	0	0	0	0	0	0	0	0

Figure 3.5 The production strategy for the make-to-order parts in a value stream.

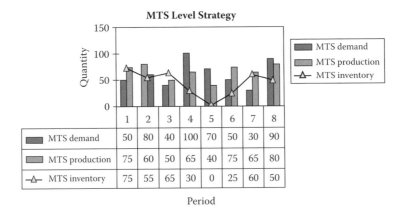

	1	2	3	4	5	6	7	8
MTS demand	50	80	40	100	70	50	30	90
MTS production	75	60	50	65	40	75	65	80
MTS inventory	75	55	65	30	0	25	60	50

Period

Figure 3.6   The production strategy for the make-to-stock parts.

Because the demand for make-to-order parts varies, and overall we want to have a leveled production, we need to also vary the production of make-to-stock parts to fit the available capacity. This then uses the inventory of the make-to-stock parts as the buffer for the value stream, as shown in Figure 3.6. The total result is shown in Figure 3.7.

Even though all of the figures show units, this is just for convenience, since it is difficult to think of inventory in terms of work content. We are really trying to level work content in this strategy, not unit production, so we would really need a way to determine how much work content was represented by each unit of production.

This strategy also requires some more robust tools than a mix-leveled value stream:

- More elaborate capacity planning is necessary due to work content variations caused by varying mixes of products being sold.
- Cross-training of operators is needed to handle required flexibility from various mixes as well as for absentees.

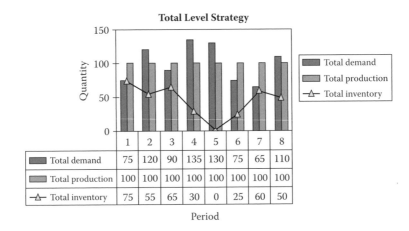

	1	2	3	4	5	6	7	8
Total demand	75	120	90	135	130	75	65	110
Total production	100	100	100	100	100	100	100	100
Total inventory	75	55	65	30	0	25	60	50

Period

Figure 3.7   The overall production strategy of using a partial inventory buffer of make-to-order parts to level work into production.

Because we will not be producing the average product mix in any period, we are vulnerable to the swings in work content caused by the various product mixes that are needed. Varying work content simply means that it takes a different amount of labor to make different parts in the value stream. In other words, we may have "floating bottlenecks" in the shop. This means that it is not sufficient to simply level the work at the pacemaker, but we also need to check to make sure that all of the other resources can produce the parts necessary to make the product mix. This requires a bit more sophistication in the capacity planning portion of the value stream.

For the same reason, it is necessary to have more fully cross-trained operators when only leveling volume, since to some extent it should be expected that operators will need to move around to where the work is for any particular product mix.

The strategy shown in Figure 3.8 is the opposite of how most people approach a high-mix value stream, in that the usual strategy is to find the high-volume items (the runners) and fill the schedule with them, then use the rest of the time for the other items (the dogs). This usual strategy will work fine as long as a few conditions are present: the market will accept variable lead time for the make-to-order items, or capacity can be flexed to keep the make-to-order lead time constant. If these conditions are not present, then the alternate strategy we have described will usually have better results. This brings us to our next buffer, lead time.

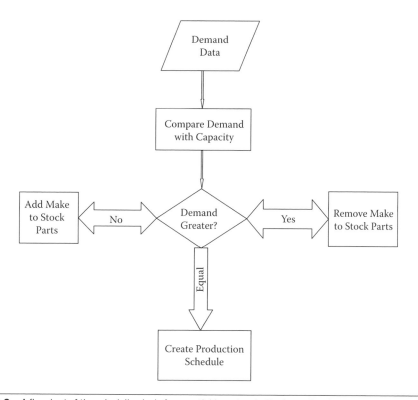

Figure 3.8   A flowchart of the scheduling logic for a partial inventory buffer in a value stream.

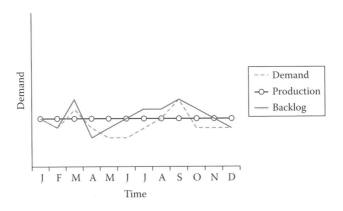

Figure 3.9   Varying backlog to buffer variable demand, keeping capacity (production) constant.

Buffer Demand Variability with Lead Time (Backlog): Make to Order

The chart in Figure 3.9 represents the strategy of buffering a value stream with a variable backlog. The slide shows that backlog will vary with the sales volume; i.e., if sales are higher than production, backlog will increase, and if sales are less than production, the backlog will get smaller. Backlog in this environment will equate to the customer lead time. Again, we are holding production level, and what will vary are the customer order backlogs, which are the orders that haven't been started in the factory yet.

BOM Shape

In the shape shown in Figure 3.10 many end items are made from a few raw materials. An example would be an injection molding company, making many different end items, all from a common resin and a few additives. In this circumstance, the demand for lower-level raw material will tend to have little difference from the volume variability for end items and would be unaffected by mix. In such an environment, it would be possible to stock the raw materials based on the volume leveled plan, then produce to the customer order.

Figure 3.10   In this shape many end items are made from a few raw materials. This shape suggests a make-to-order strategy.

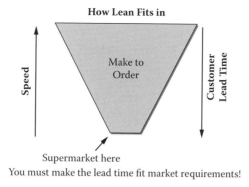

How Lean Fits in

Figure 3.11 Shows how Lean supports a make-to-order strategy based on this BOM shape.

How Lean Fits In

The key to producing to customer orders is to ensure that the production lead time is less than the market lead time (Figure 3.11). Lean obviously plays a major role here, as one of the usual results of a Lean value stream implementation is shortened lead times due to flow.

What things does Lean do to increase the speed to the customer?

- Strategically places supermarkets
- Creates flow
- Streamlines administrative processes
- Creates partnership with customer

Managing Backlog

Figure 3.12 shows that the administrative functions must also be accounted for when planning the lead time through a make-to-order value stream. This is shown here as variable backlog, which would include all of the time from when the order is first received until it is started in manufacturing. Having understood that the manufacturing lead time must be less than the market lead time, this figure suggests that it must be even less than expected. This is because the period of time from when the order is received until it is started in production must also be included as part of the lead time

Figure 3.12 The relationship between three elements of lead time in a make-to-order environment: the customer, or market lead time, the backlog, and the production lead time.

that the customer will experience. The expected amount of backlog will depend on the amount of volume variation experienced by the value stream.

What activities would be included in variable backlog? We think these activities would include order entry, credit checks, engineering design work, part creation, drawings, BOM, standard work, and schedule creation. While this is not an exhaustive list, and repeat items would not require all of these steps, it should be easy to see that any combination of these could amount to adding a significant amount of lead time to the ordering process.

Promised dates must be managed in one of two ways:

- For fixed lead time, vary capacity if backlog exceeds allotted time
- For variable lead time, govern by an aggregate view of the amount of capacity sold vs. "normal" available capacity

The promised date is the delivery date given to the customer at the time of order entry. This is especially important in make-to-order environments. Not all markets will accept variable lead times. In this case, we must make the promised dates on customer orders based on a fixed lead time, and we must make the combination of the unstarted backlog plus the production lead time less than the market lead time. These two segments of the lead time must be monitored and managed, because if the total grows to be longer than the market lead time, overtime must be worked.

In other environments, we can promise variable lead times, in which case the promise date can be made based on the amount of work already sold vs. the capability to produce the work. This must be done at the aggregate value stream level, not via something based at the item level schedule, such as available to promise commonly used in ERP systems. But that is another topic for another day.

Chase

Chase involves buffering variability with more flexible and agile manufacturing resources. This is the third strategy available to us, including varying inventory, varying backlog, and now varying capacity.

> **Chase production method:** A production planning method that maintains a stable inventory level while varying production to meet demand.
>
> —*APICS Dictionary*, **12th edition**

A chase strategy in theory has the potential to have the least waste of all of the strategies, although in practice that is not often the case (Figure 3.13). This is because the needed flexibility in both the material and capacity execution of this strategy can be difficult and costly. It should be pointed out that most master production schedule (MPS) and material requirements planning (MRP) algorithms assume that the value

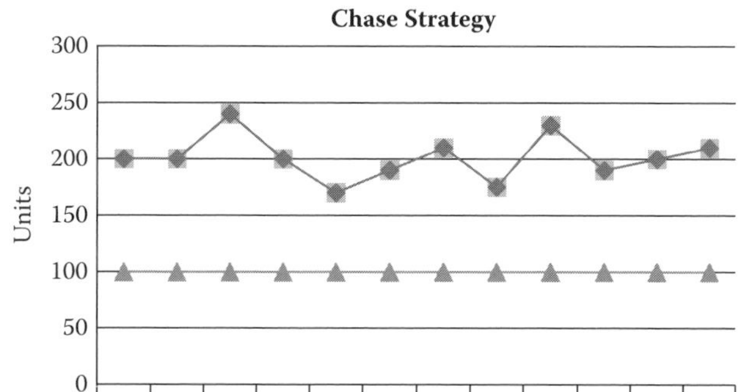

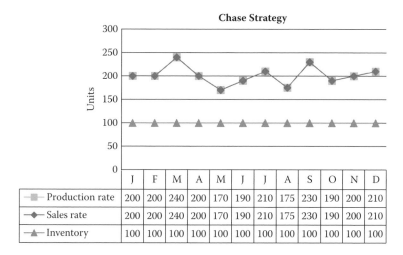

	J	F	M	A	M	J	J	A	S	O	N	D
Production rate	200	200	240	200	170	190	210	175	230	190	200	210
Sales rate	200	200	240	200	170	190	210	175	230	190	200	210
Inventory	100	100	100	100	100	100	100	100	100	100	100	100

Figure 3.13 Note that in this strategy we are holding inventory (or backlog) constant and varying capacity to match demand.

stream will be executing a chase strategy, meaning they vary the capacity via infinite scheduling and attempt to hold inventory constant as they create supply plans.

Takt Time and Chase

Because we are constantly changing the production rate, don't we need to change takt time constantly in this strategy? Not really. Takt time has a different connotation in this strategy. Think in terms of units of capacity, such as with adding production in chunks of lines, or adding time at the same rate. Instead of changing takt time, what happens more often is that we will adjust the effective working time. The initial thought with a chase strategy is that takt time will have to change all of the time because of the different production rates. However, in practice that is not usually how it is done. Most often, value streams are constructed with a base takt time and operator balance charts to set the staffing level. As the production rate changes, the working time is simply adjusted, by either working more or less hours or adding segments of capacity (another production line or one half of a line, for instance). The takt time, and therefore the pitch, stays the same in each configuration.

For instance, we could start with a line that produces 480 pieces in effective working time of 480 minutes with 40 people (takt time equals 1 minute). If demand went to 960 pieces, the most likely thing to do would be to simply add another line producing 480 pieces in 480 minutes, now making 2 lines producing 960 pieces in 960 minutes, keeping takt time at 1 minute. What we have really done is change the effective working time.

Chase requires:

- Cross-training
- A way to know when to switch jobs during the workday (controlling flow)

- Adding or subtracting labor by using:
  - Temporary employees
  - Overtime
  - Subcontractors
- Staff for peak periods and working on improvements when slow

These points show why a chase strategy is difficult in many environments. As the skill level of the employees increases, this strategy becomes more and more difficult to execute. The other issues listed here, such as cross-training and how to control flow, can be overcome more easily. The staff for peak periods, while a nice fit for a true Lean company, is rarely employed by companies who view labor as the largest controllable cost in a company.

Which of these challenges do you think would be the most difficult to overcome? Why? To some extent, it would depend on the environment, but where skill level is high or labor is scarce, the most difficult task will be adding or subtracting employees. In a union shop with strict rules it may be cross-training.

Hybrid

A hybrid strategy buffers variability with common component inventory (produce to stock) and finishes to order with flexible finishing capacity (also known as postponement). This strategy is a combination of make to stock and make to order, requiring management of an inventory buffer as well as a customer order backlog.

BOM Shape

In the shape in Figure 3.14 many end items are made out of a few subassemblies or intermediates that are themselves made out of many unique raw materials and parts. Examples include a pharmaceutical manufacturer with many package types from a

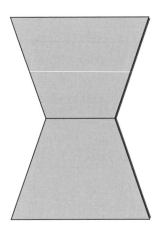

Figure 3.14 A BOM shape that suggests a combination of strategies should be used to schedule production.

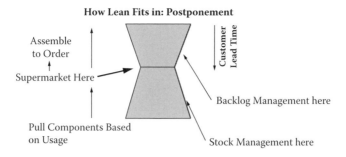

Figure 3.15 Shows how Lean supports a hybrid, or postponement, strategy.

standard product (aspirin), personal computers, and packaged chemicals. This shape lends itself to a postponement strategy.

How Lean Fits In: Postponement

Figure 3.15 shows that the postponement strategy is really a hybrid strategy, employing both backlog management (in the make-to-order segment of production) and make–to-stock management for components. Important to note is that the customer lead time will only be the assemble portion of the process (plus the administrative activities), not the entire manufacturing process. This model thus has the potential to provide a high variety of products plus quick delivery times for the customer.

MPS and Heijunka

In this section we will discuss whether the practice of scheduling end items in ERP systems, called master production scheduling, is the equivalent of the heijunka process, of the varying leveling strategies that we have described in this chapter.

Master Production Schedule

The master production schedule states requirements for individual end items and options by date and quantity. It is constrained by and supports the sales and operations plan. It "disaggregates" the sales and operations plan.

> **Master production schedule (MPS):** The master production schedule is a line on the master schedule grid that reflects the anticipated build schedule for those items assigned to the master scheduler. The master scheduler maintains this schedule, and in turn, it becomes a set of planning numbers that drives material requirements planning. It represents what the company plans to produce expressed in specific configurations, quantities, and dates. The master production schedule is not a sales item forecast that represents a statement of demand. The master production schedule must take into account the forecast,

the production plan, and other important considerations such as backlog, availability of material, availability of capacity, and management policies and goals.

—*APICS Dictionary*, **12th edition**

The master production schedule is the real point at which supply and demand are matched up at the mix level, meaning that in the planning hierarchy, up to this point, we have simply been dealing with aggregate production rates, or rates by product family.

> **Master schedule:** The master schedule is a format that includes time periods (dates), the forecast, customer orders, projected available balance, available-to-promise, and the master production schedule. The master schedule takes into account the forecast; the production plan; and other important considerations such as backlog, availability of material, availability of capacity, and management policies and goals. See: master production schedule.
>
> —*APICS Dictionary*, **12th edition**

The Master Schedule
- The main purpose is to balance supply and demand.
- S&OP deals with volume; master production scheduling deals with mix.
- There is expected to be a detailed schedule behind this.
- Timeframes are set at the master production schedule level.

This is a summary of the role of the master production schedule in a production planning and control system. It is by no means comprehensive in describing the master schedule, but is meant instead to set up the contrast between the MPS and the heijunka processes for later on in this chapter. The last two bullets probably need more clarification: in most instances, the master production schedule is generally viewed as simply driving the material requirements planning portion of the system. This material requirements planning then provides the input to a detailed scheduling process that actually provides the schedule for the factory floor. In most instances the MPS itself is often broken down to a further level of detail to become an end item, or perhaps an assembly level schedule for the factory. Second, timeframes in this sense mean such considerations as the planning horizon for visibility of future requirements as well as any firm portions of the schedule where changes are limited.

One of the primary problems with the traditional ERP approach is that the master production schedule is often overstated, meaning that it contains more production than there is capacity. Why is the MPS often overstated? Because MPS logic says supply is calculated based on the higher of forecast or real demand. The steps:

1. The forecast at the S&OP level equals the decided upon production rate. This is a good start, meaning that at the aggregate level demand and supply are equal.
2. The forecast is disaggregated to the item level and still equals the planned production rate.

3. MPS is run and the supply equals the forecast, and thus the agreed upon production rate. So far, so good.

4. Real demand begins to come into the system over some horizon. At some point 100% of the real demand is in hand.

5. For any item where the real demand exceeds forecast (about half of them statistically in a normal distribution), the supply will be set to equal the real demand. This is the normal rule for master production scheduling programs, and is designed to keep supply and demand in balance.

6. The supply is now greater than the agreed upon production rate, and should be adjusted, but it seldom is.

7. Because the MPS has no visibility of the agreed upon production rate, the system thinks everything is fine because supply and demand are in balance according to the rules.

8. Thus, the master scheduler is on her own because the system has provided no messages to guide her as to what must be done. No messages usually means no action, and the schedule stays overloaded.

The best known and probably most effective way to combat this effect is to set a "planning time fence," where the forecast can no longer drive supply. The problem with this, however, is that to keep the schedule completely clean, the time fence would need to be set to cover the exact amount of time covered by the customer order backlog. This is usually difficult to pinpoint, and may even vary by part number. So overall, this solution has a limited effectiveness for most companies.

Heijunka

Heijunka is defined as "the distribution of production volume and mix evenly over time." Heijunka converts uneven customer pull into even and predictable manufacturing processes. These are textbook definitions of the Japanese word *heijunka*. It is important to note that in its purest sense heijunka is meant to level not just volume but also product mix. Does the conversion of uneven customer pull imply push? Yes, we think it does. See the quote on page 41 from Fugio Cho for more on this.

Work Like the Tortoise, Not the Hare   The chart on the right in Figure 3.16 is more common in most value streams. What causes it to look like this? The main cause is that the value stream does not have a strategy to handle uneven customer demand. Sometimes, even if a strategy is chosen, it can be difficult to implement without the proper tools to support the strategy. Remember, most ERP systems only support a chase strategy. Because of this, it is also common that a chase strategy is implemented without conscious choice. This chase strategy causes uneven output. Other potential causes would be varying work content for the units, so that even if the number of units scheduled is constant, the varying work content of the units causes uneven unit

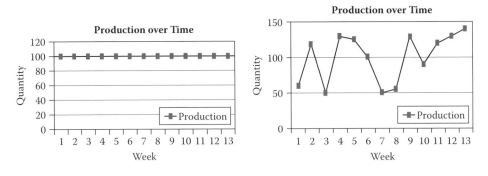

Figure 3.16   Two ways to make 1,300 pieces in thirteen weeks. Which way do you think would be more efficient?

output; uneven flow through the value stream, with large queues, causing outputs to be erratic; the quarter-end "hockey stick" phenomenon, which puts extra pressure to "make the numbers" only when public reporting is due; and quality problems in the value stream.

Obviously, the chart on the left represents the least wasteful way to make thirteen hundred units. Making one hundred per week each week will be less stressful and require less adjustment in terms of people and equipment than the chart on the right, which is erratic and would be difficult to manage effectively.

Heijunka:

- Represents the single point of scheduling for a value stream. "Schedule one point" is one of the seven principles of a Lean value stream as listed in "Learning to See" from LEI.
- Is tightly integrated with the material plan in many instances, but doesn't necessarily drive it. The execution portion of the pull system is not driven by the Heijunka schedule, but is triggered by the usage of parts.

Both of these are rather subtle points but are also very important in understanding the difference between the two production systems: enterprise resource planning vs. Lean manufacturing. In the Lean manufacturing world, a value stream has only one single schedule point, not a series of schedules represented by a master production schedule, an assembly schedule, and then various detailed shop floor schedules for each process or machine.

In the ERP process the master production schedule "drives" the material planning process, meaning that all of the material plans directly depend upon the integrity of the master production scheduling process. The result of this is that if the master production schedule is overstated, either there will be more inventory than necessary to support the production process, or priorities in the factory will be uncertain, or often both.

In the Lean manufacturing process the schedule is placed at a single point in the value stream and all subsequent, downstream processes simply work on either one-piece flow or via a FIFO process, and therefore need no schedule. Prior processes upstream of the schedule would be attached via a pull system, and would simply make what the schedule had pulled out of the supermarket that it supplies, therefore also requiring no schedule. The result of this is that all processes are basically making to the exact same schedule that was put at the single schedule point, and no inventory is built other than that called for by replacing what was used in the supermarket.

To review heijunka:

- The main purpose is to balance demand and capacity.
- S&OP deals with volume and setting takt time (production rate).
- Heijunka is then set to produce at the takt rate.
- Timeframe is an interval.
- Interval deals with mix.

This process keeps the executive S&OP production rate and the heijunka schedule in sync. The difference between balancing demand and supply, and demand and capacity is a subtle but powerful one. The latter is a much more straightforward way to look at the world, in that the job of the scheduler is to simply take customer demand and place it into the factory in the form of a single schedule. Because the heijunka process is capacity oriented, it can directly translate the production rate from the sales and operations plan into a schedule, keeping the two control processes in sync. Because of the nature of the way that Lean thinks about capacity in the terms of setup capability of the process, the timeframe for a heijunka schedule in most cases will be an interval (or every part every interval). The concept of interval defines how the product mix will be handled within the value stream.

Table 3.2 is a summary of the stated objectives of these two approaches to linking demand and supply. It would be best summarized by saying that the production planning and control environments think in terms of trade-offs in the production environment, while the Lean environment thinks in terms of continuous improvement with only perfection as the end goal. Because of this difference in attitude, the two approaches, almost by definition, have a different emphasis on how to view customer demand going into the value stream.

Table 3.2   A Comparison between the Objectives of Master Production Scheduling and Heijunka Scheduling

MASTER PRODUCTION SCHEDULING	HEIJUNKA SCHEDULING
Maintain desired level of customer service	100% customer service
Make best use of resources	No waste
Keep inventories at desired level	No inventories

Note: The heijunka objectives help drive the continuous improvement mindset. While perfection may not be obtainable, it is important to constantly work to make things better.

Concluding Observations

- System support for MPS is poor.
- It generally supports a chase strategy via make-to-stock or flexible capacity approaches, not make-to-order flex of backlog.
- Both MPS and heijunka schedule one level of the BOM only, but they are not similar in too many other aspects.
- One is not a substitute for the other.

It is a commonly held belief that the traditional master production schedule can stand in for the heijunka process in Lean. We hope that we have convinced you that this is not the case. The concluding observations are just to refocus us back on the original topic, which was to provide some insight into whether master production scheduling was an acceptable substitute in the Lean world for the heijunka process. The first point is that if the major concern is to load work to a defined capacity, then the master production scheduling process with its separate rough-cut capacity plan is not the ideal environment to work in. Many of the programs and practices grew up in make-to-stock environments and are set up to work by either trying to keep a fixed inventory level as defined by safety stock, or a flexible capacity approach where the company is committed to build to customer order and will vary capacity to meet those orders, such as in film developing. In Lean, however, we're mainly interested in trying to keep capacity fixed, while varying either backlog or inventories in response to variable customer demand. This model is often not supported in the systems that provide modules for the master production scheduling process.

While both of these approaches schedule one level of the bill of material, the master production schedule is generally accompanied by several other schedules, often driven by the material requirements plan. The heijunka process provides the one and only schedule for the value stream.

In this chapter we have described several approaches to one element of the base of the House of Toyota: leveling. While the ideal situation is to achieve true heijunka, leveling product mix over time, there are many environments where the waste that this approach would create is prohibitive. For these environments we have presented several other options, two of which sacrifice leveling mix (a partial supermarket of finished goods, buffering with backlog) but still achieve leveling, and one that employs flexible capacity to truly chase real demand. If you think of production as having two main elements, a material plan and a capacity plan, what this means is that we have stabilized the capacity plan, while the material plan will vary based on the product mix that must be produced. The shape of the bill of material will determine how much buffer is necessary to enable these strategies to be feasible.

In Chapter 4 we will explore the management of dependent demand materials in a Lean environment. The conclusion is that the most commonly used tool to manage dependent demand materials, material requirements planning, not only isn't necessary in the Lean supply chain, but is the wrong tool in almost all circumstances. Instead, we will suggest that a gross explosion of the production schedule, along with flow, pull, and visual factory, is the correct tool for the job.

4

DEPENDENT DEMAND MATERIALS

In this chapter we will cover flow and FIFO instead of BOM levels, pull systems instead of MRP, long-term planning, short-term planning and execution, and gross explosions versus netting.

All of these topics will be limited to dependent demand materials only.

Dependent demand: Demand that is directly related to or derived from the bill of material structure for other items or end products. Such demands are therefore calculated and need not and should not be forecast.

—*APICS Dictionary*, **12th edition**

We have already addressed independent demand materials in the previous chapter. This chapter presents a radically different answer to how to plan and control dependent demand material than the traditional approach supported by enterprise resource planning (ERP) systems. This new approach revolves around basic Lean principles, such as making material flow, visual factory, and pull. Combined, they eliminate the need for material requirements planning (MRP) as a primary tool for controlling dependent demand material.

We will start with an overview of flow, both one-piece and first-in–first-out (FIFO) flow. Flow is critical to this approach, as it facilitates visual control of work on the factory floor as opposed to controlling it in the computer. Further, flow shortens lead times, which enables more of the bill of material to be made within the customer's (market) lead time. Flow, especially FIFO flow, and shorter lead times allow levels in the bill of material to be eliminated, as parts will no longer be kept in stock in between processing steps. This leads to a simplification of the entire control hierarchy, from fewer transactions to fewer reports and less reliance on forecasts (Figure 4.1).

When we design a value stream we strive to obtain one-piece flow, which has the least waste of any of the methods for connecting processes. Pull is the least preferred method, as we will see later on. When material is produced in batches, inventory tends to accumulate and lead time rises, as material waits in queue for its turn to be processed. Our goal is to establish flow, ideally one-piece flow, and to synchronize process steps so inventory can't accumulate.

Continuous flow is the best method to manufacture because it has the least waste and inventory does not have an opportunity to accumulate. The power of flow is seen in many aspects of a factory, from better visibility of problems to higher quality levels throughout the factory.

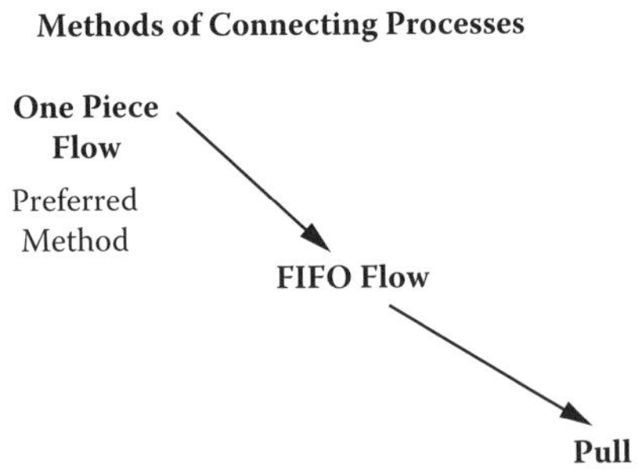

Methods of Connecting Processes

One Piece
Flow

Preferred
Method

FIFO Flow

Pull

Figure 4.1   Shows that there are three choices for how to connect processes in Lean.

True flow has the following aspects:

- The processes and machines are very close together to virtually eliminate walking and motion wastes.
- One piece at a time is processed, leading to better quality.
- Inventory does not accumulate between steps.
- The work is balanced among the operators.
- Work progresses at the pitch rate—meaning no faster or slower than the calculated takt interval.
- Everyone can see at a glance how they are doing, and easily call for help if required.
- Operators don't wander around doing out-of-cycle work like replenishing supplies.
- Waste is identified and removed using work observation and balance charts.
- Staffing can be flexed to account for changing customer demand rates.

Benefits of Creating Flow

Creating flow can be hard, detailed work, but the benefits shown in Figure 4.2 make it worth the effort. It should be your primary focus on the plant floor. These are some of the benefits of implementing flow in the value stream. Note that these benefits are realized across a variety of areas in the value stream, from better quality to reducing

A. Quality: Work is passed directly to next process with no defects	B. Productivity: Minimize wasted movement, warehouses, and double handling	C. Space: Free up floor space for new products
D. Lead Time: Shortest supply chain, highest flexibility to satisfy customer demand	E. Team Member Morale: Value of work is more visible and recognized; teamwork	F. Cost: Reduced Inventory Levels

Figure 4.2   Several of the benefits of creating flow within a value stream.

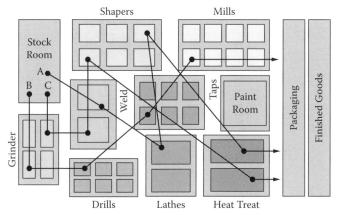

Figure 4.3 This layout is called a functional layout, and is designed to maximize the productivity of the machines and the managers. It causes excessive material movement and long lead times.

the lead time. This is why flow, not pull, should be the emphasis when you design a value stream future state.

Batch Manufacturing

Figure 4.3 shows a typical picture of how material moves through the plant when we first start a Lean transformation. Based on a functional organization, where machines with similar functions (such as welders or grinders) are grouped together, the path of each part is guided by an individual routing. This layout is designed to improve the productivity of the machines, not to improve the flow of material.

Lean Process Flow

In Lean, we attempt to get plant layouts where materials can flow quickly from one process to another. This is done by grouping parts together into product families, based on similar process paths.

In Lean, we attempt to obtain a layout that facilitates material flow (Figure 4.4). By grouping parts that go through roughly the same processes to make value streams, it becomes possible to line the machines up in the sequence in which the parts will be processed. This type of layout will help reduce the wastes of waiting, transportation, motion, and inventory. Occasionally, this type of layout calls for more machines than a functional layout, but there are solutions to this. For more about determining needed machine capacity, reference Kevin Duggan, *Creating Mixed Model Value Streams*, and the training class "Creating Flow through Shared Resources," Duggan and Associates, Inc.

Figure 4.5 is another diagram of possible plant layouts and the strengths of each. The functional layout, as mentioned before, is designed to optimize the productivity

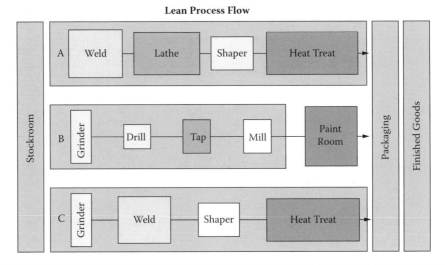

Figure 4.4   Material flow in a Lean layout. Organizing based on commonality of material processes (product families) facilitates straight-line flow.

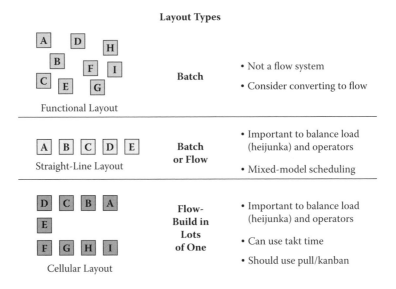

Figure 4.5   Three possible plant layouts, with the least desirable on top and the most desirable on the bottom. The cellular layout facilitates flow and is the most flexible for changing staffing.

of the machines. The other two layouts are designed to facilitate flow. The cellular layout is more flexible because it allows the operators flexibility to perform different combinations of jobs due to the fact that the walking distance between processes is short, as opposed to the other two layouts. So a single operator could perhaps perform processes A, B, and C, or perhaps A, B, and I, or A, H, and I, etc.

Figure 4.6 shows three possibilities for production cells. The shape of cells can vary depending on the available space. Machines or workstations are arranged in the particular process sequence. U-shaped cells are the basic configuration, but I-shaped

Production Cell Varieties

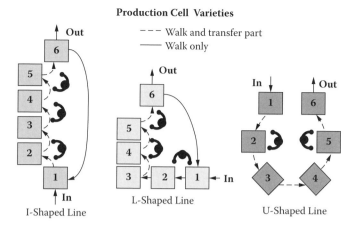

Figure 4.6 The shape of the cell is largely dictated by the space available in the plant. The U shape is the best because it has the least walking distance to start the loop again and allows greater labor utilization by allowing people to operate more than one machine. Additionally, it enables capacity flexibility by allowing capacity to flex with the amount of staffing in the cell.

and L-shaped cells are used where they would be more effective. A straight-line or I-shaped cell is often the best pattern for long, narrow buildings. The L-shaped configuration may work best for square-shaped buildings when several similar process lines are nested together. The U-shaped cell is the most common and allows the work cell to be laid out using a fairly small footprint. This design has the most flexibility and often the least walking for the operators. It is important that people who work in a cell work well together.

The key benefits of cells include:

- Facilitate visual control (on local boards)
- Create common drop-off and pick-up areas
- No wasted return transport required; material and workers end up where they began

Operator Balance Chart

Operator balance chart: A graphic tool that assists the creation of continuous flow in a multistep, multioperator process by distributing operator work elements in relation to takt time. (Also called an operator loading diagram or a yamazumi board.)

—Lean Lexicon, **4th edition**

Operator balance charts (Figure 4.7) are an important element of standard work, as they show in detail which activities will be performed by which operator, and they also make sure that no operator has more than a takt time's worth of work to do on a part. This ensures that the work can proceed at the proper pace.

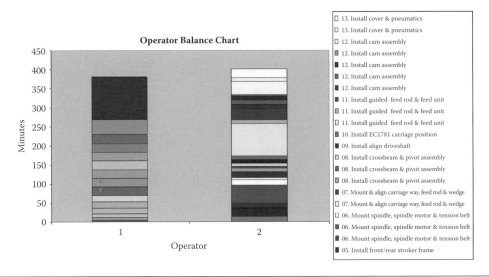

Figure 4.7   A simplified operator balance chart, showing the distribution of activities across two operators. Planned cycle time was 400 minutes, takt time was 440 minutes.

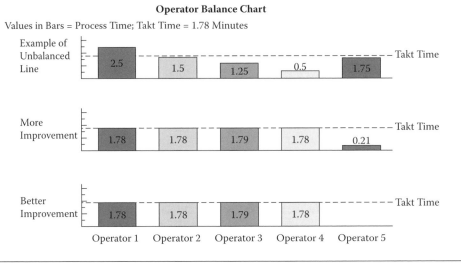

Figure 4.8   Operator balance charts—showing Lean improvements.

Figure 4.8 shows the time required for each operator in a cell. The value of each bar is the total time of all of the operations for each operator. The takt time of the process for the cell is shown as a horizontal dotted line across the top of the chart. Any deviation between the takt time bar and the operator bars represents waste—an opportunity for improvement using Lean tools.

Product flow must keep pace with takt time to avoid overproduction or late delivery. Cycle time is the actual production rate, which tells us how often we can produce a product with the given resources. The unbalanced line graph shows a cell that will have trouble meeting the takt time. Operator 1 has too much work to do on each piece, and will fall behind the takt time. Operators 2, 3, and 4 do not have enough work, and will need to help Operator 1 to catch up once in a while. Flow in this cell will be sporadic.

The more improvement graph is well balanced for the first four operators, with only Operator 5 having too little to do. The job of Operator 5 becomes to help reduce enough waste to eliminate the need for Operator 5. Flow will be good in this cell.

The final chart in the figure shows the result of the efforts of Operator 5, who has now been moved into another cell to help on the continuous improvement effort.

Batch Flow

Figure 4.9 shows the flow when five pieces are moved from one operation to the next; in other words, the batch move size is five. Assuming that the line is empty when the batch is started, each of the five parts in the batch takes one minute at a process, for a total of five minutes per batch at each workstation. Therefore, it takes a total of twenty minutes for a batch of five parts to complete the four process steps.

Historically, manufacturing companies had large batch sizes to maximize machine utilization because of long changeover times. Tools such as single-minute exchange of die (SMED) drive down changeover times and allow for smaller batch sizes. Ideally, the batch size should be one. Reducing batch sizes reduces the amount of work in process (WIP), which in turn may reduce inventory costs and lead time. Smaller batch sizes may shorten the overall production cycle, and that may enable faster delivery of customer orders. (The authors are "hedging our bets" on these improvements making any difference in a non-Lean environment. Theoretically these should reduce costs, lead time, and production cycles, but we have seen "piecemeal" improvements not really improving anything. Of course, all of these contribute to becoming Lean.)

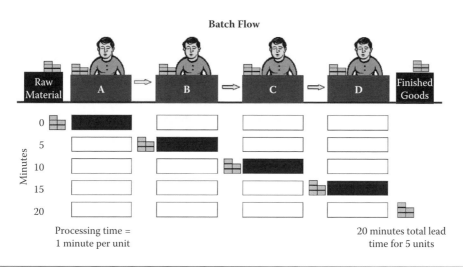

Figure 4.9 How batch size can impact lead time.

It would be nice, of course, to be able to achieve single-piece lot sizes for all items in a value stream. Because of changeover times, this is often not possible. Does this mean that one-piece flow can't be achieved in these conditions? No, here is another way to think about this: the lot quantity does not have to equal the move quantity. "The transfer batch need not, and many times should not, equal the process batch" (Eli Goldratt). It is fairly common for assembly lines to run many of the same models down the line sequentially, but because of the assembly line they do so using one-piece flow. This same concept can be extended to the connection between any two processes. Where ERP reporting still exists, however, it may still be very important to achieve small lot sizes, as many ERP systems still make it difficult to have a single material lot scattered across several processes.

One-Piece Flow

Figure 4.10 shows how the flow improves when the move quantity is reduced to one. The lead time has been reduced from twenty minutes to eight minutes, a 60% reduction. Do any of the four operators have to work harder or faster to achieve this? No. What is the cost of this? Although there are many more material moves, from four in the five-piece move to twenty in the one-piece move, does this drive up any costs in a Lean setup? This is why there is an emphasis on placing subsequent operations in close proximity to each other when you lay out the value stream.

So to reiterate: Do the lot size and the batch move size need to be the same quantity? The answer is no, with a caveat. Many ERP systems make "splitting" a batch very

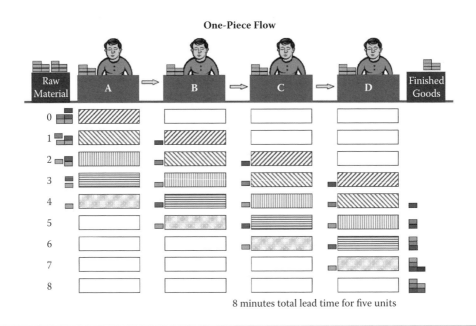

8 minutes total lead time for five units

Figure 4.10 How one-piece flow reduces lead time.

difficult, as they use the work order, tied to the lot size, as both a mechanism for guiding the order via a routing with the shop paper, and as a feedback mechanism for shop floor control. Ask: Does your current system allow the flexibility to have a work order at multiple processes at the same time? If so, make sure you differentiate between lot sizes and move sizes when designing your value stream.

First-in–First-Out Flow

First-in–first-out (FIFO): FIFO is used to regulate flow between two disconnected processes where one-piece flow is not possible. The principle and practice of maintaining precise production and conveyance sequence by ensuring that the first part to enter a process or storage location is also the first part to exit. (This ensures that stored parts do not become obsolete and that quality problems are not buried in inventory.) FIFO is a necessary condition for pull system implementation.

—Lean Lexicon, **4th edition**

Where we can't obtain one-piece flow, we try for FIFO. The idea is simply that the process performs work in the same sequence as it arrived. FIFO shares many of the same characteristics as a pull system, in that it has a maximum size, and therefore serves to prevent overproduction. FIFO is used to regulate and manage flow between two disconnected processes. FIFO is not used to store inventory. It is used to manage inventory for flow. An assembly line may be thought of as a kind of FIFO lane (Figure 4.11).

FIFO is one way to regulate a pull system between two decoupled processes when it is not practical to maintain an inventory of all possible part variations in a supermarket because the parts are one-of-a-kind, have short shelf lives, or are very expensive but required infrequently. In this application, the removal of the one part in a FIFO lane by the consuming process automatically triggers the production of one additional part by the supplying process.

—Lean Lexicon, **4th edition**

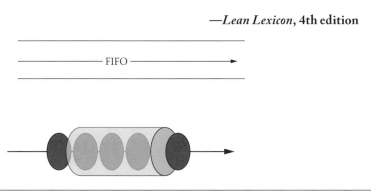

Figure 4.11 FIFO lanes are used where one-piece flow cannot be achieved. They can absorb many of the processing differences between two processes, such as different cycle times, different changeover times, etc.

FIFO lanes can be used to connect two processes that have different process capabilities, such as cycle times, setup times, up times, scrap rates, etc. Because the processes both have to be able to achieve takt time or the same interval, they will make the same number of pieces over an interval. This means that the minimum size for the FIFO lane is the greatest difference in production that would occur within each interval. How large is determined by several factors: difference in work time between processes, and difference in flow rates between processes. Regardless of formulas, however, the maximum will mainly depend on the tolerance of the value stream management for unplanned downtime.

Typical FIFO Lane Rules

- Place incoming parts in the rear of the lane.
- Use parts from the front of the lane.
- Production for the supplying process can only occur when the lane has an empty space.
- The lane should be located near the supplying process.

FIFO lanes control overproduction in the same way that a supermarket does, since production should only occur when there is an open space in the lane. Rules for FIFO lanes should be simple and easy to follow. FIFO lanes have some of the same characteristics as a supermarket: if the lane is full, then the supplying operation should not produce any more parts. This prevents overproduction in the same way that the supermarket does. There are many ways to control the FIFO lane, but it needs to be located near the supplying operation, since it is their responsibility to keep it full.

Question: What should the supplying operator do if the lane is full, besides not make any more parts? Answer: Go find out what happened to disrupt the flow of parts and help fix the problem.

Material Planning

Now that we understand a bit about flow, we will turn our attention to the material planning process for dependent demand materials. We will start with a brief discussion about the various timeframes over which materials are planned.

Material Planning Horizons

- Long-term planning
- Short-term planning
- Execution

We position this discussion at the beginning of this section because it is important to understand that these three timeframes require different levels of detail, which then implies that different tools are probably needed for each horizon. It is also important to understand that the length of these horizons will be different for different industries, with inherent challenges being different as well. For instance, the long-term planning in the aircraft industry may well cover five years, while in consumer goods it may be less than one year. (Think in terms of the industries' material planning, not their business planning.)

Long-Term Planning
- Long-term planning should be mainly for capacity and scarce materials.
- Rough cut planning or MRP?
- MRP typically understates long-term requirements. This is because inventory reductions are often overstated in the planning system.

Most long-term planning should simply be to coordinate capacity plans through the supply chain. Therefore, long-term planning should not be concerned with product mix, but instead product volumes, operating at the takt time level of planning. This should immediately bring to mind the positioning of the executive sales and operation plan, which also dealt at the product family level and not the mix level. This means that a rough-cut planning process associated with the executive sales and operations plan should provide all of the information necessary to synchronize the supply chain in this time horizon. MRP could be used, but it isn't recommended for the following reasons:

1. Because inventory is netted in the MRP process, the requirements at the purchased parts level are typically understated, unless a special MRP run can be made with the inventory that is supposed to stay, being set as safety stock in the system.
2. The MRP run implies a degree of precision that simply doesn't exist in this timeframe.
3. MRP operates at the mix level, and this is not usually necessary in the long term.

Why would you have to plan at the mix level in the long term? There really aren't many reasons to do this, but a few things that we can think of are material scarcity, where a component or raw material is not generally available, or long lead time items for special items.

Supply Chain Issues for Long-Term Planning
- The first question in this section should be: Are you buying capacity or items in the long term?
  - If capacity, rough-cut capacity from the executive S&OP plan should be used to plan this activity.
  - If items, you must decide how to reconcile this long-term plan with short-term actual plans.

When we talk here of capacity, we are equating it with the volume from the executive sales and operations planning (S&OP) plan, not the product mix handled by master production schedule or heijunka. The concept, which has been around for a long time, is that it should only be necessary to commit to a production level for suppliers in the long term, thus ensuring an uninterrupted flow of material. Mix should only be committed to at the last moment. This will create some problems if you must deal only at the mix level with your suppliers, because mix is typically more uncertain in the long term than volume is. It may be useful to remember that Toyota has solved these issues by freezing and leveling the production plan for at least two to three months, and has shortened the supply chain so that significant product activity through the entire supply chain can occur in that frozen horizon.

Short-Term Planning
  Supply Chain Issues for Buying Materials
  • Choices for material purchasing:
    • Pull
    • MRP
    • Rough-cut planning
  • All will have problems on long lead time items.
  • Mix sensitivity matters here.

The point here is that you need to select a tool that properly supports the strategy that has been chosen. On long lead time items, where there is no actual demand to drive requirements, none of the options will really work that well, so again, you should go with the one that is being used to plan the other items. The higher the mix sensitivity—in other words, the wider the bill of materials (BOM) is on the bottom— the more the leveling strategy is important, to the point where leveling mix as well as volume becomes the best strategy for managing the material. How would you decide which method to use?

The easiest is to use the same tool that is being used on the items with short lead times.

Material Planning and Pull
  • If we have only flow and supermarkets (pull) in a value stream, then MRP is not needed.
  • A supermarket wants to simply replace what was just used, so gross to net logic is not a proper approach for managing a supermarket.

This is a difficult concept for most supply chain managers to accept, but the idea is simple. If the supermarket contains the correct inventory level, then the inventory can be ignored when determining what needs to be made. In other words, we will simply do a gross explosion of requirements for planning and replace what is used in execution. If the inventory level is not correct, the pull system will have a different mechanism to correct this than MRP would have anyway, so using MRP with a supermarket is not a good solution.

Why not MRP?
- MRP is inventory centric. It treats inventory as a fixed target, while in many cases we would like to treat capacity as a fixed target.
- It is very difficult to teach MRP that we simply want to replace what was just used. MRP wants to net the inventory, because the inventory result is what MRP is programmed to worry about. We do not want to net the inventory in Lean, because the usual logic will be to simply remake the inventory, not eliminate it by using it. The inventory is there because the value stream needs it there right now.

We went over the buffering possibilities in an early chapter, and the same concepts apply to dependent demand supermarkets. For the most part, value streams have difficulty pursuing a pure chase strategy. We reviewed this approach when we talked about MPS and heijunka, and the same holds true for MRP and supermarkets.

We feel that a gross explosion of the BOM is all that is needed for both short- and long-term planning. A gross explosion assumes that whatever will be used will also be replenished, which is what we generally do in a supermarket. This solves the problem of having the inventory "net" the demand requirements and not pass on supply requirements to the supplying work center. It also solves what we feel is a problem with MRP understating long-term requirements.

We believe that the long-term requirements are understated by MRP for several reasons. First, there is rarely safety stock set on dependent demand items in most planning systems, and yet there is often significant inventory present. MRP believes that this inventory will go away, and therefore nets it out of the requirements for supply. Our feeling is that if this inventory was going to go away, it would be gone already. There are many factors contributing to the presence of this inventory, many of which cannot be solved or prevented. It would be far more accurate to plan for the inventory to be the same at the end of each planning cycle. Second, most capacity plans are set in the long term, often using rough-cut planning techniques using the production plan. This plan does not net dependent demand inventory, and therefore plans for all levels of the value stream to make the full set of parts for the full production plan. With this level of capacity in place, the MRP netted plan understates the amount of material needed to operate at this level of capacity. Since it is the job of the supervisors and managers of the plant to keep productivity high, the result is that they will need to build at a higher production level than the material plan calls for, causing shortages to appear from the plant floor perspective (not enough work) when the planner sees none.

What would you have to do to make MRP work as a driver for a pull system? Set a safety stock level to be equal to the current inventory level each time MRP is run. This effectively sets the inventory level to zero. This is difficult because it must be done one part number at a time. Ignoring the inventory will make MRP work the same way as a gross explosion, but this would be a lot of work to simply fool a computer program. It would be easier to find a more correct tool for the job. To make MRP behave with the same logic as a supermarket, we would need to have the entire supermarket inventory set as safety stock, so that whatever the usage requirements are get passed on as supply. This is generally not practical, since in most cases the safety stock is a static number set by item, which would mean that you would need to reset the safety stock number manually to match the current inventory before each MRP run. A program could be written to do this, but it would be just as easy to write a gross explosion program and skip MRP altogether.

Short-Term Supply Chain Planning   We now turn our attention to a short-term planning tool, which needs to take individual part numbers' demand and supply into account.

- Choices for material purchasing include:
    - Pull
    - MRP
    - Rough-cut planning

We will start with the last choice, rough-cut planning, as a short-term planning option. Because we have moved into the short-term planning horizon, some level of detail about mix is now required. Because of this, rough cut is not an appropriate tool for this horizon. Rough cut is typically for resource planning in the long term, and in the short term we need to deal with individual items. Rough-cut planning is mainly a tool to do long-range resource planning, and rarely contains part level detail. Because of this, even though it does not net inventory, we do not consider it a viable option for short-term planning in the Lean environment, just as it is not in the traditional planning environment.

Supermarket Pull System
Supermarket: In Lean production, a storage facility within a manufacturing facility where processes can withdraw materials, parts, components, or finished goods as needed. Restocking is triggered by actual demand. Stocks are replaced by new production only as items are withdrawn from the supermarket, which makes it easy to see what has been used and avoids overproduction.

—APICS Lean Enterprise Workshop Series

A supermarket is a managed amount of inventory that allows for a pull system: it can also be called an inventory buffer, and can contain raw materials, finished items, or work-in-process items (Figure 4.12). Supermarkets are located between processes and contain a predetermined amount of inventory. The supermarket supplies downstream processes without the interruptions caused by product variations or batch sizes. Kanbans, or signals, may be used to indicate a replenishment request.

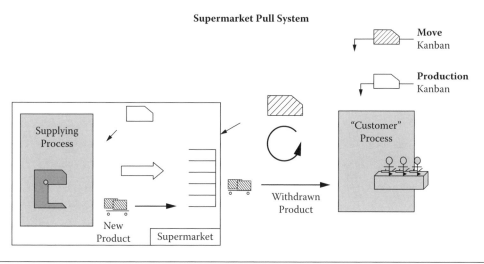

Figure 4.12   The mechanics of a simple supermarket system.

A supermarket system serves several purposes, including:

• Provides a way to control production between disconnected flows
• Gives production instruction without schedules
• Prevents overproduction (if sized correctly and rules followed)

Detailed Single-Card Kanban
Pull (system): 1) In production, the production of items only as demanded for use or to replace those taken for use. 2) In material control, the withdrawal of inventory as demanded by the using operations. Material is not issued until a signal comes from the user.

—APICS Dictionary, **12th edition**

In pull production, a downstream operation, whether within the same facility or in a separate facility, provides information to the upstream operation, often via a kanban card, about what part or material is needed, the quantity needed, and when and where it is needed. Nothing is produced by the upstream supplier process until the downstream customer process signals a need. This is the opposite of push production.

—Lean Lexicon, **4th edition**

Kanban can be used in manufacturing, material control, and distribution (Figure 4.13). The most common type of kanban is a physical card that is placed in a container of parts. When the components are used, the kanban card is removed from the container and sent back to the supplying process (including purchasing) to signal that replenishment is needed. The requests are processed in a FIFO sequence. A simple two-bin system, where a bin is refilled any time one is emptied, is a common type of kanban, with the bin itself serving as the replenishment signal.

Detailed Single Card Kanban

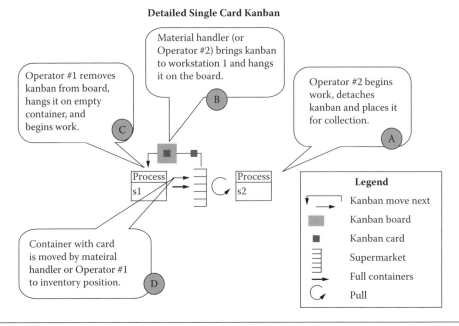

Material handler (or Operator #2) brings kanban to workstation 1 and hangs it on the board. **B**

Operator #1 removes kanban from board, hangs it on empty container, and begins work. **C**

Operator #2 begins work, detaches kanban and places it for collection. **A**

Container with card is moved by mateiral handler or Operator #1 to inventory position. **D**

Process s1 → Process s2

Legend

	Kanban move next
	Kanban board
	Kanban card
	Supermarket
	Full containers
	Pull

Figure 4.13

Simple Product Kanban Operation

Kanban: A method of Just-in-Time production that uses standard containers or lot sizes with a single card attached to each. It is a pull system in which work centers signal with a card that they wish to withdraw parts from feeding operations or suppliers. The Japanese word Kanban, loosely translated, means card, billboard, or sign.

—APICS Dictionary, **12th edition**

Figure 4.14 illustrates the workings of a kanban card operation. As a container is pulled from the supermarket inventory, a kanban card is sent to the supplying process to make a replacement quantity. Typically, the card will hang on a board next to the supplying operation. Alternatively, a kanban square can be used, which can be a

Simple Product Kanban Operation

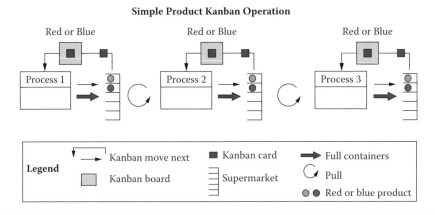

Figure 4.14   The mechanics of a simple one-card kanban system.

rectangle or square painted on the factory floor. The signal to replenish is not a card, but the fact that the square is empty. The example shows a kanban that contains two products, red and blue. If a red product is used, then a kanban card indicating to replenish red is sent back. If blue is used, then a blue kanban will be sent.

The Two-Card System   The two cards are typically a withdrawal or move card, and a production card (Figure 4.15). Note that the production card stays at a work center, cycling from back to front. The move kanban stays between a pair of workstations. In each case, there may be several cards in a loop. "If the source and point of use processes are not close, or there are multiple points of use for the material, it makes sense to define both replenishment and withdrawal loops (a two-card system)" (Christopher Gray, "The Lean Standard System").

Execution
- Kanban is both a planning and an execution tool, since the card signals both a need for replenishment of material and an authorization to replenish.
- MRP, on the other hand, relies on work orders, purchase orders, or repetitive and supplier schedules to provide the execution of the plan.

The kanban system is better able to handle incremental increases or decreases in inventory, since it is easy to add or subtract a card from the Kanban board as needed. The MRP system is more cumbersome to do this with. The long-term material plan can be based on the production plan from the S&OP process and a gross explosion later on of the heijunka schedule. This plan sets the supermarket size and the number

The Two-Card System

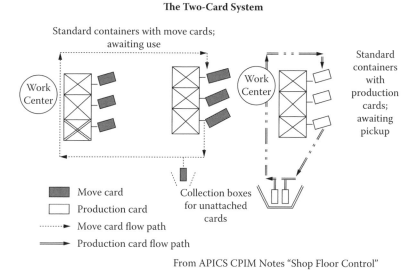

From APICS CPIM Notes "Shop Floor Control"

Figure 4.15   The mechanics of a more complex, two-card kanban system. The two-card system is used by Toyota and increasingly by many others.

of kanban that will be circulating in the loop. The short-term plan is based on the actual usage of the parts, as we have already seen.

Mix Issues

- In a pure heijunka environment, mix is much less of an issue. Because the same sets of parts are used over and over again, flow will work for supply.
- A non-mix-leveled schedule environment, where a particular item is needed next, requires some lead time.
- The key question is: Can we afford to hold all items in stock? Or can lead times to the customer be long enough, and production lead times short enough, to afford to build to order?

Pull systems will have better results in a mix-leveled environment, and conversely, the more variable the mix, the more you should try to implement flow instead of pull. The more flow is achieved, and the shorter the lead time for production, the farther back in the product structure the production schedule can be placed, and more and more of the production can be performed against real demand rather than on speculation. In the Toyota Production System, the dealers' orders are placed and fixed long enough into the future to cover a significant portion of the supply chain lead time, making for a very efficient planning environment. If you don't have that luxury, then a strategy needs to be developed to answer the questions above. Such a strategy would need to include: where the schedule will be placed, where inventory will be held, how the value stream will be buffered against demand uncertainty, and what will be our expected level of customer service by adopting this strategy.

In this chapter we have reviewed the supply chain issues around planning and controlling dependent demand materials. We began the chapter with a quick review of creating flow, which is critical in Lean, especially in environments where mix is highly variable and supermarkets are wasteful. Creating flow shortens lead times and eliminates levels in the bill of materials, lessening the numbers of items that must be planned and controlled. We have made the important differentiation between the various time horizons, allowing us to better select the proper tool for each job, namely, using the executive sales and operations planning production rate, along with rough cut planning, for long-term material planning, and gross explosion of the production schedule, flow, and pull for short-term planning and control. We also reviewed the use of materials requirements planning in these timeframes, concluding that MRP is not the correct tool to use for dependent demand material planning in a Lean environment.

In the next chapter we will cover capacity management and shop floor control. And surprisingly enough, our close friends flow and pull will again play a prominent role in the solutions offered.

5

Capacity Management and Shop Floor Control

In this chapter we will cover several very important topics that have to do with capacity planning, including capacity planning and takt time; flow, pull, and capacity control; and scheduling for capacity control. In this chapter you will, among other things, learn to compare traditional capacity requirements planning to Lean tools such as operator balance charts, understand the process of capacity planning using takt time and interval, and see how flow and visual factory replace shop floor control.

We will start with some definitions of capacity planning, and then contrast the traditional approach and tool set for capacity planning with its Lean counterparts. We will close the chapter with a review of shop floor control.

> **Capacity planning:** The process of determining the amount of capacity required to produce in the future. This process may be performed at an aggregate or product-line level (resource requirements planning), at the master-scheduling level (rough-cut capacity planning), and at the material requirements planning level (capacity requirements planning).
>
> *—APICS Dictionary*, **12th edition**

What are we trying to control, as supply chain or materials managers, with capacity planning? Hint: It is not capacity. If you look at the basics, going back to Plossl and Wight, two influential developers of the operations management profession, capacity planning is a way to control inventories. The use of capacity planning was simply a "lever" to help control inventory—typically applied in sales and operations planning (S&OP). As we have stated several times already and will several times again, the main focus of the traditional planning and control system is to manage inventory, so this should really not come as a surprise.

How a system calculates capacity is another issue that we will discuss in depth later, but at a high level, it is simply a calculation of work center "use," similar to what material requirements planning (MRP) calculates in a materials plan. In Lean, we are simply taking this same concept—using capacity to control inventory—and applying it in a different way than what you are accustomed to.

There are several other purposes for capacity planning and control:

- Do we have the resources to produce, in general, what we think we will need? This is a general approach, or what is referred to as rough-cut capacity planning. This is used only to determine if your planned level of constrained resources—machines, labor, or material—will be enough to support your chosen production rate.

- Is my plan valid? Is it attainable? The second capacity check is the sanity check on your actual schedule, generated within the detailed materials planning cycle. Here, you typically look at the load levels of your work centers and sometimes constrained resources (as above) to see if they are under- or overloaded. More or less work can/should be put into the work center as needed.

We will first deal with this section of the standard system, rough-cut planning (Figure 5.1). This is a macro level capacity check using rough-cut or resource planning—checking overall or constrained resource utilization. It is generally applied both at the executive sales and operations planning level and with the master production schedule. This is a sanity check of overall capability—based on what is known about plant, equipment, and staffing, checking to see if the rough plan can be made with some reasonable certainty.

Resource: Anything that adds value to a good or service in its creation, production, or delivery.

—*APICS Dictionary*, **12th edition**

Rough-cut planning typically is only performed on the critical resources, the ones that will determine the capability of the value stream to achieve the production rate desired. This resource list is not limited to the machines and people in the value stream, but may include such items as suppliers' value streams, transportation, or money.

To accomplish this capacity check, we need just a few pieces of information: the production plan, stating how many units of product are to be made in each time period, and a bill of resources.

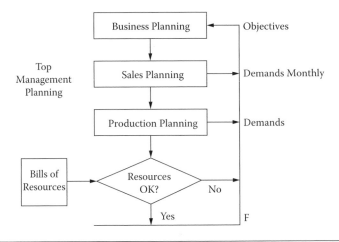

Figure 5.1   The long-term section of the traditional planning and control hierarchy.

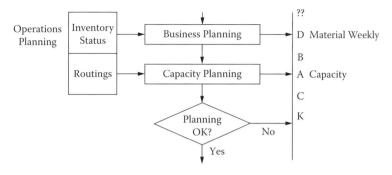

Figure 5.2   Diagram of the detailed level of planning and capacity checking.

Bill of resources: A listing of the required capacity and key resources needed to manufacture one unit of a selected item or family.

—APICS Dictionary, **12th edition**

The bill of resources approach sets factors for resource usage per unit of production, using simplifying assumptions about the detail (mix). This factor is multiplied by the units of production in the production plan to yield an amount of the resource that will be used by the plan. This is compared to the amount of each resource available, and a determination of the feasibility of the plan is made. It is our feeling that this process is applicable to both the traditional and Lean environments. For instance, we may determine that every unit of production in a product family would require one person working in the value stream; people could be defined as a resource and a factor of one could be entered in the bill of resources.

We will also cover the more detailed section of capacity planning, shown in Figure 5.2. This is a micro-view of planning—the sanity check we mentioned—using the plan generated by MRP and seeing how the plan impacts the work centers or resource use. We see that the output from MRP feeds into capacity planning, so labor hours or machine capacity is exploded (via routings) into a capacity plan.

Detailed capacity planning starts with inputs at the work center level. These include shop calendar information—when the work center is working overall, how many machines—as well as factors such as utilization, efficiency, and average queue and wait times.

Utilization: A measure (usually expressed as a percentage) of how intensively a resource is being used to produce a good or service. Utilization compares actual time used to available time. Traditionally, utilization is the ratio of direct time charged (runtime plus setup time to the clock time available).

—APICS Dictionary, **12th edition**

Efficiency: A measurement (usually expressed as a percentage) of the actual output to the standard output expected. Efficiency measures how well something is performing relative to existing standards.

—APICS Dictionary, **12th edition**

To perform detailed capacity planning, we need the following data:

- Work center data: Rated or calculated capacity, the amount of work that the resource can do. At this point there is typically some divergence of opinion regarding how much capacity is really available in the work center. Theoretical capacity can be discounted for planning because it rarely can be achieved.

Theoretical capacity: The maximum output capability, allowing no adjustments for preventive maintenance, unplanned downtime, shutdown, and so forth.

—*APICS Dictionary*, **12th edition**

However, this can be used as a target for Lean activities. Demonstrated capacity does have some advantages, but can be misleading if not calculated and used correctly.

Demonstrated capacity: Proven capacity calculated from actual performance data, usually expressed as the average number of items produced multiplied by the standard hours per item.

—*APICS Dictionary*, **12th edition**

It has been established that the use of calculated or rated capacity is ideal. This is simply available work time × utilization × efficiency (all for that specific work center).
- Routing data, containing setup and runtimes for each operation. Routing data are another input that details the path that the work order (planned or released) will take through the shop.
- Work orders, containing the part numbers, dates, and quantities of planned production (from MRP).

The output of capacity planning is projected capacity utilization, typically by work center. As we mentioned previously, the actual work orders, quantities, and dates complete the data needed to calculate capacity requirements, and this output is typically some sort of load profile by work center that details by shift/day how much of the available capacity for the work center is planned on being used. Unfortunately, the planning portion of most systems treats capacity as infinite, so the work order inputs will either use all of the available capacity, exceed the available capacity, or underuse the available capacity. However, this is where the skills of a master scheduler/planner come in.

The next step involves doing something with the MRP output that includes both material and capacity (labor/machine) availability. This step in the formulation of production activity control (PAC) is a close-in look at actual work order scheduling using the results of the dependent demand calculations in MRP —both buy and make.

Production activity control (PAC): The function of routing and dispatching the work to be accomplished through the production facility and of performing supplier control.

PAC encompasses the principles, approaches, and techniques needed to schedule, control, measure, and evaluate the effectiveness of production operations.

—APICS Dictionary, **12th edition**

This can take the form of daily or weekly schedules that may extend out over the short-term planning horizon—a few weeks to several months, depending on the environment.

PAC is used to control the release of shop/work orders into the shop, again based on the balancing act that the master scheduler/planner performs (assuming that there are typically priority conflicts, as well as material and labor/work center constraints or shortages). We'll discuss shop floor control in more detail toward the end of this chapter.

Issues with Traditional Capacity Planning

The largest issue with traditional capacity planning is that the system allows for infinite capacity. When looking at the system logic for this, it really was an easy way to approach this issue. Traditionally, there are too many variables for most systems to try to account for, so in this case, the easiest answer was to have the user oversee priority control/capacity management. For example, don't schedule more work than can be handled; if capacity is 7.6 hours, then don't schedule more than that. The upshot of this, however, is that by the time a problem is identified in the capacity planning process, a large amount of the planning process has been completed. This raises two other issues: when a problem is identified, it is often difficult to identify the source, in particular which master production schedule orders are contributing to the capacity problem, and second, since the planning process is often quite time-consuming, there is a reluctance to start over again. The temptation caused by both of these issues is to simply leave the problem and move on, hoping for the best and making adjustments in execution as needed. Unfortunately, there are constant deviations from what was planned, and these changes often require the established schedule to be changed. The more unstable an environment—poor schedule attainment, unreliable suppliers, etc.—the more challenging it is to make a long-lasting, single schedule. This drove a significant amount of users to not use scheduling per se, but to rely more on expediting. Although this seems like a good idea, it only makes things worse.

Unfortunately, many organizations have struggled with trying to control capacity manually from the master production schedule, mainly from having difficulty in hiring or training a good master production scheduler or not being able to effectively control their priorities, as sales-focused companies don't like to say no to customers, even if there is no possible way to fulfill a customer order as desired. Master production scheduling is a difficult job, especially if you are not pursuing a chase strategy, as explained in Chapters 2 and 3, in which case the planning system gives you very little support. If you are pursuing a variable inventory or a variable backlog strategy, you are mostly on your own, which in many environments, where there are lots of end items or variants, this is very difficult to manage effectively.

As computing power became cheaper, finite planning became popular, at least within the higher-end systems. The biggest issue here was that all the variables could not be configured and many companies that invested in these modules simply wasted their money.

Another significant issue is that traditional capacity planning focuses only on the machines, while in many environments the real constraint is the number of people and their skill sets. This is especially true in high-mix environments, where there are often more machines than people to run them. This people constraint is sometimes difficult to model in traditional capacity requirements planning (CRP) systems, especially as the skill sets for performing the work become more and more specialized.

The bottom line about capacity requirements planning: While far from scientific, the following may provide some real insight on the effectiveness of traditional capacity requirements planning. Over a short period of time, Bill has asked his audiences at several of his talks, covering the APICS International Conference and several other meetings of materials management types, "How many of you run/use capacity requirements planning?" So far this informal survey has covered about two hundred professionals, and no one has raised their hands to say they run CRP. Surely someone somewhere runs CRP, but it would seem they are in the minority. Further, in reviewing the Operations Management Body of Knowledge Framework published by APICS, there is only one section on capacity planning, and no section at all on CRP. While there are lots of mentions of capacity planning and control, there is virtually no detail on CRP in this important reference on operations management. We think this speaks volumes about the effectiveness of the CRP process.

Capacity Planning in Lean

In its simplest form, capacity planning in Lean does resemble the capacity planning that you are used to, so this may be a pretty simple "translation" (from ERP to Lean) for you. Your first iteration of capacity planning will be in planning your value stream. Can you produce to takt?

The day-to-day capacity planning will be dependent on whether you can achieve flow in the value stream. If you can, then capacity planning is moot because of the way your value stream is set up, with all processes balanced to takt and connected via flow. However, most companies will not be able to achieve flow across the entire value stream, mainly because of machine setups. In the case of value stream loops that have significant setup times, the interval that is set will determine the capacity required. We look at flow as being one-piece or continuous flow, or first-in–first-out (FIFO) flow. One-piece flow can be between two or more work centers, where the cycle times plus setup times of the processes are less than takt time, so no work in process (WIP) is required between the activities (work centers). In most manufacturing operations, flow is used internally, between processes, where we can control the production schedule using buffers, and balance work to takt time. Flow between value streams is extremely difficult, especially trying to achieve flow to the customer, because demand patterns and lead times do not match takt and process lead times. Just because you can produce at takt does not mean your customers will order at that exact rate or in the quantities that you can produce with your current capacity. That is why most Lean organizations use a finished goods supermarket, or other buffer against variability of demand. The fact that Toyota achieves flow in the extended supply chain is a sign of just how strong the Toyota Production System is. We can attribute this to the Heijunka process, which completely levels mix, and the frozen horizon on the Heijunka schedule.

Let's look at a completed value stream map and see where flow is appropriate (Figure 5.3). Before we do anything else in planning our future state, we should first check to see if the overall process can meet customer demand. To do this, we compare takt to process times. Takt in this example is 1.78 minutes and cycle times are all under takt. (We will cover this in more detail later in this chapter.) We don't need to look at operator balance charts in this example because we are going to focus only on areas where we can flow. Where do you think we can implement one-piece flow, based on the map data? There is one place where we can do flow, and that is at assemble and pack. The cycle times are the same and there is no setup. Items can go directly from assembly to pack, without any inventory queue. In this example, this removes 1,512 units of inventory and six days of lead time from the process (Figure 5.4).

Value Stream Loops

The concept of a value stream loop was created to make implementation easier, since it broke the value stream into segments and allowed the implementation team to tackle one segment at a time, starting with the pacemaker loop (attached to the customer). All processes within a loop are connected via flow, either one-piece flow or FIFO flow. (From a purist's point of view, however, any processes connected by one-piece flow should be considered and managed as though they were a single process, so the previous statement should really just include FIFO flow.)

Because in Figure 5.5 each loop terminates in a supermarket, and a supermarket is where inventory is present in a value stream (FIFO inventory should be considered WIP for our purposes), it can be equated that the end of each loop should be represented by a new item number; treat this as an assembly item, although technically it is a phantom item, because we will not be netting its inventory in MRP. This means that the supermarket will represent a new bill of materials (BOM) level. Conversely, as we connect more and more processes with flow, levels in the BOM can be eliminated (as well as the item numbers, if possible; if not, these item numbers should be marked as "phantoms" in the bill of materials).

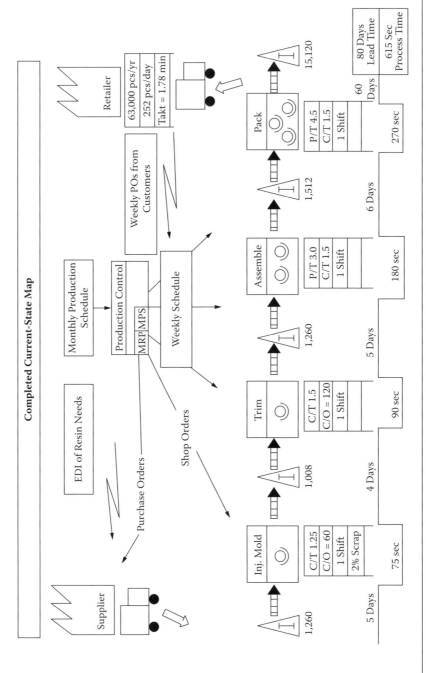

Figure 5.3 A completed current state value stream map. Value stream mapping is an important technique for planning improvements in value streams.

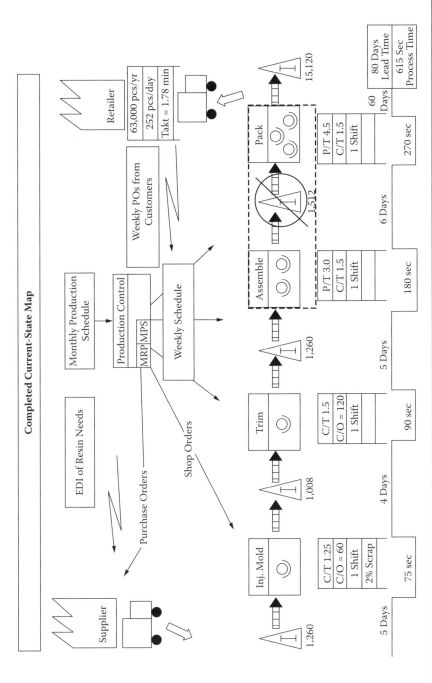

Completed Current-State Map

Figure 5.4 The decision to combine the assembly and pack process steps into one process with two steps connected by one-piece flow, eliminating the inventory between the two processes.

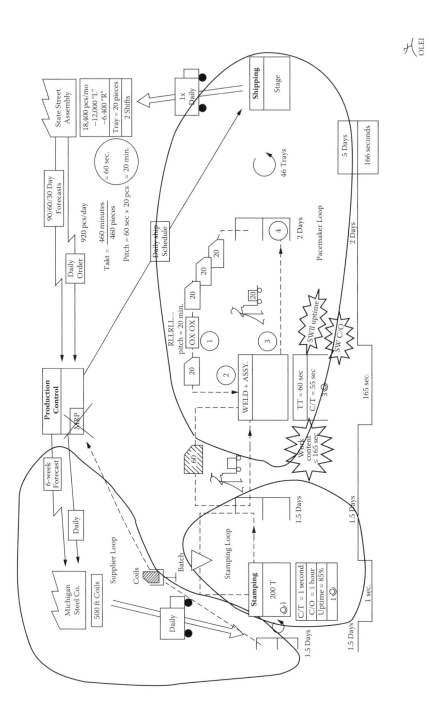

Figure 5.5   The value stream map has been broken down into loops for ease of implementation. (Courtesy of the Lean Enterprise Institute.)

Loops should be managed as a unit at some levels. This point will become more obvious when we discuss interval and capacity shortly. For now, though, take this to mean that each loop should only get one production signal (heijunka schedule or kanban signal), and should have a single lot size for the parts in the loop. What this means in terms of capacity management is that all of the processes in a loop can be managed as a single entity, since they will all be producing to the same interval; therefore, all of their capacities will be in balance as long as the interval for the loop can be achieved. Because of this, a simple but important correlation can be understood: the more flow in a value stream, the simpler capacity planning will be.

Capacity and Pull

When people think of Lean, they should think of flow. Unfortunately, flow is not always possible in a lot of environments, but that does not mean that Lean is not possible. You just have to go about it differently. Pure, one-piece flow is possible when you can produce exactly at the pace of demand. It is tough but possible. For example, there is a defense contractor that produces and ships assemblies to the Department of Defense exactly at takt, with no finished goods inventories. It helps that there are no demand fluctuations and only one customer. However, demand fluctuations spread across multiple customers can make operating "Lean" more difficult. However, look inward first to make this determination. As we have been saying, anytime two consecutive processes have cycle times plus setup times less than takt time, one-piece flow can be implemented. For most other instances, where cycle time is less than takt but cycle time plus setup time are greater than takt, FIFO flow can be used to connect two processes.

This leaves us with our third method of connecting two processes: pull. In our view, we think pull should be used in the following instances: where demand is unknown (independent demand from customers), and the market does not allow for all of the process steps to be completed to order; as a buffer from demand variation, as described in Chapter 3; where two processes or loops of the value stream will have less overall waste by producing to different intervals; and where logistics of connecting two processes preclude using a FIFO lane, such as material from a supplier who cannot deliver in the desired sequence of production.

In general, pull systems work on the principle of "replace as used." In other words, as parts are withdrawn from the supermarket, a signal is sent back to the supplying loop to make more parts. At its simplest, the parts to be made are the same ones that were used, but there are systems that will alter this logic. Because of this relationship, where one part is replaced when it is used, in general all of the loops in a value stream will be in balance, meaning that as long as the pacemaker loop is scheduled to capacity, the other feeding loops should also be planned to the correct capacity. There are exceptions, where mix is not leveled and work content varies greatly in the lower levels of the bill of materials according to the mix sold, but in general the pull system helps to simplify capacity planning.

We will now turn our attention to some of the elements of capacity planning and control in a Lean environment, starting with standard work, which is the basis of Lean capacity planning and control.

Standard work: Establishing precise procedures for each operator's work in a production process, based on three elements:

1. Takt time, which is the rate at which products must be made in a process to meet customer demand.
2. The precise work sequence in which an operator performs tasks within takt time.
3. The standard inventory, including units in machines, required to keep the process operating smoothly.

Standardized work, once established and displayed at workstations, is the object of continuous improvement through kaizen. The benefits of standardized work include documentation of the current process for all shifts, reductions in variability, easier training of new operators, reductions in injuries and strain, and a baseline for improvement activities.

—*Lean Lexicon*, **4th edition**

If you were to look at standard work in terms that most of us are familiar with, this is simply the time study part of Lean, in an attempt to find the best way to perform the work. Specifically, standard work wants to separate what the person does from what the machines do in the work centers. The main purpose of this is to drive labor productivity. A recurrent theme in Lean is that machinery can be idle, but people never should be. This also allows us to track the capacity needs of both the equipment and the people, which, as stated before, is important in many environments.

Standardized work originated with Henry Ford, and more important for Lean, Training Within Industry. Training Within Industry was a military program taught to the Japanese after World War II. The emphasis is that the best way is discovered in a joint effort between the foreman and the workers.

The most time-consuming part of establishing standard work is the work sequence because this requires studying the work being done. Traditionally, within a Lean environment, the area supervisor and factory engineers will initially perform the studies, with the area supervisor and the most experienced operators maintaining the information after that. The ongoing maintenance of the work sequence process does not require an industrial engineer, although one could be helpful in the initial setting up of the sequence. So, once again, Lean takes a technical turn and is much more than just 5S and kanban cards.

Work standards got a bad name through the application of Frederick Taylor's scientific management. Taylor's theory treated the standard as a fixed item and did not want the workers involved, because he essentially thought the workers were incapable of being helpful and left the development of work to the "experts," which is sort of how Six Sigma treats the majority of workers, as often only people with "belts" are thought to be capable of being involved. Lean takes some of the basic time study concepts of scientific management and adds kaizen to the process. Standard work in Lean is very much different from simple work standards. The key point is that Lean applies the small group concept (kaizen) to this process. The small group takes over ownership for the baselined standard process and works to continually improve it.

There are several components to calculating standard work. The first, takt time, has already been touched upon previously. Takt time calculates the pace of finished items that need to be completed at an even pace during the workday.

The work sequence lists the individual elements of the process (typically within a work center). The observation sheet allows you to record your observations of the work center: Are the elements really being done, in the sequence detailed, or are there any missing elements, and what are their times? We will cover this in more detail below.

Standardized work in process includes units in machines, required to keep the process operating smoothly. As we mentioned, work may not flow evenly through the value stream. Typically, unrestricted inventory is allowed to pile up between work centers, but as we will discuss, there is a better way to control this WIP.

A common misperception is that standard work is the same or similar to best practices. A best practice is often described as an industry best practice that implies that no other company in the industry has a better way to perform the task. We feel that this is misguided and somewhat similar to futile "benchmarking" practices that we often see. Our misgivings about these two practices are similar; be careful who you compare your company to or you'll end up as "the best-dressed bum." Companies that are interested in developing sustainable competitive advantages develop their own best practices and benchmark against all industries, not just their own.

Another potential issue is the typical "standard times" bureaucracy: Typically, when you discuss standards, most people look at this as being negative and coercive. Tightly controlled standards often were developed in conjunction with incentive pay in order to motivate employees to produce more products. Often, these environments are very rigid, tightly controlled, and adversarial. They are characterized by strict enforcement of extensive written rules and smothering hierarchic control. We are not necessarily condemning these practices, but simply looking at a different way to achieve the same results.

Instead of the rigidity, involving people in the process, especially through the small group process, will get you better results. Empowered employees are a powerful tool in improving a company, and the Toyota Production System gives you a framework from which to work from. Once you engage the workforce in maintaining and improving standard work, you can position standard work as a set of rules and procedures to enable continuous improvement, and construct a management hierarchy that supports organizational learning.

Standard work assumes that the work being studied is repeatable. Why is this important? If the work is not repeatable, then trying to standardize it would be very difficult. Standardization is just creating a baseline for going forward; it sets the initial conditions for measuring improvement. How would you know if you improved something if you didn't measure it? Most work is set up to be repeatable, but it would be wrong to make a blanket statement that all work is repeatable. The next two items are closely related: the equipment/process is relatively stable and reliable and can generate good parts the majority of the time. Why is this important? This is a multipart answer. If your equipment or processes are not stable or reliable, you probably should not be trying to do Lean, or at least your first effort should be to stabilize the process. Aside from the obvious, trying to standardize a process that is not standard in reliability or process output would be like trying to hit a moving target. Again, standardization implies that there is stability to the process and the output. If the equipment is constantly breaking down or the parts are constantly out of specification and are rejected, there is no standardization.

The observation sheet (Figure 5.6) is critical to completing the standard work process. As you can see, a number of the tasks needed to complete your standard work profile are included on this sheet.

Reference points include:

1. Takt time (calculate as shown): time available divided by units required.
2. Make a drawing of the work area and record the work element sequence; example shows 1, 2 done at table, 3 walking to board, 4 recording, 5 walking back to table.
3. Record three random observations of the total sequence—elements 1 to 5.
4. Record the work element steps on sheet.
5. Record the time it takes to do each element—ten observations of each element.
6. Record tasks that are outside the regular work elements but have to be performed periodically.
7. In the Low column, record the lowest time for that element. Repeat this for each element. Do the same for the High column, using the highest time for that element. Subtract low from high to get the fluctuation result and record that number in the Fluctuation column.
8. Complete totals for the Low and Fluctuation columns.

So what do these data tell you? First is that takt is 12 seconds and, if everything is going well, you currently may be able to do the job at 14.6 seconds. So, 14.6 seconds is your new standard. Unfortunately, you are still over takt. Many people may want to question this, but the purpose of standard work is to break each part of the work down to its elements, then replicate the conditions that made that time achievable. So, realistically, you might be running anywhere from 14.6 and 17 seconds, or an average of 15.8 (50% of the fluctuation). The important point is that you now have a starting point to work from.

Next, not performing to takt would be the next item to tackle. What could you do to improve this? By moving the erase board closer to the work area you would reduce the walk time. By cutting this in half, you would now be under takt. You could also

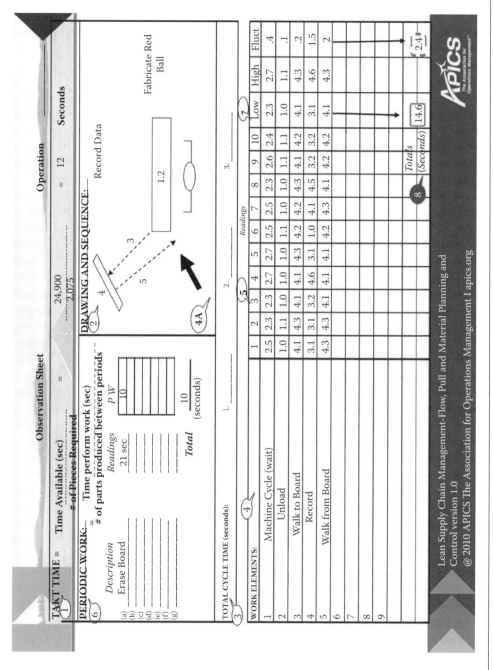

Figure 5.6 Example of a standard work observation sheet.

offload the periodic work to someone else. Periodic work can be defined as labor time that is spent on tasks that are not directly involved with making each piece, but take place on a predictable, periodic basis (delivery of material, quality checks, loading/unloading hoppers, etc.). So how does periodic time figure into this? Obviously, every so often, the board needs to be erased. However, this has no bearing on the task at hand and is for informational use only. Even better would be to remove the need to erase the board by the worker or only have to do it once a day. The most common solution is to assign this task to someone who is not responsible for cycle work, often known as a water spider. The water spider is responsible for material handling in a fixed-time, unfixed-quantity material handling system, based on pitch, and can also be tasked with some periodic activities along the route.

> **Water spider:** An expert worker who makes the rounds of workstations and provides assistance, as needed. The water spider knows all processes well enough to take over if needed. At Toyota, this position is a prerequisite to supervision and management positions.
>
> —*APICS Dictionary*, **12th edition**

How work moves through the factory also has a significant impact on work planning and capacity. As we see in the first example in Figure 5.7, the functional layout, the machines and operators are positioned according to their function. For example, all lathes would be placed in the same area. This is advantageous for batch processing but not for flow or pull because of the need to move items from functional area to functional area. Of the three examples, the top one would potentially use the least machines and the most people. This is because having the machines grouped together by type would provide for the best utilization of the machines, but this same grouping typically encourages the one-person-one-machine arrangement discussed earlier, as well as requiring more support for moving parts between functional areas.

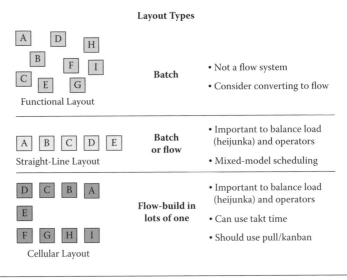

Figure 5.7   Three possible layouts for production.

The second and third examples in the figure show how machines and operators are set up according to their value stream. These are more conducive to flow. Which of the layouts you use, straight line or U cell or something similar, depends largely on your building configuration and space availability. The second and third examples would both potentially use more machines than the top functional layout, but both would probably use less people and potentially less floor space.

Standardized Work in Process

Standardized WIP may seem to be an odd concept, but as we have mentioned, one-piece flow is not always possible. Our second option is to connect two processes with first-in–first-out flow. Standardized WIP simply sets a target for the level of WIP that should be maintained between processes, with the goal of not exceeding this amount—the typical "letting WIP get out of hand." So we can think of standardized work in process as the amount of material that should be in our FIFO lanes to connect two processes.

When do you need to use FIFO?

- Processes are not close to each other, and therefore moving one piece at a time is impractical.
- Cycle times between processes are too varied and you have not come up with a way to balance the work.
- Changeovers can also cause problems when changeover time varies among the processes, even if their cycle times are similar.
- Any time two processes do not produce parts at the same rate, for whatever reason, such as defects, cycle time differences, changeover time differences, uptime differences, etc., we will need standard work in process between the processes.

We now equate standard WIP to what we have been calling FIFO inventory. This inventory acts as a buffer between processes that have dissimilar process characteristics that can't be "fixed." When we reviewed line balancing, we often oversimplified the fact that it is not easy to even these process characteristics out. FIFO is the preferred method of connecting two processes when you can't create one-piece flow.

Sizing of the FIFO inventory is important so you have the right amount of inventory in place (Figure 5.8). As mentioned, this is used if there is an imbalance between two processes that need to be connected. Calculating this is similar to safety stock, and there are no exact calculations. Having said that, in the spirit of being exact where

Figure 5.8 Value stream mapping icon for first-in–first-out flow.

no real exactness is either required or possible, we will show you at least a starting point for how much material to plan for when sizing a FIFO lane.

MACHINE A	MACHINE B
C/T 60 seconds	C/T 70 seconds

Takt time is 60 seconds, based on a single shift of 440 minutes. It has been decided to run Machine B extra time to make the correct number of pieces until the cycle time can be reduced. The question is, then: How much inventory will we need to keep in order to allow Machine B to operate in this manner. In this case, it is a simple math problem. In the one shift, Machine A will produce 440 pieces, 1 per minute. Machine B will produce 377 pieces (440 minutes multiplied by 60 seconds per minute divided by 70 seconds per piece). So there will be 63 pieces between the 2 machines at the end of the shift. This is the minimum size of the FIFO lane. It will take Machine B another 73.5 minutes (63 times 70 seconds divided by 60 seconds per minute) to complete these pieces. This is the minimum amount of material for the FIFO lane, but there are many factors that enter into how much material is actually needed to be held, such as machine uptime, setup times for the machines, and scrap rates.

Shop Floor Control

> **Shop floor control:** A system for using data from the shop floor to maintain and communicate status information on shop orders (manufacturing orders) and on work centers. Shop floor control can use order control or flow control to monitor material movement through the facility.
>
> —*APICS Dictionary*, **12th edition**

Now we get to the real weak part of most ERP systems. Shop floor control in most systems consists mainly of a list of orders in sequence of their due dates. We have thus finally left the world of planning and entered the world of scheduling. Theoretically, this detailed scheduling would work if everyone executed their schedules as printed, but we know that that simply does not happen. Often, many things do not happen as scheduled, and most scheduling systems do not keep up with these off-schedule problems. Last, people simply don't like to follow directions that may not be logical. In many cases, schedules that come out of a system may not make sense on the shop floor, as they may miss some opportunities for increased efficiency. Also, as mentioned before, sales-driven organizations will tend to overpromise, committing to system dates that are not attainable due to capacity. Principle 53 (Plossl and Wight): The more input is controlled, the less output has to be controlled. This fits the Lean environment very well.

Traditional elements of shop floor control include:

- assigning priority of each shop order;
- maintaining work-in-process quantity information;

- conveying shop order status information to the office;
- providing actual output data for capacity control purposes;
- providing quantity by location by shop order for work-in-process inventory and accounting purposes;
- providing measurement of efficiency, utilization, and productivity of the workforce and machines.

—APICS Dictionary, **12th edition**

The normal way of trying to deliver this control is via controlling the shop orders that authorize production. Each production order contains information necessary to complete that particular batch of material, including the component material required (in the form of a bill of materials); the processing steps required, including which work centers should be used (in the form of a routing); and other items, such as required tooling.

A whole set of rules and techniques have been created to support shop floor control and perform detailed scheduling:

Longest task time (LTT) heuristic
Least changeover cost
Advanced planning and scheduling
Automatic rescheduling
Back scheduling
Block control
Central point scheduling
Constraint-oriented finite loading
Critical ratio
Dispatch list
Due date rule
Earliest due date
Earliest operation due date
Earliest start date
Finite forward scheduling
Forward flow scheduling
Forward scheduling
Gapped schedule
Input/output control
Lead time scheduling
Least changeover cost
Manufacturing execution systems
Material-dominated scheduling (MDS)
Mixed-flow scheduling
Operations finite loading
Overlapped schedule

Probable scheduling
Processor-dominated scheduling
Rate-based scheduling
Resource leveling
Resource-limited scheduling
Reverse flow scheduling
Shortest processing time (SPT) rule
Undercapacity scheduling

All of these techniques are aimed at doing one thing: taking the orders created by MRP and doing the detailed scheduling of the shop floor to produce the material. What this is really saying is that all of the processes in the planning and control system up to now have been about planning. Once we reach the shop floor level we enter the realm of scheduling, and as is obvious from the list of scheduling approaches, chaos begins to reign. While we are the first to say that each situation in production is somewhat unique, it wasn't meant to mean that they each should have their own scheduling approach. But even with the variation in production environments, it should be obvious that a handful of techniques that actually work are all that would be needed. So, the implication is that most of these techniques don't really work all that well, and most of them confuse the shop floor environment to the point where the schedule is often ignored.

Whichever the technique, they all, generally, share one characteristic: they will produce an individual schedule for each work center in the facility. The idea is that if every work center executes the schedule correctly, then material will flow from one step to the next according to the rules, and eventually the product will be built and the customer will be satisfied, or at least inventory will be replenished. Often, many things do not happen as scheduled and most scheduling systems do not keep up with these off-schedule problems. Rescheduling more frequently, as some systems have attempted as a fix for this, simply injects more chaos into the factory, and fails to address the real issue, which is that this is less of a scheduling problem (although this level of scheduling doesn't really help the situation), but is really a problem with execution and control. And that is what Lean is all about.

Heijunka, Flow, and Visual Control as Shop Floor Control

Scheduling, and capacity controlling the schedule, is easily done with a physical heijunka box. It can be an actual box, as discussed in Chapter 3 or better yet, a dry erase board that is divided into the scheduling pitch increments (time buckets) represented as an empty space on the dry erase board. You write the parts to be made (part number) and their quantities within the appropriate pitch spaces on the board.

The pacemaker process is the place in a Lean value stream that receives the heijunka schedule.

Pacemaker process: Any process along a value stream that sets the pace for the entire stream. (The pacemaker process should not be confused with a bottleneck process, which necessarily constrains downstream processes due to a lack of capacity.) The pacemaker process usually is near the customer end of the value stream, often the final assembly cell. However, if products flow from an upstream process to the end of the stream in a FIFO sequence, the pacemaker may be at this upstream process.

—Lean Lexicon, **4th edition**

So if the pacemaker is not the bottleneck, how can it be the pacemaker? The answer is simple: because it will run parts at takt time, and all subsequent processes will therefore need to run at takt time. This concept is critical to shop floor and capacity control in Lean, so let's explore it for a minute.

The pacemaker process would be the first process in the pacemaker loop, defined as the loop attached to the customer, or the finished goods inventory, and then continuing upstream until the next supermarket is found. The process after this second, upstream supermarket is the pacemaker process. By definition, all processes downstream of the pacemaker will be connected by flow, so they will all work on a first-in–first-out basis, thus needing no schedule. Further, by operating the FIFO lanes within the rules, meaning that no parts are produced unless there is an empty space in the FIFO lane, we can ensure that all of the processes are producing at the same rate as the pacemaker. If they produce faster, the FIFO lane where the process draws parts from will run out of parts and the process will have to stop, and if they run slower, the FIFO lane that the process feeds will run out of parts and the subsequent process will have to stop, which will then result in an investigation of why flow was interrupted. So the shop floor control part is pretty straightforward in the pacemaker loop: one schedule, the heijunka schedule given to the pacemaker process, then simply monitoring flow for interruptions.

And how do we make sure that the pacemaker is making parts at the correct rate? Pitch refers to how often we release work to, and take work away from, the pacemaker. This is a way to check to see if we are obtaining takt and to measure how we are doing. Pitch is often implemented at the pacemaker via a process called paced withdrawal.

Paced withdrawal: The practice of releasing production instructions to work areas and withdrawing completed product from work areas at a fixed, frequent pace. This practice can be used as a means of linking material flows with information flow.

—Lean Lexicon, **4th edition**

So by implementing paced withdrawal at the pacemaker, we can quickly detect if the pacemaker is under- or overproducing. Pitch (the fixed, frequent pace referred to in the definition) quantities are typically packing quantities for the specific item, so if takt time is 1 minute and a container holds 30 parts, then a good pitch time would be 30 minutes. We could have the water spider collect a full container every 30 minutes. If a full container is available, all is well, and another kanban is given to the pacemaker process. If not, the pacemaker has not produced to takt, and corrective action is called for.

The use of heijunka does not necessarily keep you from scheduling more than what can physically be done in the work area, as with normal ERP. However, you will only get as an output what the work center/cell can do because the workflow is controlled at the pacemaker. If you recognize this as a truism, then it ultimately makes no sense to schedule more work than there is capacity for.

Staffing and Takt Time

Figure 5.9 shows the relationship between takt time and the number of people required to run a cell. Note that customer demand rose from 16 to 24 units in the bottom graphic, so the number of operators was increased from 2 to 3. In both examples shown, all of the process times are set at 5 minutes. Therefore, the machine and labor times are actually balanced.

For both examples, the total lead time is 60 minutes and the available time is 480 minutes. In the top example, the customer demand is 16 units. Therefore, the takt time is 30 minutes (480/16 = 30). Based on the process, the takt time is met with 2 operators (60 minutes total process time divided by 30 minutes takt time). In the bottom example, customer demand increases to 24 units. Correspondingly, takt time decreases to 20 minutes (480/24). The process design that is U-shaped provides the

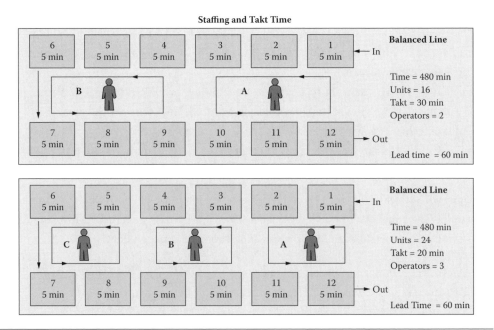

Figure 5.9   There is a direct relationship between takt time and the number of people needed to perform manual operations.

flexibility to add another operator. Thus, customer demand can be met with 3 operators (60 minutes total process time divided by 20 minutes takt time).

Operator Balance Chart

Once we have determined how many people are needed to run a workstation or cell, we then need to determine how to distribute the work elements among the operators. This is done with an operator balance chart, shown in Figure 5.10.

This line balance chart shows the time required for each operation within a cell. The value of each bar is the time required for that particular operation. To be effective, the bar chart must also show the takt time, which is represented by a horizontal line on the chart. Any deviation of the operation bars to the takt time is waste—an opportunity for improvement using Lean tools.

This chart shows how the frontloading of operators so that their operations' process time reaches the takt time better balances the line, eliminating waste and allowing an operator to go to another line. Even though these are machine operations, what we are balancing is the operators' time, not the cycle time of the machine. This is an important distinction (remember the jidoka principal of separating the person from the machine?). Product flow must fall in pace with takt time to avoid overproduction or late delivery. Cycle time is the actual production rate, which tells us how often we can produce a product with the given resources.

These four graphs show varying relationships between operator process time and takt time. The top graph shows two of the five operators with process times running

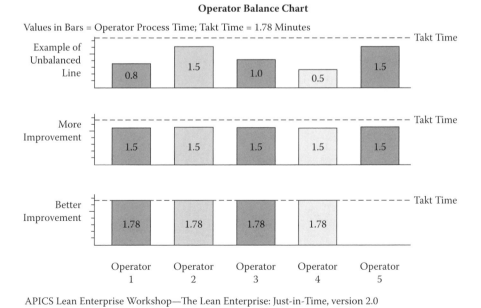

APICS Lean Enterprise Workshop—The Lean Enterprise: Just-in-Time, version 2.0

Figure 5.10   Three examples of operator balance charts, which are used to distribute work activities to operators within a process.

very close to takt time, whereas the other three operators are underutilized. The second graph shows a slight improvement in that the operators are a little more balanced. There is not as large of a gap between the five process times. However, note that there is still a gap between the process times and the takt times. We would try to never have the "more improvement" configuration, because the operators would overproduce. The third graph shows even more improvement since all of the operator process times are now equal and we are now using fewer operators for the process. The "better improvement" is what we would go for, or at least to always have one operator have a takt amount of work. The better improvement shows the "least operator" concept in which you frontload the operators by bringing them up to or close to the takt time. This can help drive continuous improvement by reducing total cycle time and moving the work to the front. Eventually the final operator will be displaced to another cell.

The least operator concept states the cell should be frontloaded, and all waiting time and waste should be allocated to the last operator. The other operators should be fully loaded to takt time. This makes the waste, the waiting time, visible. It also exposes the opportunity for improvement at the last operation. Natural work, grouping the activities by function or machine, has the operators at various loads. The traditional approaches to work setup have the operators at equal loads; however, this is usually not at takt time, and may cause overproduction. Additionally, in Lean we can calculate resource requirements easily. The total number of operators required is equal to the sum of individual operator process times divided by the takt time. So we can see how we can use heijunka scheduling, takt time, and pitch to plan and control the manpower necessary to run a value stream.

In this chapter we have reviewed traditional capacity planning and shop floor control, again probably the weakest area of ERP and control systems. In contrast, this is one of the strengths of the Lean planning and control system, offering straightforward, easy-to-understand and -administer tools and techniques. Further, the same set of processes are used to both plan capacity and manage the shop floor, namely, the heijunka schedule, gross explosion, standard work, flow and pull, and visual factory. So instead of a plethora of tools and techniques to schedule the factory, we have a single schedule, accompanied by pull and flow to control the production in the value stream.

In Chapter 6 we take on the heart of the ERP system, inventory management. And, surprise again, we find that Lean will have a completely different take on what inventory management is all about.

6
INVENTORY MANAGEMENT

In this chapter we will describe the differences between the traditional approach to inventory management and the approach taken by Lean.

Is this chapter really necessary in a book about Lean? Contrary to popular belief, inventory management is still very necessary within most Lean environments. Why? In spite of our best efforts, inventory will still be present in even the best value streams. Can you think of any manufacturing environment that could operate with no inventory at all? If not, then inventory management will be necessary. It is thus important to put the proper procedures and controls in place to make sure that the inventory that is present is truly needed for the operation to function well.

Most folks envision Lean as some magical process that allows you to make exactly what customers want, when they want it. Although this would be ideal, it is simply not practical in most cases; for a variety of reasons, companies cannot produce exactly to demand through the entire value stream. We reviewed many different production strategies in Chapter 3, and many of them involved having an inventory buffer somewhere in the value stream. Even those environments where inventory is not being used for customer service will undoubtedly have inventory in process, so it is really difficult to think of a production environment that will not need to manage inventory.

We will start with a brief review of traditional inventory management topics and approaches, then move into the Lean approach to inventory management.

- Traditional inventory management topics
  - Importance of good inventory management
    - Costs relevant to inventory decisions
    - Inventory is on the financial statement
  - Functions that inventories perform
  - Objectives of inventory management
  - Inventory metrics
- Lean inventory topics
  - Inventory as waste
  - Inventory management in Lean
  - Kanban sizing
  - Production loops and inventory reduction

We will cover the main differences between Lean inventory management and traditional inventory management in this chapter. There are, of course, many other subtle differences that we will not cover, but the above list touches on many of the major differences.

Let's start with a definition:

Inventory: 1) Those stocks or items used to support production (raw materials and work-in-process items), supporting activities (maintenance, repair, and operating supplies), and customer service (finished goods and spare parts). Demand for inventory may be dependent or independent. Inventory functions are anticipation, hedge, cycle (lot size), fluctuation (safety, buffer, or reserve), transportation (pipeline), and service parts.

—*APICS Dictionary*, **12th edition**

A second definition is given: "2) All the money currently tied up in the system" (*APICS Dictionary*, 12th edition). As used in theory of constraints, inventory refers to the equipment, fixtures, buildings, and so forth that the system owns—as well as inventory in the form of raw materials, work in process, and finished goods. This second definition, while specific to the theory of constraints, is also applicable to Lean, although the semantics are different. We will not refer to anything such as buildings or machines as inventory, but Lean will certainly pay attention to managing all of these assets. In this chapter, however, we will stick to discussing inventory as defined in definition 1.

As you can see from this definition, inventory serves many purposes in a company. From one viewpoint, inventory covers up problems. For most people this would be considered a good thing, but for a Lean thinker problems must be surfaced so they can be fixed, so any inventory beyond what is immediately needed is bad and should be removed.

Traditional Inventory Management

By *traditional*, we mean the inventory management techniques generally taught in operations management classes and supported by most enterprise resource planning (ERP) systems. We will start our discussion with a brief review of traditional inventory management theories and practices as a way of establishing understanding of the differences in the Lean approach.

The Importance of Inventory Management: Customer Satisfaction and Company Financials

Aside from keeping your job, why is inventory management so important? Number one is that inventory management should work to first satisfy customers. Customers will quickly abandon you if you cannot supply them with the goods they want, when they want them. In many companies this customer service focus has led to holding huge amounts of inventory, and in the authors' view, we see more inventory being held than is necessary—even for non-Lean companies. This has been caused by many factors, such as an increasing number of SKUs to make the same sales volume, meaning less volume per item and more erratic demand for each item; longer supply chains created by the current wave of outsourcing production to the Far East; and poor capacity management via the executive sales and operations planning process (or lack of one); among many other things. And although keeping lots of inventory has been a well-used strategy in the past, few companies nowadays can afford to tie up working capital (cash) in inventory. So managing inventories in light of the company financials is important as well. If you look at where inventories are placed within your company's financials, they are placed in the asset section of the balance sheet. So, inventory is looked at as a good thing, financially.

Logically, this makes sense, but it also is a distortion of reality because inventory may not always be readily sold and converted to cash, and as we all know, some inventory items on "the books" may not sell at book value or have any value at all. This bad situation is often made worse by companies securing debt (borrowing) on the value of the inventory. In this case, the more money you have in inventory, the more money you can borrow. How receptive would such an organization be to reducing inventory? In some cases reducing the inventory level in a company will put the company at financial risk, as the collateral basis for the loans disappears. What does not make sense in this whole line of thought is that since inventories are eventually converted into cash, isn't it better to have cash than inventory? Because, after all, if you had cash, you wouldn't have to borrow it. Cash is, when all is said and done, much more flexible than inventory.

So inventory management is a balancing act of keeping just enough inventory available for customers, without having too much. It is not an easy task, and APICS members have done a great service to their firms by doing this. Unfortunately, for every APICS professional, there are one hundred amateurs in the workplace costing their companies untold amounts of money. (Unfortunately, most of this is self-inflicted by company management because they are too short-sighted to see that these professionals save them money, instead of costing them a salary.)

Concepts of Traditional Inventory Management

1. Segmentation: Break the inventory down into different types or purposes. This allows different techniques of control to be employed for each type or purpose. Types: Raw, work in progress (WIP), finished. Functions: Anticipation, fluctuation, lot size, transportation, hedge.
2. Balance cost of carrying with cost of ordering: This is a lot sizing guideline. The idea is that the correct order quantity will have the least total cost, which occurs at the point where the cost of carrying inventory (meaning that the order will leave some inventory on the shelf after the immediate need is fulfilled) and the cost of placing the order (creating the order itself,

performing the setup, etc.) are equal to each other. This is called the economic order quantity.

3. Order quantity: As stated in number 2, quite a bit of effort in inventory management is spent in trying to determine the correct amount to order at one time. There are many formulas available to do this, plus many rules for determining which formula to apply to what type of item.

4. Order timing: The idea is that if the order is launched at the correct time, it will arrive in inventory at the right time and all will be well. Of course, it was quickly recognized that disruptions are inevitable, and a whole system of maintaining priority control evolved to try to get the highest need items into inventory as soon as possible.

5. The real action of inventory management occurs at the item level, not at the aggregate level: The idea is to get the correct order policies and lot sizing rules in place for each item. We will spend some time discussing this later in the chapter.

We can begin our discussion of inventory segmentation with one type and one function: finished goods and fluctuation inventory. The essential thought behind the traditional strategy for finished goods inventory is the bell-shaped curve (Figure 6.1). We start with the general assumptions of finished goods inventory:

- The more erratic the demand, the higher the inventory level will need to be to provide a certain level of customer service.
- We can accurately measure the variation of any item using a standard deviation calculation.
- There is a diminishing return to keeping higher levels of standard deviations, but in general, if I keep more inventory, I will achieve higher service.

Because of this set of assumptions, we have traditionally taken a very "inventory centric" view when it comes to planning our value streams, for the most part. What this

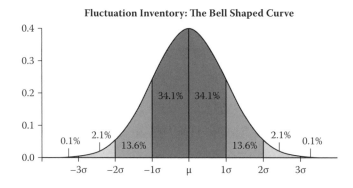

Figure 6.1 This is the classic bell-shaped curve representing a normal distribution of demand around the mean (average). Each one of the vertical bars represents one standard deviation from the mean, and the percentage shows the percent of events that would fall within that number of standard deviations. For instance, 68.2 of all events fall within ±1 standard deviation of the mean.

means, again, is that the primary objective of the ERP planning system is to maintain the proper level of finished goods inventory, with the promise that the desired level of customer service will follow. This is basically done by setting the desired inventory level by part and having the system balance demand and supply to obtain this inventory level.

Other functions of inventory include:

- Anticipation inventory is inventory built up ahead of an expected spike in demand, such as from a promotion or busy season. It can be kept at any level of the product structure, although it is most common as a finished goods inventory. Anticipation inventory should be controlled in the executive sales and operations process described in Chapter 2.
- Fluctuation inventory is carried as a buffer against forecast error. To some extent, this is similar to the safety stock described in the finished goods inventory discussion in Chapter 3.
- Lot size inventory is simply the amount of inventory build that is not immediately needed for the next process, mainly for cost reasons. We will discuss the thoughts behind traditional lot sizing approaches in the next section. In Lean we try to eliminate this inventory.
- Transportation inventory is inventory that is in transit between two locations. It is also called pipeline inventory. Obviously, the closer together the supply chain links are, the less transportation inventory there will be.
- Hedge inventory is extra inventory to protect against unfavorable events, such as a labor strike, price increases, government interventions, and other disruptions in material flow.

The second topic in this discussion is the model of balancing cost of carrying with cost of ordering (Figure 6.2).

Although economic order quantity is not as popular as when it was first introduced, it still is a consideration for most lot sizing approaches. Lean recognizes the relationship

Figure 6.2 Classic chart showing the trade-off of carrying cost and ordering cost, which is at the heart of the thinking in traditional lot sizing.

between lot size and capacity as the most important one, and has a lot sizing rule, interval, which accommodates this view. Interval will be covered in depth in Chapter 7.

The thought behind traditional lot size management is the trade-off between inventory carrying costs and the cost of ordering, shown here in graphic form. The idea is to find a lot size where the cost of inventory and the cost of ordering equal each other, which is the point of least total cost. Lean, as we will show in Chapter 7, worries less about the cost and more about the lot size in terms of its impact on capacity.

Order Quantity

There are three basic types of order quantity rules: economic order quantity, shown above, which is an attempt to balance the cost of ordering with the cost of carrying inventory; fixed order quantity, where the same quantity is ordered no matter how large or small the demand; and period order quantity, where a supply order is created to cover a certain number of periods of demand. Lean, as we shall discuss in the next chapter, has two simple lot sizing rules: one piece and every part every interval.

When to Order

There are three common systems in use to decide when to place an order:

- Order point system. The order point system involves calculating an inventory level based on demand during lead time plus safety stock, and then placing an order any time the inventory falls below this level. The theory is that since the inventory level was based on the lead time to replenish, releasing a replenishment order when this inventory level is reached should give adequate time for the replenishment order to be built. The order quantity, which certainly can affect the lead time to replenish the inventory, is addressed separately in this system.
- Periodic review system. On a fixed basis, the inventory is monitored, and an order is placed to bring the current inventory up to a target level. This is a fixed-period, variable-quantity system.
- Master scheduling. Master scheduling is a process of balancing supply and demand at the item level.

The master schedule is a format that includes time periods (dates), the forecast, customer orders, projected available balance, available-to-promise, and the master production schedule. The master schedule takes into account the forecast; the production plan; and other important considerations such as backlog, availability of material, availability of capacity, and management policies and goals.

—*APICS Dictionary*, **12th edition**

Once the order has been scheduled, a start date is calculated based on the due date minus the lead time for the item. The system will signal to the scheduler when items have reached their start dates, and the scheduler must then take action to release the orders to the value stream.

In Lean, we have either the heijunka schedule, which, as described in Chapter 3, is the counterpart of the master schedule but isn't really the same, or the signals from the pull system.

The real action of inventory management occurs at the item level, not at the aggregate level. Management must establish decision rules about individual inventory items:

- Importance of inventory items: This refers to segmenting the items into ABC classification based on usage. The higher-level usage items, the As, then get the most attention and typically the strictest inventory policies.
- How they are to be controlled: This refers to how the inventory status will be reviewed (via material requirements planning [MRP], reorder point, time-phased reorder point, two bins, master production scheduling, etc.) and how a replenishment order will be triggered.
- How much to order at one time: This refers to the lot sizing rule to place on an item.
- When to place an order: This refers to the lead time of an item and trying to determine the correct time to launch an order.

All of these policies are assumed to be able to be determined independently for each item, with little interaction with the other items in the value stream. If you really stop to think about this assumption, it is obviously a bad one to make as you determine how a value stream will be run (primarily due to value streams being set up to accommodate groups of items that require similar processing).

In traditional inventory management, inventory is measured in a few ways. Inventory turns measures how often the inventory turns over (is sold) during a period of time, usually measured annually. Inventory turns measured overall is helpful, but it is an even better measurement using dollars instead of units. This is because quantity data can skew the overall results, either good or bad. Inventory turns measures the velocity of inventory; in other words, the lower the turns, the more the inventory sits around and does nothing. Lean has the equivalent measurement, only it is the inverse, measuring the amount of inventory in days of sales. In this case, when the number of days of inventory goes down, it is a good thing, which seems to make more sense to most people than inventory turns.

Gross dollar—in other words, just the raw dollars without comparison to some usage amount—is not that helpful unless used to show amounts in some sort of classification, like ABC, but even then, what does it really tell you? Dollarizing overall turns can be very helpful in gauging excess working capital tied up in inventory. Once you know what one inventory turn is worth (or a fraction of a turn), in inventory money, you can benchmark yourself against your peer group to determine how much of an opportunity you have to free some of this cash.

Measuring obsolescence can provide important clues to the effectiveness of inventory policies.

Obsolescence: 3) The loss of usefulness or worth of a product or facility as a result of the appearance of better or more economical products, methods, or facilities.

—APICS Dictionary, **12th edition**

In industries where product life cycles are short, such as fashion and electronics, significant investment in finished goods inventory will often result in high obsolescence levels.

Lean Inventory Management

We will now turn our attention to how Lean approaches and manages inventory. As you have probably figured out by this point in the book, Lean has a very different take on inventory management.

Inventory as Waste

As opposed to the traditional view of inventory, which views inventory as an asset, any inventory beyond what is immediately needed should be looked at as waste. This may appear to be harsh, but it really is a mind frame that people have to get into when adopting Lean. Inventories are waste, but we have to have inventory to operate, even in a Lean environment. While inventory has value, it may not have the same value as it ages, as obsolescence sets in. If your money's tied up in inventory, that's less money you have to work with. Is this contradictory? Not really, if you look at your job as relentlessly trying to reduce inventory, instead of a traditional set-and-forget (inventory levels) mentality.

Inventory is one of the eight deadly wastes in Lean. It is caused by overproduction (producing more than is immediately needed), but in turn it causes several other wastes. How does excess inventory manifest itself?

- Extra space—A common problem with companies experiencing growth. You may appear to outgrow your facilities, but how much of the inventory that is using up storage space is excess?
- Extra people—More space and inventory usually results in having to have more people to move it around, count it, etc.
- Waste of conveyance—Inventory that is greater than what is immediately needed for production or sales must be stored, and therefore must be transported to and from the storage area.
- Extra costs—Aside from space and labor, most inventories are built on borrowed money, so the cost of capital has to be added. You can also add other costs, such as taxes and insurance.

Inventory Management in Lean

Inventory management in Lean is built around the same principles that govern most Lean activity: create a simple set of tools that can be used directly in the workplace that will help surface problems so that they can be addressed. Inventory management is thus quite different in Lean, starting with the view of inventory as waste rather than an asset. From a practical viewpoint, what this means is that inventory reduction is built into the fabric of the system, just like it is for any other waste. Because of this, there are typically no special efforts or programs aimed at reducing excess inventory. Reducing inventory is part of everyday work life.

Visual Control

The idea behind visual control is to enable the people working in the value stream to have the tools at hand to make decisions and facilitate continuous improvement. In place of computer reports are displays on the factory floor, such as first-in–first-out (FIFO) lanes and pitch boards that indicate whether production is proceeding at the correct pace (pitch). One of the objectives of visual management is to have "going and seeing" take the place of reports and data, encouraging familiarity with the work being done, which is necessary to make improvements to the work.

This is significantly different than the approach of ERP systems that seek to gather detailed information from each operation and then produces a series of status reports on everything from where parts are currently located in process to the productivity of individual workers.

Visual control has been around for quite some time, and it is a core part of managing inventory in Lean. One manifestation is kanban, and we'll discuss that later. However, most inventory control people are familiar with two-bin systems where there are two bins of parts. When the first bin is empty, the second is open and parts are then ordered to fill the empty container. In this case the empty bin itself serves as the kanban signal for replenishment of the part. This is often done with consumable parts—small nuts, bolts, hardware. Stuff you don't want to count because of low value. The same concept can be used for "regular" parts, but the size of the container becomes more of an issue. You don't want too many, nor do you want to run out.

Plan for every part is an important element of visual control (Figure 6.3). It is a basic database containing all the key data on parts such as supplier names and locations, order frequencies, container types and dimensions, shipment sizes, transit times, etc. This set of data allows the value stream to control the delivery, movement, and presentation of each part. With each part having a designated place in the work area, it is easy to see at a glance if anything is missing. Plan for every part may seem like a great deal of detailed work, and it is. The payoff is how much easier it makes execution. We'll discuss this in more depth later in this chapter.

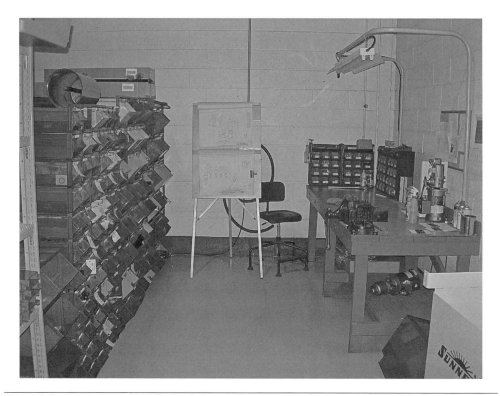

Figure 6.3   An example of point of use storage as well as plan for every part and visual control. The operators are responsible for maintaining the inventory control of their area. (Courtesy of Sunnen Products Company.)

Approaches to Reducing Inventories

When we discuss reducing inventories, there are a lot of ways to approach this. As we have been stressing all along, Lean is primarily a cultural change process that will take many years and a lot of effort. Pure Lean adoption requires you to take a framework, like the Toyota Production System, and adapt it to your company. However you do it, inventory reduction should be a part of normal operations, not a special project.

Let's start with a simple fact: inventory reduction happens when you either buy or produce less than you sell (or use). Sometimes the truest things sound the stupidest. Somehow, though, we have lost sight of this simple fact and have evolved into elaborate schemes to reduce inventory, mainly involving activity at the item level. Unfortunately, these do little to address the fundamentals of our simple truism. This simple fact is a reality that is completely overlooked by the traditional approach, which emphasizes managing inventory by setting ordering and lot sizing rules at the item level. This approach often places the inventory policies in conflict with the capacity, in that the ordering policies do not produce the correct amount of work for the employees. When this happens, we get a face-off between two distinct choices: if the amount of work is less than the capacity agreed to, then we get a conflict between productivity and inventory reduction. Since productivity is one of the primary objectives of front-line supervision, inventory reduction usually loses this battle. If the amount of work is greater than the capacity, then the conflict is between inventory and priority in the value stream. A winner in this case is less easy to predict. Sometimes priority is sacrificed to capacity and inventory is decreased, and sometimes priority is the winner, in which case we get the unseemly picture of overtime being worked while inventory is increased or stays the same.

Because of this simple fact, that inventory reduction occurs when you produce or buy less than you sell, effectively managing inventory reduction needs to happen in the planning phase, namely, during executive sales and operations planning. If this is done correctly, the execution system should be able to remove the inventory without any special effort. In Lean, of course, the objective is to provide the value stream with an amount of work that equals the agreed upon production rate, which was used to set takt time, which was then used to set the capacity of the value stream. The schedule for the value stream is governed by the takt time, which avoids the conflicts listed above, and ensures that the decisions made in the executive sales and operations planning (S&OP) meeting in regards to inventory will happen in execution. Flow, pull, and visual factory will help make it so.

Supermarket Sizing as a Way to Reduce Inventory

Being wise guys at heart, we would like to say that there *is* a correct level of inventory in Lean. In fact, there are two correct levels: less and none. Because of this, to some extent, calculating the size of a supermarket is theoretical. There are lots of algorithms for calculating the size of a supermarket, many of them similar to sizing a finished goods inventory. However, this can only calculate what the inventory should be under the current conditions, and does not foster a continuous improvement mindset. After all, if the inventory is at the correct, calculated level, what more is there to be done? In Lean, then, the correct level of inventory is less, and the system must help drive toward this goal. This is one of the primary jobs of the kanban system.

Further, when first establishing a supermarket, inventory of the parts usually already exists (often more than is theoretically needed). The choices are thus two: wait until the inventory reaches the calculated level of the supermarket, then implement the kanban system, or implement the kanban system with the present inventory and build a mechanism into the kanban system to reduce inventory. If option 2 is chosen, and we think this is the logical choice, then the theoretical inventory level is irrelevant, since the job of the kanban system will be to reduce inventory until a problems occurs, fix the problem, then continue the process of reducing inventory until the next problem surfaces. This process does not stop once a calculated level of inventory is reached.

Having said all of that, however, the theoretical size of the supermarket can help with decision making on such issues as how fast to reduce inventory, which helps to set takt time for producing loops in the value stream, so we will show a few equations on how to size supermarkets.

Kanban Sizing

One of the primary focuses for many companies as they implement kanban is the proper sizing of the number of containers used. You may wonder, why not the number of pieces, but the piece quantity is really determined through these calculations—how many pieces fit in the container is a part to the equation. There are two basic methods for doing this: constant quantity, nonconstant cycle (timing), and constant cycle, nonconstant quantity. The choice of which method is appropriate depends largely on the mix variable of the value stream loop feeding the supermarket. The higher the mix of parts and the more mix variability, the more the constant cycle, nonconstant quantity should be used. In this case the interval is the fixed cycle for production.

It should be noted that in the mix-leveled environment there is a third type, namely, constant quantity, constant cycle, since the same parts will be used in the same quantities in the same timeframes (interval) in this environment. Also note that there are many kanban sizing formulas and all can be useful. However, don't get hung up on the formulas and concentrate more on removing kanbans/inventory.

Constant Quantity, Nonconstant Cycle (Timing)

$$\# \text{ of kanbans} = \frac{E + (DD + SS)}{CC}$$

E = monthly demand/monthly number of setups
DD = daily demand
SS = safety stock
CC = container capacity

This formula is used typically when starting Lean efforts. It should be modified to the following when setups are reduced significantly (impacts E) and the travel distance between operations is short:

= average daily demand × lead time × (1 + safety coefficient))/container capacity

The ideal, of course, is to get to 1. (Note: A safety coefficient is used instead of SS in this latter calculation. This is to move from a fixed amount to a percentage.)

Constant Cycle, Nonconstant Quantity

$$\# \text{ of kanbans} = \frac{DD \times (OC + LT + SS)}{CC}$$

DD = daily demand
OC = order cycle – time interval (days) between production orders
LT = processing time + wait time + conveyance time + kanban card collection time
SS = safety stock

As mentioned earlier, this is typically used in conjunction with the every part every interval (EPEI), or when there are milk runs—set up either by your company or by a group of suppliers. The key here is that there is a constant fixed cycle of parts deliveries, but the quantities may vary.

Supermarket Sizing Add up all of the kanban quantities for all of the parts in the supermarket and this will be the supermarket total. This seems fairly simple, but is one of the only places in Lean where we will derive an answer by adding up the results of item level calculations. Again, this is okay because this inventory level is theoretical, and is meant to be used to help in decision making, not to set a target to be aimed for. To repeat, the only goal is to have less than what you currently have.

WIP Inventory: FIFO Management

FIFO is used to connect two processes that cannot be connected by one-piece flow. The rules of FIFO are similar to those of a kanban system, in that they both have a specified maximum for inventory, at which time the feeding process must stop making parts until there is usage and room is created for more parts. As such, both kanban and FIFO control inventory and production. The major difference between the two is that the FIFO lane will contain only parts that have been scheduled to be produced, while the supermarket will typically contain all of the parts produced by the feeding production loop. There is thus less waste in a FIFO lane than in a supermarket (Figure 6.4).

FIFO is an integral part of visual management in Lean, as it provides a signal when something has gone wrong with the flow of material. If the lane fills up, either the feeding process overproduced or the using process didn't meet takt (or both). If the lane empties, the opposite has occurred. In either case, the process must stop, either from lack of parts or from no place to put more parts, and the operator should go to either the previous or the next spot in the value stream and try to help determine the cause of the problem and fix it so it does not occur again.

Reducing inventory in a FIFO lane is similar to reducing inventory in a supermarket in that they are both physical activities. But whereas in the supermarket we will remove a card or other signal to reduce inventory, in a FIFO lane we will physically reduce the size of the lane so that less parts can be located in the lane. If no operating

The balls are used in the same sequence in which they
were produced.

Figure 6.4 First-in–first-out flow.

problems emerge after this, reduce the size again. If problems do arise, solve them and continue on.

Reducing Pipeline Inventory: Kanban—Visual Card

Pull systems are used to connect two processes that cannot be connected via flow. The basic mechanism of a pull system is to replace parts that have been used from the inventory. The usage of inventory authorizes the feeding process to make more parts. As such, kanban controls both inventory and production. This is important to remember when you think back to the basic rule of reducing inventory: inventory reduction happens when you produce less than you sell (or use) (Figure 6.5).

As we discussed in Chapter 4, kanban is simply a signaling card, a signal to do something—typically to make something, as shown in the single kanban system discussed next. The one-card system works well when your work areas are close together and the handoff of cards is easy. In this system, the kanban card is attached to or in the container of parts, and when the subsequent work center takes the container, the card is removed and sent back to the previous work center to authorize production (Figure 6.6).

There are two card systems in which one card signals a move and the other a make. As discussed, this is usually done when the work centers are far apart. In this system, the production cards stay in the work center and a move card from the next work center authorizes the taking of the container to the next workstation. When the container is taken, the "unassigned" production card authorizes new production.

The no card system is very simple and is represented by what we discussed in Chapter 5, FIFO inventory. Product is only produced when there is an empty space

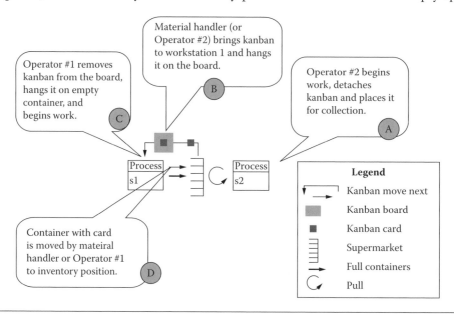

Figure 6.5   Single kanban card operation.

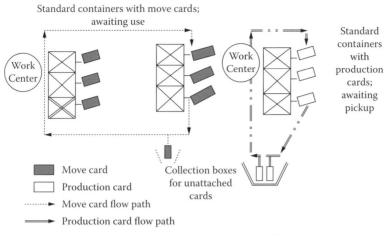

Standard containers with move cards;
awaiting use

Standard
containers
with
production
cards;
awaiting
pickup

Work
Center

Work
Center

■ Move card
□ Production card
········► Move card flow path
══════► Production card flow path

Collection boxes
for unattached
cards

From APICS CPIM Notes "Shop Floor Control"

Figure 6.6 Two-card kanban operation.

in the FIFO lane. This implies that the FIFO lane should be close to the supplying process so that they can easily see the status of the lane.

Inventory Reduction through Reducing Lot Sizes

The formula for calculating average inventory is half of the lot size plus safety stock. The lot size inventory is thus a significant portion of any inventory, and should be aggressively attacked and reduced. Reducing lot sizing can be accomplished in a lot of ways, depending on the "logic" used in the initial setting of these levels. Most of the time, lot sizes are large, just because they have always been large; in other words, there is really no good reason for them to be at the level they are. If this is the case, these lot sizes can be cut dramatically without causing real problems on the shop floor.

In the cases where lot sizes were increased to offset the impact of lengthy setup times, arbitrarily reducing lot sizes will cause nothing but trouble. This is where setup reduction can be beneficial, and most successful setup reduction processes follow Shingo's single-minute exchange of die (SMED) methodology. Here, it is not unusual to experience immediate 15 to 30% reductions and 90% long-term reductions in setup times. Setup reduction can be the turning point in becoming Lean in many companies. This allows them the flexibility to easily move from one product to another, with minimum downtime (waste). Even if you were not to fully implement Lean, setup reduction can allow many companies to lower costs and increase agility.

The basics of setup reduction revolve around separating the steps that must be done while the machine must be stopped (internal elements) and those that can be done while the machine is still running (external elements). Once they are identified, you should attempt to do all of the external elements while the machine is running, work to reduce internal times, and shift internal items to external where possible. The best way to visualize what a setup should look like is to watch a pit stop in an auto race. What you will see is lots of preparation being done while the car is still running on the track, a flurry of activity while the car is stopped, with very little wasted motion, then another round of preparation for the next pit stop. A pit stop may be the best example of the power of standard work, which is readily available for everyone to study.

By reducing overall setup time, from hours to minutes, you will be able to set up more often, shortening the interval and thus running smaller batches.

To complete this chapter, we would be remiss if we didn't at least mention two other inventory management techniques that have become popular over the last few years: vendor-managed inventory and sharing of point of sale data.

> **Vendor-managed inventory (VMI):** A means of optimizing supply chain performance in which the supplier has access to the customer's inventory data and is responsible for maintaining the inventory level required by the customer. This activity is accomplished by a process in which resupply is done by the vendor through regularly scheduled reviews of the on-site inventory. The on-site inventory is counted, damaged or outdated goods are removed, and the inventory is restocked to predefined levels. The vendor obtains a receipt for the restocked inventory and accordingly invoices the customer.
>
> —*APICS Dictionary*, 12th edition

Vendor-managed inventory is a very successful retail strategy, where the supplier gets increased control of product availability and display space on the retail shelves, while the retailer gets decreased costs. A classic win-win. Further, we are dealing with a true level of independent demand in a retail environment, so the strategy of keeping a certain level of inventory does indeed equate with a certain level of customer service in many cases, especially since this is an environment where an empty shelf results in no sale. In the retail environment the demand is conveyed via point of sale data, meaning it is based on actual usage. In essence, a pull signal. So the basis for VMI is a sound one in this environment.

Now we turn our attention to VMI in industrial settings. In this environment, it becomes harder to find the benefits for the supplier, since shelf life management and shelf placement are no longer issues from which the supplier can benefit. Indeed, there have been many abuses of companies using vendor-managed inventory to simply transfer cost and worry to the supplier. So we need to find some benefit for the supplier for this to be truly effective for the supply chain, because simply pushing responsibility and cost down in the chain is clearly not going to result in long-term improvement. That is the first hurdle in making this work.

Also, we are now dealing with dependent demand inventories, so we need to be sure that the replenishment signals make sense. And here the ironies begin. For in most ERP systems, the cornerstone is that we will be providing a forward look into demand, via forecasting and master production scheduling, and that we will buy materials and build components in anticipation of the end item schedule. And because there is rarely a mix-leveled schedule in these environments, there will undoubtedly be conflicts between what the recent usage has been and what the future projection of need will be. For example, if we build a product only once every two months, and at that time we build two months' worth, the last six weeks' usage data showing zero usage is worth very little. In this case, we need to have at least two months' worth of product on hand. A rule where we would have, say, thirty days of average usage on hand at all times would be doomed for failure. Conversely, there would be lots of waste if it was decided to carry two months' worth of material all of the time so that we would be ready at any time to build our two months' worth of product. So there is an inherent conflict in the simple demand based on usage that is used in VMI and the future-based (granted, usually based on a forecast) demand projection from ERP. In a Lean environment, however, the vendor-managed inventory mechanics closely resemble a pull system, if we simplify the rules to be that the supplier should simply replace what has been used. This eliminates the need for the supplier to monitor the inventory level, and makes the concept no different than implementing a pull system. Further, because of the partnership relationship that a Lean company should have with its suppliers, this program could be evaluated in light of whether there will be less waste for the supply chain. If the answer is yes, then we implement VMI. Note that we are not advocating eliminating the monitoring of inventory for the retail environment, where VMI, as stated, is a win-win situation and the management of the shelf inventory is an important element for the supplier.

Point of Sale Data

As we just saw, sharing point of sale data is an important element of vendor-managed inventory, where it serves as a pull signal in retail environments. But what of sharing point of sale data farther down in the supply chain, where the demand is dependent on the production schedule each step of the way through the chain? The answer is, as should be obvious, the more levels away from the point of sale date, the less valuable it is. This is because each level either has a chance to create a production schedule that doesn't match up with recent sales history, or will be trying to make an adjustment to inventory level, which will mean that the point of sales data will be either overstated (if a company in the chain is reducing inventory) or understated (if a company in the chain is increasing inventory). And remember, the materials requirements planning process will reduce or increase the inventory right away in the planning horizon, not on a rate basis, so that any inventory change will be reflected immediately in the planning and ordering driven by the material requirements planning (MRP) system. At this point the short-term data based on the point of sale data will look radically different than that provided by the ERP system.

So we come full circle to our initial position on inventory management in Lean: inventory should be managed as though it were waste, and the best strategy is to simply replace what was used. If changes in inventory levels are desired, these should be closely coordinated with all parties involved in the supply chain to determine the effect on all partners before making the adjustment. If this approach is followed, point of sale data driving a vendor-managed inventory approach are feasible through many levels of the supply chain.

In this chapter we have reviewed inventory management, both from a traditional perspective and from a Lean perspective. As expected, there are significant differences in most all aspects of the practices, starting with the contrasting views of inventory as an asset (traditional) vs. inventory as waste (Lean), continuing through managing inventory at detailed part level vs. in aggregate, and proceeding using MRP vs. pull systems for replenishment.

In Chapter 7 we will cover another aspect of planning and inventory control: lot sizing. This is an area that is very complex in ERP systems, with many algorithms and techniques for determining how many to order at once. In Lean lot sizing is simplified, with two basic choices: one-piece lot, the ideal, or EPEI, each of which has significant advantages over most other lot sizing rules.

7
LOT SIZING

In this chapter we will review the issues of how to determine lot sizes for production in Lean. We will cover lot sizing — every part every interval (EPEI), interval and cost, make to order interval, and lot sizing and capacity.

Lot Sizing in Lean

There are really only two valid choices for lot sizing in a Lean value stream: one piece, the preferred method, as it provides a basis for leveling workload in the value stream (heijunka), and EPEI, used where runtime plus setup time is greater than takt time.

These are two lot sizing policies that are demand sensitive, meaning that there will be no remnants of the lot size left over at the end of each production cycle. Both of these policies have their corresponding policies in the enterprise resource planning (ERP) world, namely, lot size of one and period order quantity. Having only two possibilities for lot size calculation seems limiting, but Lean is not trying to balance the cost of setting up and carrying inventory, but is instead trying to improve the flow of material. These two lot sizing methods help do that.

One Piece

If the runtime plus setup time for a part is less than its takt time, then the lot size can be one piece. This is most common in manual operations, such as assembly, where setup between parts is often minimal. It is also common in low-volume job shops, where the customer order is often for one unique unit and cannot be combined with other items, so one-piece orders are common in production.

This condition of low setup times would commonly be found where there are manual processes, such as assembly steps, where there are no machines present, just tools and perhaps fixtures. Low-volume job shops may have no choice but to make one piece at a time, because they often only sell one piece, and it is a custom piece, which may never be ordered again, so making more than one is risky and wasteful. The irony here is that while we often associate one-piece flow with high-volume value streams, in extremely low-volume shops one-piece flow is often possible, mainly because takt time is often long, so that the setup and runtime combined is less than takt time.

Barriers to achieving one-piece flow include:

- Long setup times.
- The increased cost of creating and managing many small work orders in the ERP system. This must be solved, perhaps with repetitive functionality.
- For purchased parts, the logistics cost of shipping one unit at a time.

Every Part Every Interval (EPEI)

EPEI (or simply interval) is defined as the longest lead time to make any product variation within a product line. (The elapsed time from the receipt of one lot to the receipt of the next lot of the same part.)

> The frequency with which different part numbers are produced in a production process or system. If a machine is changed over in a sequence so that every part number assigned to it is produced every three days, then EPEI is three days.
>
> —*Lean Lexicon*, **4th edition**

The EPEI is often a difficult concept to grasp, but it is a powerful and important concept in Lean. EPEI refers to the capability of a process to make the volume and setups required to cover the demand for all of the parts that the machine produces. The basic idea is to fit the runtime and the setup time into a specific timeframe, with the basis of the idea being that the volume that is required in any time period is fixed (based on the sales and operations planning [S&OP] production rate), and that the variable to how much work will be done is the number of setups that will be done.

Interval should be thought of as a form of period order quantity.

> **Period order quantity:** A lot-sizing technique under which the lot size is equal to the net requirements for a given number of periods (e.g., weeks into the future). The number of periods to order is variable, each order size equalizing the holding costs and the ordering costs for the interval.
>
> —*APICS Dictionary*, **12th edition**

The chart in Figure 7.1 shows weekly demand for all of the parts in a product family. We will start with the simplest case, where all of the parts in the family have demand in each period, no matter how small the period. This environment is the one existing at Toyota and other manufacturers who are able to level mix in their value streams.

Because the weekly demand totaled 4,200, we have set the value stream to produce at a constant rate of 840 per day. Figure 7.2 shows a weekly EPEI, meaning that the lot size covers one week's worth of demand. Another way of thinking of this is that each part is set up once per week, and it takes a week to make all of the parts. Note that the daily quantities are all 840, which represents the total capacity of the value

Easter Island Line	
Production Name	**Weekly Demand**
Large moai	1,000
Medium moai	1,000
Small moai	1,000
Bird man	200
Rongo rongo tablet	400
Glowing moai	600
Totals	**4,200**

Figure 7.1 This chart starts our exploration of every part every interval by showing customer demands for one week.

Easter Island Line						
Product Name	**Weekly Demand**	**Monday**	**Tuesday**	**Wednesday**	**Thursday**	**Friday**
Large moai	1,000	840	160			
Medium moai	1,000		680	320		
Small moai	1,000			520	480	
Bird man	200				200	
Rongo rongo tablet	400				160	240
Glowing moai	600					600
Totals	**4,200**	**840**	**840**	**840**	**840**	**840**

Figure 7.2 The schedule that would result if we were to build in a weekly interval.

stream. The lot size, no matter the method, has to fit within the capacity available in the Lean system.

Figure 7.3 shows a one-day EPEI, meaning that each part is set up and run each day. This approach will give much better part availability, and therefore a better service level, with less inventory, than a one-week interval. Again, note that in each day the quantity to build equals 840. To achieve this smaller interval, a significant reduction in setups would need to occur, since we are now doing five times as many setups as in the one-week interval.

Why Should We Strive for Smaller Intervals?

The smaller the interval, the smaller the lot size, which in turn:

Easter Island Line						
Product Name	Weekly Demand	Monday	Tuesday	Wednesday	Thursday	Friday
Large moai	1,000	200	200	200	200	200
Medium moai	1,000	200	200	200	200	200
Small moai	1,000	200	200	200	200	200
Bird man	200	40	40	40	40	40
Rongo rongo tablet	400	80	80	80	80	80
Glowing moai	600	120	120	120	120	120
Totals	4,200	840	840	840	840	840

Figure 7.3   The schedule that would result if we were to build in a daily interval.

- Reduces lead times
- Increases flexibility to build the right product at the right time
- Reduces inventory on the floor
- Reduces space
- Improves quality
- Reduces surges of work upstream
- Provides more practice doing setups (practice makes perfect)

Setup reduction is the key to reducing the intervals and becoming more responsive to the customer. A common definition of setup is the work required to change a specific machine, resource, work center, or line from making the last good piece of Unit A to the first good piece of Unit B. Note that this is the elapsed time, not the total work content to do the setup, just like in a NASCAR pit stop. If a NASCAR pit crew could add another person to cut one second off of the pit stop time, would they do it? The usual answer is yes, because keeping the car on the road is critical to winning the race. In Lean, keeping the machine ready to make parts when they are needed is the goal, and that is different than making more parts. We should only make enough parts to satisfy customer demand, which means that the benefit from setup reductions can be realized in smaller intervals.

Reduced setup time equals reduced intervals and smaller lot sizes, which in turn means shorter lead times, less work in process, and potentially more output if it is needed.

How can we realize savings from reduced setups?

- Keep lot sizes the same, reduce labor: This makes the cost per piece go down.
- Keep labor the same, reduce lot sizes: This means more setups (but same overall time) to make the same number of pieces. This means that part cost doesn't change.

Option 1 seems more attractive, but it can be demoralizing to the Lean effort. Since Lean requires a company-wide, all levels of employees effort to make continuous improvement happen, reducing labor, specifically by laying people off based on setup (or any Lean-related) improvement will be counterproductive. Option 1 may be attractive if labor is scarce. This would allow you to redeploy the labor to other value streams.

Option 2 is the one we advocate, since there are many residual benefits from this approach. Remember, with option 2 we are gaining all of the benefits of smaller lot sizes that we discussed previously. Further, the higher the mix variability, the more option 2 makes sense. This is because a small interval allows a broader range of products to be produced in any given timeframe.

So, we vote for option 2, keep labor the same and reduce lot sizes: Why would we do this?

- Better flow. Since flow is one of the primary goals of Lean, this alone makes a compelling case for reducing lot sizes.
- Better response to product mix changes. Adjusting the frequency with which parts show up in the schedule is much easier than trying to fit large lot sizes into a schedule.
- Faster throughput, based on the fact that the parts can spend more time being processed and less time waiting in the setup queue.
- Shorter lead time based on shorter queues of parts waiting while a setup is performed.
- Achieving a mix-leveled schedule, or full heijunka, since a completely mix-leveled schedule is our ultimate objective, and reducing lot sizes is a critical activity in achieving this. This also allows us to have more even capacity requirements across work centers, and a more even material usage plan (helps supply chain).
- Inventory reduction across the value stream.

So How Do We Determine the Interval?

We would compare the total time needed to run parts to the effective working time per interval. Any leftover time can be used for changeovers.

The dark section in Figure 7.4 represents the time needed to process parts on the workstation or total run time. The light section is the leftover time in a time period or the time remaining for setups. Effective working time is the sum of both of these and should be the same number used to calculate takt time (does not include break and lunch time). What we would do is to see how many setups could fit into the leftover time period. This graphic begins to show that the interval calculation is based on available capacity, and that the more capacity available, the smaller the interval will be (the more setups that can be done). This is not the traditional way to approach lot

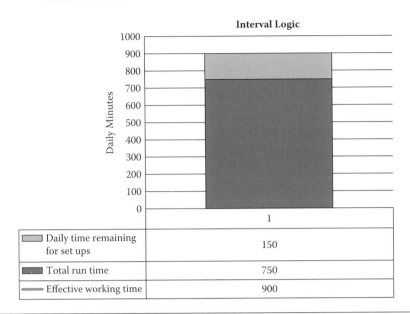

	1
Daily time remaining for set ups	150
Total run time	750
Effective working time	900

Figure 7.4 Diagram depicting the Lean approach to lot sizing, namely, the interval.

sizing, which typically tries to balance the cost of inventory with the cost of placing an order (including setup).

An Example: Murphy's Toys Trim Data

Cycle time: 1) In industrial engineering, the time between completion of two discrete units of production. For example, the cycle time of motors assembled at a rate of 120 per hour would be 30 seconds. 2) In materials management, it refers to the length of time from when material enters a production facility until it exits. Syn. Throughput time.

—APICS Dictionary, **8th edition**

For our purposes, we will use the industrial engineering definition any time you see cycle time in a Lean environment. The materials management definition shown simply serves to confuse things, as this also can be called throughput time. The runtime column is the yearly volume for each piece multiplied by its cycle time.

Figures 7.5 and 7.6 show an easy way to calculate the interval for a process. In this case we have taken the daily runtime and compared it to the daily effective working time available for the process. We have then added up all of the setup times for all of the parts and they equal 750 minutes. When we divide the minutes remaining for setup (the leftover after runtime is subtracted from effective working time) by the total setup minutes, we determine that we could perform all of the setups in the family an interval of one week. In consultation with the continuous improvement team, it is decided to go for an interval of one-half week, which means that the setup times must be cut in half. This goal becomes the driver for the kaizen efforts to improve the process and setups.

Easter Island Line	Process	3D Carver		3D Carver
Product Name	Daily Volume	Cycle Time Min	Run	Changeover Min
Large moai	200	1.5	1.5	120
Medium moai	200	1	1	120
Small moai	200	0.5	0.5	120
Bird man	20	1	1	120
Rongo rongo tablet	40	1	1	150
Glowing moai	60	1.5	1.5	120
Totals	720			750

Figure 7.5 Chart showing the data that we will use to calculate an interval for a fictitious company, Murphy's Toys.

Interval	3D Carver	Unit of Measure
Effective working time	900	Minutes per day
Total run time	750	Minutes per day
Daily time remaining for setups	150	Minutes per day
Total setup time required for family	750	Minutes per day
Interval	5	Days

Figure 7.6 Calculation of the interval for one process at Murphy's Toys.

To get to the target setup time, we know that the current setup time for all of the parts totals 750 minutes. Since we want to cut the interval in half, from one week to one half week, we need the setups to be cut in half to 375 minutes. With six parts in the family, this means around sixty minutes per part for setup.

Other factors besides setup that determine interval include:

- Cycle time
- Volume of parts
- Number of items
- Uptime
- Available work time
- Yield/scrap

Most of these factors affect the runtime required to produce the parts. Obviously, the available work time can also be manipulated, which is often a more attractive option than may appear at first glance.

We could also change any of these factors to achieve smaller intervals. If we shorten the cycle time of the items, then the runtime needed will be reduced, leaving more time for setups. We could also create a parallel process to produce some of the volume of parts, again reducing the runtime required. We could move some of the items to another product family, again reducing the volume of parts to produce. If we improve the availability of the process, through improvements in machine uptime (availability) via total productive maintenance (TPM) techniques, for instance, we will have more time available in the process, again leaving more time for setups. We could add work time to the schedule with the same effect, although this involves additional expense. Finally, we could gain more available time by reducing the yield or scrap rate, via something such as Six Sigma (which will be discussed in Chapter 9).

Interval and Capacity

Balancing Work (Operator Balance Charts)

For manual processes, or processes with no changeovers, we will balance the work to the takt time. For processes that have changeovers, we will balance the work to an interval. This is an important distinction, not often made in the Lean world. Once setups enter into the picture, it is necessary to abandon the idea of takt time (really just the rate of production) compared to the work content to determine the amount of labor needed for a process.

The interval is necessary to determine how much work will be spent doing setups. Please note that the process time for an operation is not necessarily the same as the cycle time, and the setup time used to calculate the interval may not be the labor content of the setup. A setup time of an hour with two operators will obviously contain two hours of labor.

This simply means that the operator balance chart for the process should include the activities for an interval worth of work. The interval thus sets the amount of labor needed to run processes that have setups, since the work includes the process time for the part plus the labor setup time required.

Interval is limited to the available capacity. One way to approach the interval is to set a capacity of machines and people, and then make the intervals fit the available capacity as a starting point. Then discussions about alternatives can be held, including what improvements in flow could be made if more capacity was available, what setups should be targeted for reduction, etc. This approach fits into the idea that the interval is a goal-setting exercise as much as it provides a single answer to the lot sizing question.

The logic goes like this: The amount of product to run stays constant in any period (based on the S&OP production rate.) Therefore, the more capacity available, the more time that will be left for setups, and therefore the shorter the interval will be. This seems self-evident, but EPEI is the only lot sizing approach that recognizes capacity constraints up front, not after the schedule has been created. Other lot sizing techniques try to balance the cost of carrying inventory and the cost of ordering. Capacity testing happens later in the planning cycle. The interval approach recognizes limited capacity as part of the initial calculations. Many problems in manufacturing today are caused by schedules that call for more capacity than is available.

Due to the complexity of the typical planning run in most systems, it is rare that a poor result in the capacity planning portion causes people to rerun the plan. Indeed, in the authors' experience, many companies ignore rough cut and capacity requirements planning (CRP) altogether. It is extremely difficult to project what changes will be seen in capacity requirements based on lot size changes in the current ERP setup. Lean, with the product family/value stream organization, plus clear standard work and a robust heijunka process, makes these changes much more transparent and predictable.

Lot Sizing as Part of Scheduling

The difference in the interval approach is that the lot size is determined before the schedule (not as part of the scheduling calculations), and the schedule that falls out of the process will always fit the available capacity. This is the essence of how the heijunka process is different than traditional scheduling. We have already determined how many setups and how much volume will fit into the capacity available, so the job of the schedule is to simply put enough work in the schedule to fill the capacity. The schedule will always be achievable because the capacity available is built into the scheduling template—as long as the rules are obeyed, of course.

Applying the EPEI to Traditional Planning Systems: The Period Order Quantity

In period order quantity (POQ), the lot size is equal to the net requirements for a given number of periods. The quantity of any single part can change in each interval as long as the total runtime and the total setup times equal the capacity available. Thus, as demand changes on any single part, the quantity can be changed to meet that demand, as long as the number of parts being produced and the total quantity being produced remain constant. The number of planning periods included within the ordering period can be determined based on the EPEI calculation. The intent is to eliminate remnants.

This is the most demand-sensitive lot size. Even though we are equating the POQ with the EPEI, keep in mind that this is only in the mechanics of executing the calculation of the actual lot size to build, not in the way the lot sizing rules are arrived at. Calculating the EPEI is very different from arriving at a POQ, which typically still involves trying to achieve a balance between inventory carrying cost and the cost of ordering.

Note that in Figure 7.7 we cannot answer the question marks in periods 7 and 8, since we don't have any demand visible for periods 9 and 10, which we need to

		Periods							
		1	2	3	4	5	6	7	8
Gross Requirements		130	160	120	260	130	120	185	115
Scheduled Receipts									
Projected Available	370	240	80	590	330	200	80	?	?
Net Requirements									
Planned Order Receipts				630				?	
Planned Order Releases		630				?			

		Technique
Order quantity		POQ
Safety Stock:	80	Fixed
Allocated quantity:	0	POQ
Lead time:	2	Periods
Low-level code:	2	

Figure 7.7   A classic display of demand and supply showing the mechanics of the period order quantity lot sizing rule.

determine the lot size for the order due in period 7. The lesson to be learned is that the demand visibility must be at least the lead time plus the interval for the lot sizing to work. Thus, a longer interval extends the time that customer orders must be in house before they are processed. This is a bad thing, and another reason to drive for short intervals. The longer the POQ, or the interval, the longer demand must be visible to determine the lot size. In a make-to-order environment this becomes a critical point, as it causes the lead time to the customer to extend.

Mix Issues

Up until now in this chapter we have dealt with environments where it is feasible to make each part in a value stream in every interval, no matter how small the interval may be. This is the essence of EPEI in the Toyota Production System. For many manufacturers, however, this is either not possible or not practical. We will now spend some time describing the meaning of interval in environments where a high product mix variability makes building to an EPEI very wasteful.

In a mix-leveled environment, all parts produced in the same process will be produced in each interval, and the quantities will be dictated by the projected usage of each item. The quantities will thus be fixed in each interval. Leveled mix is made possible by an inventory of all the finished goods items. Can you imagine the power of using the same set of materials over and over in the same pattern? This is the ideal situation, since leveling mix means that both the same capacity and the same materials (through the entire bill of materials [BOM] structure) will be used in each interval.

Toyota does this without a finished goods stock by having firm orders from the dealers out beyond the production lead time, indeed beyond the lead time for much of the supply chain. Because the dealers do not have real demand this far in advance, any forecasting mistakes end up on the dealer lot as finished goods, but this doesn't mean that all parts will be in the finished goods inventory, although the possibility exists for any model and option combination to end up in finished goods.

For manufacturers without this kind of future visibility, however, the usual approach is to keep finished goods of all items and use this as a buffer to be able to produce a mixed-leveled schedule, using the inventory as a buffer between forecast and actual demand.

In a high-mix environment, as stated in Chapter 3, this strategy of keeping all finished items in stock may be prohibitively expensive. In this case, we can adopt a strategy where we will make many parts to order and buffer with some high-usage parts. In this strategy we must define the interval in which the pacemaker will run the mix of products. Because some items (or maybe most) will be made to order, the actual quantity of these items will vary in each interval based on actual demand. In a make-to-order, high-mix environment, it would be more wasteful to build all of the products each interval in a mix-leveled manner than to simply build what was sold and change the parts produced each interval.

Having a lot of part numbers does not constitute a high mix in this context. The issue is how variable the part mix of sales is, in other words, how frequently the items within the family of items sell. If you have two thousand parts, but each sells every day, this would not be considered a high-mix environment as we are discussing it here. On the other hand, if you have 435 items as an example, and 296 of them sell once per year, that could be considered to be a high-mix environment. The less frequently an item sells, the more compelling the argument to make it to order, as opposed to making it to stock.

Volume Variability

Figure 7.8 shows a relatively stable volume over this period, meaning that we could potentially handle this value stream with a fixed crew. This would mean using a buffer of backlog in the case of a high-mix value stream, or of inventory in the case of a low-mix value stream.

Mix Variability

Figure 7.9 shows a high degree of mix variability, in that 296 out of 435 pumps had demand in only one month out of nine, and only one pump had demand in all nine months. It would seem that having an interval of nine months, as silly as that would

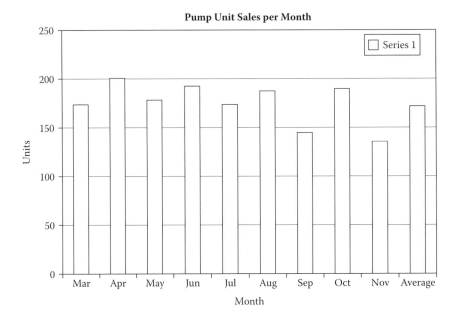

Figure 7.8   Graph of volume variability, shown as work content per interval based on the customer orders.

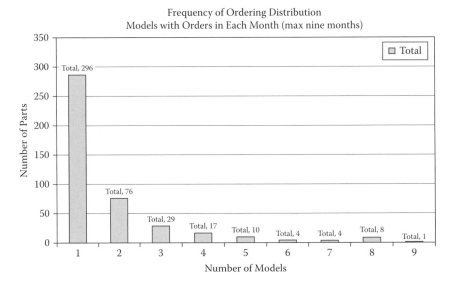

Figure 7.9   Chart showing a high degree of mix variability, as most of the items only sold one time in the last nine months. This calls for a make-to-order strategy with a make-to-order interval.

Month	Mar	Apr	May	Jun	Jul	Aug	Sep	Oct	Nov	Avg
Units	174	201	178	192	150	187	145	190	135	172
Part No.	90	98	72	92	77	91	84	92	72	85

Figure 7.10 Summary of the sales for a product line of pumps over the last nine months. For each month, we have listed the total pumps sold and the number of different part numbers that were sold.

be, would handle this situation, but it wouldn't recognize that the value stream sells more than 435 of this type of pump, so that there are many other items that weren't even sold during this nine-month sample.

The chart shows that only one pump sold in all nine months, and eight more pumps sold in eight of the nine months. These could be considered high-frequency items, meaning that they are ordered in all or most of the intervals. It is worth noting that only twenty-seven pumps sold in more than half of the months, allowing this value stream to be classified as a high-mix value stream. Indeed, most job shops don't see any more mix variation than this. Two hundred ninety-six items had a sales order in only one of the nine months, meaning that well over half of the items were sold only once in the last nine months.

Making Sense of High-Mix Value Streams

What Figure 7.10 shows is that even though there are 435 parts in this value stream, only 85 Part No. are sold on average each month. To design a value stream, we could plan to make each item each interval (say a month), and thus we could plan to do 172 pumps per month (for takt time) and 435 changeovers per month, which would be the classic definition of EPEI. It is also plainly foolish, as it would be physically impossible, to do more changeovers than parts. The alternate is to prepare to make a volume of 172 pumps per month and 85 changeovers per month, or about 8 pumps per day and 4 changeovers per day.

What Do We Gain by Increasing the Interval?

Figure 7.11 shows the relationship between interval and number of setups required in a high-mix value stream. Conventional logic says that doubling the interval will require half as many setups to produce the volume. Because of the high-mix variability in this value stream, however, we see that this is not the case. We can see based on the data that doubling the interval from one month to two months results in an average of a 13% setup reduction (11 divided by 87, as shown in the average column). This much smaller reduction in the setup work often doesn't warrant the increased inventory and decreased flexibility experienced with the larger lot size.

AMU	Mar	Apr	2-Month	May	Jun	2-Month	Jul	Aug	2-Month	Sep	Oct	2-Month	Average
Monthly interval	90	98	188	72	92	164	77	91	168	84	92	176	87
Two-month interval			157			144			149			157	76
Setups saved/month			16			10			10			10	11

Figure 7.11 The gain made by increasing the interval from one month to two months using the detailed data from the previous chart. As you can see, the gain is minimal from doubling the lot size.

Pump example:
  One-month interval:
    Volume = 172 parts per month, 87 setups per month
  Two-month interval:
    Volume = 172 parts per month, 76 setups per month

Doubling the lot size by doubling the interval only saves eleven setups per month. In a low-mix environment we would expect the setups to be cut in half, while in a high-mix environment, as we can see, this is not the case. This is the advantage of the demand-driven lot size, because if there is no demand, or demand is small, then the lot size will also be small. Why is this?

The reason for this is that most of the parts are sold very infrequently, so that the same items are rarely in the sales mix for consecutive periods. The higher the mix variation, the less increasing the interval helps. This is because the items show up infrequently as demand, so that including more periods in the interval doesn't combine many setups.

We would do better spending our efforts on reducing the setup times and reducing the lot size by reducing the interval. In a low-mix environment, where most or all parts are sold in each interval, a doubling of interval will equal a halving of setups. The higher the variability of the mix, the less payback there is in increasing the interval, and conversely the less the penalty will be for decreasing the interval. As always, smaller is better when thinking of lot size.

Interval as Goal Setting

Let's assume that we were at a two-month interval and realized that this was not that beneficial (from above), so we are going to add eleven setups per month in going from a two-month interval to a one-month interval. Suppose that the setups currently take one hour each. We are thus adding eleven hours of time. To get it back, we need to reduce each setup by 11*60/87, which equals about 8 minutes (7.58 actually). Thus, each setup must be reduced to fifty-two minutes. This would be the kaizen target. So to cut the interval in half, the setups don't need to reduce to thirty minutes, but only to fifty-two minutes. Thirty minutes may not seem possible, but fifty-two minutes should seem achievable (eighty-seven is the number of setups we plan to do based on a one-month interval from above).

It is obviously important to go through this kind of analysis before making plans, as otherwise it would be assumed that the setups need to be cut in half, which may not seem possible. Eight minutes of reduction seems much more reasonable, and will provide a significant improvement when achieved.

High-Mix Interval

Interval is critical in high-mix environments. However, interval will not be used to make all products in a family, only the ones sold in an interval. We will call this the make-to-order interval. To determine the interval in this environment, you cannot use average usages or such, but instead must use real sales history.

As we have stated before, EPEI is every part every interval. This refers to the capability of the process to make the setups required to cover the demand for all of the parts that the machine produces. It is a reflection of process capability and flexibility. Processes that can achieve smaller intervals are much more capable of responding to changes in customer demand, whether from volume changes or mix changes, than processes that have long intervals. The amount of mix present in a value stream does not change any of this.

In the case of high-mix value streams, however, it is often more wasteful to think in terms of making every part every interval, since many parts may sell infrequently. In this case we want to find out how many part numbers would typically sell in a time period and prepare to make that many setups. This will be the make-to-order interval.

In job shops we may have an interval that covers the parts that the customer has actually ordered over a period of time rather than an interval that covers making all of the items in a family. This is because it is very common to find many items that have low demand and infrequent customer orders. In some instances it is there-fore not feasible to completely level the mix within a value stream. In these cases we make sure that we level volume, and make the products that the customer has ordered first.

This has the same calculation as the EPEI, only we need to determine how many parts will be sold in any single timeframe, which makes this more of a dynamic calcu-lation than the standard EPEI.

Average usage inflates the number of setups required, because it assumes that all parts will be made in each interval. The make-to-order interval will be expressed as number of setups plus amount of output. It can also be expressed by hours available: hours run required = hours of setup possible. Interval is still a goal-setting activity, meaning that the purpose of the interval is still to set objectives for setup and other waste reduction.

Determining the Interval

The interval must be measured not only through the machine, but also by the man-power required to produce the setups. Many shops are constrained by labor capacity, not machine capacity. We thus need to check the required capacity in both machines and people. We will often find that the machines can make a smaller interval than is currently being run, but this would require more labor than the current interval.

This is an expansion of what people are traditionally doing with interval, and is an important distinction with this approach. Remember, we are usually constrained by people in a high-mix shop.

The number of people in a job shop is often the constraining factor, as opposed to the machines, which are often plentiful, as opposed to the number of trained operators. This means that you should use something like operator balance charts to check the number of people needed to perform the work called for by the interval, both in the planning stage and in the execution portion, when actual demand is scheduled.

Interval in Value Stream Loops

A value stream loop is all of the processes between two supermarkets. As a general rule, all of the processes within a loop must run the same interval. If you have two adjacent processes that have different intervals, the choices are: keep them in flow and run the larger interval of the two, or separate the two processes with a supermarket and run them at two different intervals. To some extent, the difference in the interval size between the two processes would steer this decision. If it is desired to run two different intervals at two processes, then they must be separated with a supermarket.

This is because of the physical difficulty of separating various lot sizes within a first-in–first-out (FIFO) lane, which would be how all of the processes between processes would be connected. Imagine that the first process produces three days' worth of product at a time (three-day interval), but the next process wants two days' worth for its interval. One day's worth of product would now be left at the front of the FIFO lane, and would have to be either moved or ignored, making the FIFO rules difficult to execute. The same would be true if the next process wanted a five-day interval worth of parts. The supermarket avoids this kind of problem.

In a FIFO lane, the parts are placed in order as they are produced. If I place a week's worth of parts in the lane, and the next process is running a two-week interval, they will have to go further up the lane to find the second week's worth of parts, a violation of FIFO rules. The opposite is true if we put two weeks' worth in the lane and the interval of the using process is one week: they need to leave half of the parts unprocessed until next week. Thus, a supermarket is needed to manage this. An interesting way to think of this is to think of the steps within the loop as routing steps, which in conventional logic cannot have their own lot sizing rules. The supermarket would be represented by a new level in the BOM, which could then have a new lot sizing rule.

In this chapter we have explored lot sizing in both the traditional planning and control environment and in the Lean environment. In most instances, the Lean approach is much simpler, and more directly addresses one of the real weak spots in ERP planning and control, namely, capacity planning and control. In the ERP environment lot sizing is done individually part by part, typically with an attempt to get the least total cost for the part by balancing setup costs and inventory carrying costs. The effect of changing the lot sizing rules, even though they can be significant, is not known until capacity requirements planning is run, after the materials planning portion of the system is run. As mentioned before, by the time issues are found at this stage, it is often too time-consuming or too difficult to find the source of the issue to correct the problems, so they are left until next time. As we have described, the Lean approach to lot sizing is closely tied to the available capacity, and thus avoids this problem. Further, since the setup time and the lot size are directly related to each other in the EPEI lot sizing method, and the benefits of reducing lot sizes are so clear in a Lean value stream, lot size reduction becomes a significant driver of kaizen activity in a value stream.

We have also described a significant extension to EPEI, namely, the make-to-order interval. Because there are many environments where completely leveling mix in the production schedule would be very wasteful, it is necessary to determine the quantities based on how many part numbers, and total quantities, will be produced in each time period. This combination determines the make-to-order interval.

In Chapter 8 we will talk about two topics that often spring to people's minds when they think of supply chain management: logistics and warehousing.

8

Warehousing and Logistics

In this chapter we will cover two important topics for the supply chain, warehousing and logistics. We will cover the traditional view of physical control of inventories, then the relationships between the warehouse and the organization, and then we will review traditional logistics activities. In the second half of the chapter we will review distribution requirements planning, Lean warehousing and Lean logistics.

Traditional Physical Control of Inventories

Let's start the warehousing portion of the session with discussing what warehousing is all about. In basic terms, it is all about the physical control of inventories, typically finished goods inventories. One major tool that typically has been used to help maintain this control is ABC. The ABC principle states that effort and money can be saved by applying looser controls to the low-dollar-volume class items than the high-dollar-volume class items.

> **ABC classification:** The classification of a group of items in decreasing order of annual dollar volume (price multiplied by projected volume) or other criteria. This array is then split into three classes, called A, B, and C. The A group usually represents 10% to 20% by number of items and 50% to 70% by projected dollar volume. The next grouping, B, usually represents about 20% of the items and about 20% of the dollar volume. The C class contains 60% to 70% of the items and represents about 10% to 30% of the dollar volume. The ABC principle states that effort and money can be saved through applying looser controls to the low-dollar-volume class items than will be applied to high-dollar-volume class items. The ABC principle is applicable to inventories, purchasing, sales, and so on. Syn: ABC analysis, distribution by value. See: 80-20, Pareto analysis, Pareto's law.
>
> *—APICS Dictionary*, **12th edition**

ABC has been widely used and is a great tool to help prioritize how inventory is treated; certain SKUs in the warehouse are more important than other items. As previously mentioned, ABC analysis is used to help manage inventories in the warehouse. This is typically done by using the ABC to set up cycle counting cycles, with A parts being counted more frequently than C parts; the A parts are clearly more important than the C parts. Although this is true on a general level, care must be taken not to

Example of a Warehouse Layout

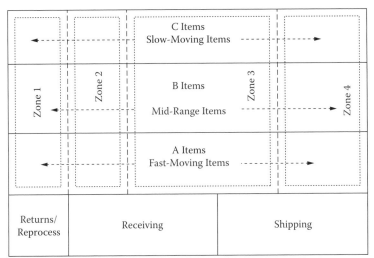

Figure 8.1   A typical warehouse layout, optimized for ABC.

ignore the B and C items; the lack of C items can shut you down just as quickly as an A item would.

Additionally, many warehouses use ABC to help set up physical inventory locations, with A parts being set up either close to the shipping area (front of warehouse) or primarily in the golden zone—shelf area typically thigh to shoulder high, an area that minimizes stooping or reaching. Let's look at a typical example of this (Figure 8.1).

In Figure 8.1 we see a typical overhead layout of a warehouse, and how ABC can be used. Nothing fancy, but it can help in minimizing travel time of put-away and picking.

Traditional Relationships

We will now discuss how the warehouse is typically viewed within the entire organization. Now it might seem odd to talk about the relationship between the warehouse and the rest of the organization, but as you will see, this relationship does have a profound impact on how a typical warehouse operates. Traditionally, the warehouse is a place where new people are hired into or, in some cases, are "put out to pasture." Also, the warehouse is often looked at as a place to escape the drudgery of the office, where you can go and grab a smoke and goof off with the warehouse guys. Additionally, not much thought is put into how the warehouse is set up and run. Once it is set up, it is rarely changed. Although these are not necessarily bad things, they can "set the stage" for how the inventories and warehouse are managed.

Issues caused by the traditional approach to the warehouse as a "second-class operation."

Packaging—Readying an Item for Shipment

Packing and marking: The activities of packing for safe shipping and unitizing one or more items of an order, placing them into an appropriate container, and marking and labeling the container with customer shipping destination data, as well as other information that may be required.

—APICS Dictionary, **12th edition**

Packaging is often ignored, but it can have a significant cost impact. How are units packaged in production? Typically, you will see either a full case or individual pieces. What may not be done is to see how the customer actually uses the items, and then package accordingly. Another packaging issue is in overpack sizes. This is sometimes a critical issue, especially with small parcel shipments, specifically with UPS and its oversized dimension surcharges. Extra dimensional inches can cost you dearly, and this cost doesn't show up at your meter in the warehouse unless you impose the surcharge yourself. The surprise comes when you get your final invoice.

Unitization is consolidation of several units into larger units for less handling. Instead of shipping one or two boxes to a customer, you could be shipping many more, each with an additional box, shipping, and labor cost. It is rare that you will see a warehouse (company) change how items are packaged or unitized once these are set up in the shipping process, although adapting either or both of these to the needs of the customer and the mode of shipping can increase customer satisfaction and often reduce overall shipping costs, including labor and materials.

Overall Warehouse Setup and Item Locations

Last, but certainly not least of the issues is in the overall setup of the warehouse. Some companies have an experienced warehouse engineer design their layout, but many just put up racks in the available space. This can be due to many things, but to not fix a bad layout is inexcusable. Even worse is assigning physical inventory locations once and then never changing them with demand constantly changing. It is not uncommon to have to change inventory locations yearly, and those with pick to light systems may have to do this seasonally—several times a year. Demand for SKUs can and will change as time passes; therefore, where items are located in the warehouse will need to change as well.

Traditional Logistics

Switching gears now, we are going to look at what we refer to as traditional logistics.

Logistics: 1) In an industrial context, the art and science of obtaining, producing, and distributing material and product in the proper place and in proper quantities. 2) In a military sense (where it has greater usage), its meaning can also include the movement of personnel.

—APICS Dictionary, **12th edition**

Logistics, within most firms, is given more attention because these costs are often negotiated with several carriers, and whether we are Lean or not, we all love to beat up carriers on pricing. So the focus is on reducing costs by shipment/lane, and all of the factors that impact "the lane" are often ignored. When discussing lanes, this refers to the point-to-point service cost, typically zip code to zip code. Little thought is given to accessorials (add-on service costs) or if the goods are in the correct "starting point."

Logistics Skill

Logistics is the keystone to supply chain management success. It is not about shipping or warehousing; it is logistics. The logistics focus is:

- The movement of product. This is more than transportation of goods. The modes and carriers selected must complement the supply chain strategy and must be responsive to the needs of customers and the entire chain.
- The movement of information. Information technology is key to being responsive. It must be both internal—the enterprise—and external, with customers and suppliers.
- Cost. This is the cost of the entire supply chain, both operating and capital. It is not just the cost of discrete cost factors such as freight or warehousing.
- Time/service. Supply chain management is tailored to and responsive to each customer. To gain a competitive advantage, service and time compression are vital to keep customers replenished and inventories under control.
- Integration. The integration of systems and people, teamwork, must be both internal and external. If it is not, then there are gaps, potential for delays and errors, and failures in the supply chain process.

Freight Cost

The freight cost is the total cost incurred in moving goods (by whatever means). It includes packing, palletizing, documentation, loading/unloading charges, transport (carriage) costs, and insurance costs.

Traditional logistics can cause a typical suboptimization problem, where the people within certain functions work to reduce costs within that function without regard to the total costs of the organization. The logistics people can reduce the hundred weight costs (basis for less than truckload [LTL] freight costs), but the hundred weight cost is only one factor that should be considered. Another misguided effort in logistics is in obtaining a higher discount percentage. The real issue is the base rate from where the discount is taken. Is it this year's tariff or from five years ago? Seventy percent off

Shipment Weight and Transit Days (201–900 pounds)						
Origin States	Small Package Transit	1 Day	2 Days	3 Days	4–6 Days	Truckload
MD, DC (Local)	1 day	EXCEL	EXCEL	N/A	N/A	N/A
CT, MA, MD, NH, NJ, NY, PA, RI, VT	2–3 days	New Penn	New Penn	N/A	N/A	CFI or Schneider
ME	3 days	New Penn	New Penn	New Penn	N/A	CFI or Schneider
DE, OH, VA, WV, NC ZIPs: 270–282	2–3 days	Yellow Freight	Yellow Freight	N/A	N/A	CFI or Schneider
AL, FL, GA, IL, IN, MI, MO, SC, TN, WI, MO, NC ZIPs: 284–289	4–5 days	Emery/ Menlo	Yellow Freight	Yellow Freight	N/A	CFI or Schneider
AR, IA, KS, LA, MN, MS, ND, NE, OK, SD, TX	5–7 days	FedEx 1 day	FedEx 2 day	FedEx 2 day	Yellow Freight	CFI or Schneider
AZ, CA, CO, ID, MT, NM, NV, OR, UT, WA, WY	5–7 days	FedEx 1 day	FedEx 2 day	FedEx 2 day	Yellow Freight	CFI or Schneider
AK, HI	N/A	FedEx 1 day	FedEx 2 day	N/A	N/A	N/A
Note: For shipment over 9,000 lbs., truckload movement, shipments requiring special handling, or shipments between suppliers, contact your buyer for special instructions.						

Figure 8.2 This example shows a typical routing guide. Again, higher costs in certain lanes can be a trade-off for this simplicity.

a current tariff may be more expensive than 30% off a tariff that is years old. Again, the lane pricing is more important than a discount percent.

One tool that is often used in traditional logistics is the routing guide. Routing guides are often set up by shippers or larger buyers, and list which carrier will service specific lanes or service areas by weight/dim weights. The guide instructs the shipper how to ship the item. This is set up by origin or destination point (sometimes both), and the instructions can further specify which carrier to use based on the weight and service level (overnight, one day, two days, etc.) desired.

Unfortunately, there are usually trade-offs in attempting to simplify logistics to this level. Often, carrier rates can vary significantly by weight range and lane, and this detail is usually ignored by a routing guide; it would make it too complicated. Often, routing done by a transportation management system (TMS) will do a better job than a routing guide (Figure 8.2). Additionally, using online transportation consolidators can help manage this process as well.

Distribution Requirements Planning

One traditional tool that relates to inventory control at the warehouse level is distribution requirements planning (DRP). DRP is a term that has been around for a while but is often ill understood. Much of that is due to how systems approach replenishment at a warehouse level, and DRP is not often an option.

> **Distribution requirements planning (DRP):** 1) The function of determining the need to replenish inventory at branch warehouses. A time-phased order point approach is used where the planned orders at the branch warehouse level are "exploded" via MRP logic to become gross requirements on the supplying source. In the case of multilevel distribution networks, this explosion process can continue down through the various levels of regional warehouses (master warehouse, factory warehouse, etc.) and become input to the master production schedule. Demand on the supplying sources is recognized as dependent, and standard MRP logic applies. 2) More generally, replenishment inventory calculations, which may be based on other planning approaches such as period order quantities or "replace exactly what was used," rather than being limited to the time-phased order point approach.
>
> —*APICS Dictionary*, **12th edition**

Andre Martin, the director of Materials Management, Abbott, Canada, pioneered DRP as a part of the quick response initiatives of the 1970s and 1980s. His book, published by the Oliver Wight Company, is considered the "seminal" work of the subject.

One way to think about DRP is simply as another planning level that manufacturing resource planning (MRPII) and enterprise resource planning (ERP) often leave out. Many, if not most, companies may operate or ship to multiple warehouses/distribution centers. Traditional ERP plans at a higher level have really gross requirements (at a finished goods level) considering a traditional supply chain. DRP simply adds on another planning level, considering each stocking location and a lead time offset to cover transportation to that location. Net requirements by stocking location, with lead time offsets to service (transportation) those locations, are the key difference between MRPII and DRP. It is a subtle but significant difference, and some systems handle this as is, but others do not.

In the example in Figure 8.3, the central supply replenishes the three warehouses, A, B, and C. The process starts with each of the warehouses doing a gross-to-net requirements calculation. The calculation creates a planned order receipt anytime inventory falls to negative or falls below safety stock. The planned order receipt date is offset by the lead time for the item, yielding a planned order release date. These requirements are then passed on as the central supply gross requirements, which are summarized for each time period, and the gross-to-net process would be performed again. This would continue through all of the layers of the supply chain. This is an improvement on MRPII, but it is still MRP netting logic; therefore, it is still problematic, as we have discussed in previous chapters.

Lean Warehousing

Now that we've discussed warehousing and logistics in a traditional setting, let's discuss what these look like when Lean is applied. First, we are going to talk about

Warehouse A

Warehouse A	Week							
	1	2	3	4	5	6	7	8
Gross requirements	80	80	80	70	80	90	90	90
Schedule receipts								
Project on hand 90	10	30	50	80	0	10	20	30
PLO receipts		100	100	100		100	100	100
PLO releases	100	100	100		100	100	100	

Warehouse B

Warehouse B	Week							
	1	2	3	4	5	6	7	8
Gross requirements	30	30	30	20	30	35	35	35
Schedule receipts								
Project on hand 90	60	30	0	30	0	15	30	45
PLO receipts				50		50	50	50
PLO releases		50		50	50	50		

Warehouse C

Warehouse C	Week							
	1	2	3	4	5	6	7	8
Gross requirements	60	60	70	70	80	80	90	90
Schedule receipts								
Project on hand 170	110	50	80	10	30	50	60	70
PLO receipts			100		100	100	100	100
PLO releases	100		100	100	100	100		

Central Supply

Central Supply	Week							
	1	2	3	4	5	6	7	8
Gross requirements	200	150	200	150	250	250	100	0
Schedule receipts								
Project on hand 550	350	200	0	150	200	250	150	150
PLO receipts				300	300	300		
PLO releases		300	300	300				

	Quality	Lead Time
Warehouse A	100	1
Warehouse B	50	2
Warehouse C	100	2
Central supply	300	2

Figure 8.3 Example of DRP mechanics.

Lean warehousing and how it builds on some of the best practices that many warehouse people already do. Although the setting of inventory levels is an important part of warehousing, we've already discussed that subject, so we are going to assume that the inventory levels are "proper." So, what are some of the key items, other than inventory, that are important to manage in the warehouse. Note that not all items that need to be controlled are critical; this list can be viewed as the major cost drivers in the warehouse.

- Inventory—There is no doubt that this is cost driver 1, but we've discussed how inventory levels are set. A warehouse is just another "supermarket" where goods are held for sale, and you only have a supermarket if you cannot match when and where customers want product with your ability to supply the goods on a timely basis. In most cases, shipping lead time is a normal expectation for customers, so you also have to consider the additional manufacturing or supply time. Can you deliver product to the customers at or under the lead time that they expect? If customers expect immediate or near-immediate order fulfillment, then you may need one or more warehouses. The process for identifying where these need to be located is not changed in Lean. However, how much inventory is held will be calculated by the same rules we discussed in determining supermarket size.
- Space—Typically warehouse space is assigned on a square foot basis and is probably cost driver 3. Many organizations find themselves with too little space, given that space is used inefficiently and growth is usually not planned for. Symptoms of this are leased trailers or outside/off-site warehouse space.
- Labor—This is cost driver 2 and, as we will discuss, is probably the least controlled.

Lean warehousing looks at space use as being a critical issue to deal with. Space usage is commonly referred to as slotting, but it goes beyond the concept of where items are placed within the warehouse; it also takes into consideration how much inventory is put into the location and attempts to create a handful of standard location sizes.

Slotting is a simple concept: put higher-velocity items closer to the point of use, then slower-velocity items. The reason to do slotting is that it can do more to save labor costs than just about anything else. How? By reducing the travel time—walking or driving in the warehouse. If your faster-moving items are closer to their point of use, either receipt or shipping, then people will be traveling less to put away or pick these items. One of the biggest issues is in how to do slotting. Some people think that slotting can only be done with a warehouse management system, but most warehouse management systems, especially those included as standard in most ERP systems, generally available do not do slotting (Figure 8.4).

The example is an excerpt from a monthly turns report that has been edited (Note: The turns are totally fictitious). The key here is that we are looking at year-to-date (YTD) issues (Figure 8.5). Make sure that you have at least six months of data, which

SKU	Description	Current Inventory	YTD Issues	Turns	Days Lead Time	Last Year's Sales Units
30-5681T	a	187	2,073	11.085	1	9
73-1650	b	108	194	1.796		416
CAW-23	c	83	194	2.337	1	2,062
E-59X	d	11,520	6,912	0.600	120	0
LABEL-2	e	48,144	7,056	0.146	1	4,911
LAM-182	f	417,739	445,261	1.065	1	3,249,541
M20G	g	2,079	7,003	3.368	1	25,090
MDF12-68A	h	45	194	4.311		123
PEN-WH	i	3,622	2,069	0.571	1	14,079
PS-43	j	107	2,046	19.121		18
TUBING-6	k	63,000	337,000	5.349	1	960,800
VPF-19	l	436,100	316,300	0.725	1	4,013,883

Figure 8.4 Slotting in Excel starts with gathering data.

SKU	Description	Current Inventory	YTD Issues	Turns	Days Lead Time	Last Year's Sales Units	Slot
LAM-182	f	417,739	445,261	1.065	1	3,249,541	
TUBING-6	k	63,000	337,000	5.349	1	960,800	
VPF-19	l	436,100	316,300	0.725	1	4,013,883	
LABEL-2	e	48,144	7,056	0.146	1	4,911	
M20G	g	2,079	7,003	3.368	1	25,090	
E-59X	d	11,520	6,912	0.600	120	0	
W-184F	m	2,640	6,888	2.609	100	120	
30-5681T	a	187	2,073	11.085	1	9	
PEN-WH	i	3,622	2,069	0.571	1	14,079	
PS-43	j	107	2,046	19.121		18	
73-1650	b	108	194	1.796		416	
CAW-23	c	83	194	2.337	1	2,062	
MDF12-68A	h	45	194	4.311		123	

Figure 8.5 The next step is simply sort descending on the YTD column. This can guide you on where to slot.

should be enough to be a representative sample unless the majority of your items are short term or seasonal type items. If that is the case, you may want to set up two slotting areas: one for seasonal items and the other for nonseasonal. As you can see, the excerpt has a wide range of YTD issue quantities.

The next step is to simply sort descending, on the YTD column. This can guide you on where to slot. Next, add a slot column to help. The slot column is where you will fill in where you plan to put that item. This requires that you have a logical warehouse location system. This is typically done with a mix of alphanumeric characters that represent:

- Aisle
- Rack
- Shelf
- Bin

For example, A12R2 can represent Aisle A, Rack 12, Shelf R, and Bin 2. This should match the location system used in your warehouse picking program and is one of the few places where the use of a system is actually helpful. (Typically, finished goods [FG] inventory is added into the FG inventory in a system and located. We will discuss where and when to use and not use ERP components in Chapter 11.)

One thing to make sure you do is spread out your highest-velocity A items, so that you don't cause congestion; spread these among many racks. You also may want to incorporate the location sizing as well, which we will discuss later.

In many warehouses, one or two items can have "high velocity" (turn very quickly). In these cases, we can often save a great deal of labor time by setting up what we like to call cross-slotting. In larger-scale and automated warehouses, cross-docking can effectively be applied. However, in smaller, nonautomated warehouses, cross-docking is not usually practical. In these cases, cross-slotting may be applicable (Figure 8.6). You simply set up these SKUs in a position near the shipping door, so items can be readily available for picking/pulling. The items in this cross-slotting location can change as seasonal demand changes, and there may be times when this is not necessary—gain due to seasonal demand.

Let's look at the example in Figure 8.7. In this picture, you can see that there is a large stack of product, staged at the dock (you can see the doors in the background). This is vinyl siding, and each box you see is about 100 pounds and 12½ feet long. Receiving this, putting it away, and then pulling it as orders come in is very labor-intensive, especially during the busy summer building months. Cross-slotting during the busy summer months has eliminated the need to expend labor to put away and pick one specific SKU that happens to make up the majority of the sales during that period. At other times, the stock is put away and subsequently pulled from racks or floor locations in the warehouse.

Cross-Slotting

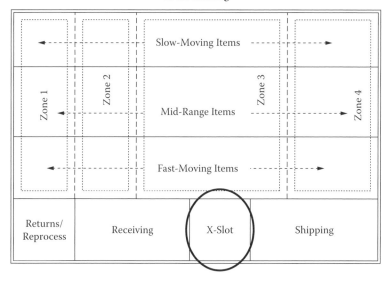

Figure 8.6 As you can see from the diagram that we reviewed in traditional warehousing, we have made one change.

Figure 8.7 An example of cross-slotting at a theoretical warehouse.

Controlling Space

A common problem for many companies is the lack of space. Most companies fail to properly plan for even a small amount of annual growth, year over year. Even with modest growth, a company can find itself out of space. This is why sizing your inventory is important. Again, this is related to inventories, and we have already had this discussion. Now, the issue is in how to manage the space that you have. In many companies, the entire inventory of a SKU is typically put into the same general location. This ties up an excessive amount of space and should be discouraged.

In order to control space better, consider these:

- Grouping similar items together. This is based on the size of the item/SKU. This brings some uniformity and better space utilization.
- Making sure that discrete items have their own separate location. Don't put more than one SKU in a physical location. Although this is warehouse 101 stuff, it is surprising that the most elementary warehouse disciplines are not enforced.
- The same can be said for clearly marking aisles, racks, shelves, and bin locations. This can turn simple picking into an Easter egg hunt.
- Using common sense in your inventory location schema. Just because you have thirteen characters in the field doesn't mean you have to use them. We have actually seen a location of 0000000000001, possibly the dumbest and worst location logic possible.
- Storing items vertically refers to storing items so their longest dimension is vertical. As we will discuss in the next slide, we use the longest length to determine standard shelving height, and come up with some standard heights in order to easily set up an area and use it for random storage. Sizing by at least one dimension is a better use of space than using a standard pallet-size setup for every location. This does not guarantee good cube use, but it is much more efficient than a one-size-fits-all setup.
- Most well-run warehouses will have primary picking locations, based on an ABC classification, sized for a day's or less worth of demand and bulk storage for the excess. These primary locations are then replenished.

Next, we discuss how to calculate the size of a location (Figure 8.8). Let's review some of the data requirements first, by column.

A—SKU.
B—Size grouping of SKU. This example shows Sbox or Small Box; user defined, this is example of any box smaller than 12 × 12 inches.
C—Lead time for SKU in days.
D—Safety stock level for SKU in days.
E—Days of supply: calculation C + D.
F—Average daily demand.
G—Stocking quantity (locations): calculation E × F.
H—SKU length in inches. Note: One important factor is that "length" will always be the longest dimension of the SKU.
I—SKU width in inches.
J—Minimum location size in square inches: calculation G*(H × I). Often, this may be easier to do in feet; just change your input and reference in J3.

Note: If you do have a lot of items that are lengthy (long in length compared to more of a box shape), then setting up racks to accommodate the length using the shelf

		Location Calculation—Stocking Quantity and Area Required								
A	**B**	**C**	**D**	**E**	**F**	**G**	**H**	**I**	**J**	1
SKU	Group	Lead Time Days	Safety Stock Days	Days of Supply	Average Daily Demand	Stocking Quantity	SKU Length	SKU Width	Min Location Area Sq In	2
										3
(Formulas)				C4 + D4		E4*F4			G4*(h4*14)	4
A324	Sbox	28	3	31	3	93	12	10	11,160	5
B459	Sbox	21	3	24	1	24	10	7	1,680	6
S547	Sbox	10	2	12	2	24	9	2	432	7

Figure 8.8 A quick method to calculate the space requirements for a location.

depth is probably wise, even if you have to double up the shelf depth. Otherwise, store these items vertically.

It is impractical to customize space for each item, so standardizing location sizes is recommended. Three to five sizes based on the results will get you started. Using the example above, you could create three small box location sizes: one to accommodate 12,000 square inches, one to accommodate 2,000, and the last to accommodate 500.

Controlling Labor

Labor takes front stage in Lean warehousing. If we look at traditional manufacturing cost of goods sold (COGS), labor is a small part. However, the goal in the Toyota Production System (TPS) is to make sure that your labor is fully utilized, as opposed to fully utilizing the machines. This subtle outlook helps control inventories, doing away with the silly notion that machinery must be fully utilized. In warehousing, machinery is a lesser issue and people are typically not tied to specific machines or lines. Here, labor is a major cost, and therefore must be managed in order to control costs.

Controlling warehouse labor can be accomplished without a great deal of technology, but it does take some effort. What we are attempting to do is to control labor in the warehouse by employing what is known as short-interval scheduling or man loading. All that this does is to look at the basic time it takes to do a task, like picking orders, and multiply this time by the number of orders to be picked to come up with a staffing plan (Figure 8.9).

Workload Planning (in minutes)				
Total Time		Breaks, Nonproductive Time		Total Available Time
480	minus	30	equals	450
Day's Lines		Standard Lines		Batches
500	divided by	5	equals	100
Total Available Time		Batches		Pace
450	divided by	100	equals	4.5
Standard Cycle Time		Pace		Pickers Needed
20	divided by	4.5	equals	4.4444444

Figure 8.9 Example of picking workload planning.

Let's look at some of the data that will be needed to do this:

- Standard lines: This is simply the average number of lines per customer order.
- Cycle time: How long does it take to pick? This can be based on existing labor records or can be calculated using informal time studies. This would be a good task for a kaizen group from the warehouse.
- It is recommended to do this planning in seasonal buckets—lines per order or cycle times may change during seasonal periods, and orders will have more lines or the lines will have more units, or both. This usually isn't a linear increase, so having actual data or studies is helpful.

First, we determine the total available work time by subtracting planned breaks, etc., from the total shift time. Next we look at the demand (day's lines) divided by what we found to be an average number of lines per order, and this results in the number of planned batches, often referred to in Lean as pitch. All this does is capture the amount of work anticipated to be released into the warehouse. Next, we divide the total available time by the batches to come up with a pace that is the pace of planned work completion. Next, we look at this calculated pace against our labor standard of 20 minutes per 5-line order; the result is that we need 4.44 pickers to do that day's workload. We need to round this up to 5 pickers, anticipating that other work can/ should be assigned when the pickers are finished with the day's workload.

Now that we have that information (we need 5 pickers), what do we do with it? The question here is how can we best manage these 5 pickers? Do we just turn this information over to the supervisor and expect him or her to deal with it the best way he or she knows how, or do we adapt some Lean tools from TPS into the answer?

We've discussed the use of visual control in order to help manage a number of things, such as production and inventories. Let's look at using it in the warehouse. Visual control is used in conjunction with the workload leveling. It provides an easy to see and use visual tool to monitor performance and to organize off-schedule conditions. In traditional management we used to focus on the individual, while in visual control we focus on the causes of variances. We still monitor the team's performance if necessary, and can drill down to the individual pickers if needed. Let's walk through this process.

In Figure 8.10 we have assigned 5 pickers as planned in the workload leveling. Our visual control board has time-related intervals of control, in this case hourly buckets. Now, how do we come up with the plan? Each anticipated order should take 20 minutes; that translates to 3 orders per hour times 5 pickers. So, in the hourly intervals outlined above, they should pick 15 orders per hour, and after the second hour, they should have 30 and so on. Now the actuals will vary, but this is where Lean management comes in. The time slots cover picking time increments. In the example, the first period is from 8:15 to 9:15 and there are order increments of 1 to 15; these represent how many orders that could be picked in that time frame.

Warehouse Operations Control Board			Pickers—Jim, Bob, Mike, Karen, Debbie			
Time	Plan	Count	Actual	Variance	Comments	Action Items
8:15 to 9:15	15/15	~~1 2 3 4 5 6 7 8 9 10 11 12~~ ~~13 14~~ 15 16 17 18 19 20	14/15	−1	Slow start	Have orders ready
9:15 to 10:15	15/30	1 2 3 4 5 6 7 8 9 10 11 12 13 14 15 16 17 18 19 20				
••••••••						

Figure 8.10 Warehouse visual control board.

So, the pickers pick up their orders and pick them. As they finish one order and return to pick up another, they simply cross off the next uncrossed number in the count column. This shows everyone, including the supervisor, how well they are doing during that time slot. At the end of the time period, the supervisor writes in the actual count, calculates a variance, and writes down what caused the variance (may have to ask) and a plan for eliminating the variance cause in the future. This continues to the end of the day—simple, easy, and most importantly, visual.

Lean Logistics

Lean logistics covers a pretty broad number of items, and we'll cover these during the remainder of the chapter. Lean logistics is the application of Lean principles within the logistics part of the supply chain to help optimize the entire supply chain.

> **Lean logistics:** Pull system with frequent, small-lot replenishment established between each of the firms and facilities along a value stream. Let's suppose that Firm A (a retailer) sells directly to the end customer and has been replenished by large and infrequent deliveries from Firm B (a manufacturer) based on a sales forecast. The adoption of lean logistics would involve installation of a pull signal from the retailer, as small amounts of goods are sold, to instruct the manufacturer to replenish exactly the amount sold. The manufacturer would in turn instruct its suppliers to replenish quickly the exact amount sent to the retailer, and so on all the way up the value stream. Lean logistics requires some type of pull signal (EDI, kanban, web-based, etc.), some type of leveling device at each stage of the value stream (heijunka), some type of frequent shipment in small amounts (milk runs linking the retailer with many manufacturers and the manufacturer with many suppliers), and in many cases, various cross-docks for consolidation.
>
> —*Lean Lexicon*, 4th edition

Lean logistics as a terminology has been around for some time, but it is largely associated with transportation firms—LeanLogistics or LeanCor (the latter was founded by one of the pioneers of Lean logistics—Robert Martichenko). Unfortunately, if you look for concrete examples of Lean logistics, you won't find much detail, but the

Lean Lexicon definition does capture the essentials. Our hope is that we can start to build a framework from which to work and build on. It is important to work toward optimizing the entire supply chain while applying Lean logistics concepts, so you don't suboptimize the chain to perform some Lean logistics activities.

We are going to discuss Lean logistics in two ways. The first has to do with the things you can do to reduce waste/minimize costs for you and your customers. The second has to do with addressing common logistics problems that plague you and your customers. If you asked most customers about the logistics problems that they experience, it usually comes down to two things: items are not delivered as promised and poor communication/visibility regarding the shipment. So, we are going to address improving your logistics processes so that you deliver your service as promised.

What do the customers want vs. what are they willing to pay for? Obviously, what the customers want and how they want it has a big impact on your logistics. However, this should not stop you from offering more efficient (cheaper) alternatives to the customer. It is not uncommon that the customers will change their buying wants/habits if you can offer them a better (lower) overall landed price.

- Shipping costs: Because shipping is often an add-on price on the invoice, your customers may not be aware of the true landed cost. As we will discuss in the next chapter, many firms have no idea what their real total landed costs are, so coming up with ways to help them lower these can foster the type of relationship that Lean means to develop—getting away from the hiding of information and not doing the right thing by your customers.
- Areas for Lean logistics: Lean logistics covers a pretty broad number of items, and we'll explore these in the remainder of the chapter.
  - Inbound logistics
  - Controlling costs
  - Outbound logistics

Inbound Logistics

When we talk about inbound logistics, it really comes down to who is controlling the costs of shipments inbound to your facilities. It has been a fairly long-term practice that a supplier will ship items for "free," at some order total ($) level. Does anyone really think that this is free? In our experience, freight is not only not free, but it is rarely even a pass-through expense, where you are paying only the costs that the supplier pays. Most of the time, freight is marked up, so the supplier is making a profit on the transportation portion of the overall part cost. Eliminating this factor can help reduce the overall part cost by 1 to 2%; that may not sound like much, but this goes right to your bottom line or can help reduce your costs and make you more competitive.

An important part of product costing, whether or not you are Lean, is in understanding exactly what you are paying for, so your purchasing people must "guide" your suppliers into breaking down and realistically assigning these costs. This will be covered in the purchasing section, but it simply comes down to getting item pricing from your suppliers that excludes any shipping costs. Shipping costs then can be looked at discretely and decisions regarding these costs can be determined.

If we were to break this down into an example, we would first need the cost for the units, without freight built in. Next, calculate the transportation cost for a typical order or order minimum. You can easily do this at the website of your transportation provider (will need freight class and possibly dim weight) or at a web-based freight broker. You will need to talk to your transportation provider to see if the added volumes (you are shipping) will have an impact on your tariff—better discounts or more favorable classifications, e.g., freight-all-kinds (FAK). (Having an FAK rate allows you to ship everything under one freight class, simplifying the process. However, you must make sure that this is favorable to you and not just the freight company.) Also, have your supplier provide you with a quote as well; even if they mark it up, they may have a better discount than you.

Other costs need to be considered. For example, what are your costs for handling the transportation now? These costs should be based on an activity-based or value-stream costing model and not just some percentage thrown in. For simplicity, will your transportation department be able to handle the additional load without having more people (based on the assumption of simplicity, we will assume that you have a transportation group and that they can take on additional shipment volumes) so the real costs may be marginal and can be ignored? Add these up and you will get a rudimentary total landed cost. Compare this with your supplier and act accordingly.

When we talk about other ways to control costs, some of these may not be new to you; again, Lean does not have a "corner on the market" in good business practices.

- Milk runs: Milk runs are used extensively by Toyota—mainly taking advantage of the close proximity of its suppliers to the assembly plant. This entails the sharing of transportation expense by many suppliers as a truck makes its way, supplier by supplier, and ends up at the assembly plant. This may not be practical in all applications, but do you take advantage of the opportunities to use truckload service this way? Would it be less expensive to move freight from an LTL carrier to a TL carrier and make one or more stops to pick up freight? This would include combining inbound loads with companies within your general vicinity (your supplier may be able to help you identify companies in your area that it ships to).

- Merge in transit: If suppliers are close to each other and not necessarily close to you, can they merge their shipments to you at one facility, so the freight can be combined and give you a lower cost? This was common practice for Bill when he worked in the bicycle business, where many of the components at that time came from Taiwan. Thus, the suppliers were close to each other but far away from our plant in Tennessee. The practice had the advantage of filling containers that otherwise would not have been well utilized. For instance, a container of bicycle chains would reach maximum weight before the container was full, and conversely, a container of handlebar grips would fill the container well before it reached the maximum weight for the container. Combining these two items into one container utilized both the maximum volume of the container as well as the maximum weight. Note that it is doubtful that your suppliers will know about other suppliers in their area, so your logistics people will have to do this. Freight consolidators are also available to help with this. Consolidation can be coordinated so the freight does not linger at the supplier. If you have enough leverage, you can do this merge at the LTL cross-dock; the timing is much more critical because the freight companies don't want freight "lingering" on their dock.

- Buy the service that you need: One obvious but overlooked cost control is in buying the service that is really needed. We've walked into many warehouses and have seen boxes, pallets, crates, etc., sitting there after being air freighted in. As with manufacturing, if you have to expedite on a regular basis, there is something seriously wrong with the way you operate. Another cost savings area is moving freight via rail or intermodal. Obviously, it may only make sense for freight traveling long distance, but recent improvements in rail on-time shipment performance may make this a smart move, especially for large/bulky and heavy items.
- Last is another obvious method—consolidate your transportation expenditures with one national carrier and a handful of regional carriers: The more dollars you spend per carrier, typically the better the discount off of tariff rates.

Outbound Logistics

As with inbound logistics, outbound will focus on cost management. However, before you can worry about things like cost, service expectations must be dealt with. Obviously, what the customers want and how they want it has a big impact on your logistics. However, this should not stop you from offering more efficient (cheaper) alternatives to the customer. It is not uncommon that the customers will change their buying wants/habits if you can offer them a better price.

Service will determine cost, and your customers should be given choices regarding service—talk to your customer. This should be approached in a true partnership frame of mind, as you should remember that the shoe is on the other foot regarding transportation costs; you should be prepared to separate transportation costs out of your product costs as well.

Although service (in days) is generally better nowadays, faster delivery times usually result in higher costs. As with inbound transportation, "overbuying" service (paying for service not needed) should be reviewed with your customers. Again, how much savings can you and the customer realize if delivery is delayed? Although this is obvious, how many of you do the analysis and share it with your customers? Many of the things we talked about in the inbound section will apply here—milk runs, merge in transit, buying the service that you need, and consolidating your spend, both inbound and outbound.

Zone Skipping

Zone skipping is used with small packages, typically shipped via UPS or FedEx. Shipments to a specific area are combined into one shipment, at a bulk type rate, and then the shipment is broken down and shipped from the area, by box, using point-to-point rates. Contact your local UPS or FedEx rep to run the numbers.

Packaging

Another little used but obvious cost driver in outbound logistics is packaging. Unfortunately, packaging can be driven by many illogical factors, such as "We've always done it that way" or the more mysterious carton of 12 and case of 144. By dealing with what the customer wants, some of these traditions can be changed for the better in delivering what the customer wants.

Packaging is often handled in two ways, selling in either "eaches" or case quantities. This overlooks two important factors. One is how the items are used. Are they typically used by the customer one at a time, or are they used with some other item? Packaging items that are typically used or sold together can lower shipping costs and can add some convenience to the customer. Two is a pure shipping cost consideration. Does your customer even need the item formally packaged or overpacked? It is not unusual to see instances where items have to be unpackaged before use. This creates two wastes: waste of inventory and the waste of overproduction.

What is the velocity of your product usage by your customer? Wouldn't that be helpful to know before packaging is designed? This could have a direct impact on the size of box, carton, and even pallet, and all of these will have a direct impact on the transportation cost. This is not to say that you can or should have custom packaging for every customer, but what does this do to overall supply chain costs for your customer? Not knowing is no longer good enough.

Product Availability and Its Effect on Logistics

Product availability is often a problem for not only you (the availability of the products you buy from your suppliers), but it is also an issue for your customers. As we all know, demand management is rife with problems and forecasting; no matter how good we get, we will usually be wrong. Toyota goes to great lengths in trying to stabilize

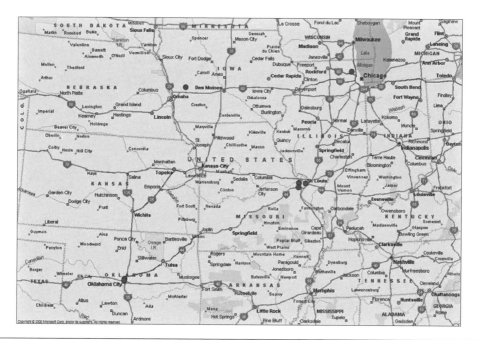

Figure 8.11 An example of a map created by MS Streets and Trips. This is step two. The first was determining that the current logistics setup would not satisfy customer expectations.

demand, so that the bullwhip effect is minimized through the supply chain. To be sure, Toyota does stack the deck a bit in its favor by limiting options, etc.; however, to dismiss what is really going on would be short-changing the learning experience and benefits to be gained. However, if you have determined that you cannot meet your customer expectations, as far as inventory availability—for example, customers want it next day, but you do not have an economical way of shipping next day—then the next step would be to start an analysis regarding where the inventory may need to be.

How to do this? A great tool to help you with mapping where your customers are is Microsoft Streets and Trips (Figure 8.11). (Microsoft Map Point has more features but it is more expensive.) You simply import an Excel file with all of your customer zip codes and they will be mapped out as shown. The obvious densities of customers can help you start an overall analysis to determine if your inventory is in the right area. The next step would be to look at sales dollars or volume sales (units), using the same process. Being close to the customers is important, but dollar sales and volume will have a greater impact on the decision. You simply want to make sure you take care of the customers that buy more dollars or units.

Scenarios can be built to compare total costs side by side; one example is no change in shipping methods from what is done currently. The other would be to compare costs of setting up inventory in a dedicated or public warehouse, with all costs broken out.

One note on customer expectations that was mentioned earlier: These can be shaped by working with customers by discussing service levels and associated costs. For example, do the customers know that they can save money by accepting three- to five-day delivery vs. one- or two-day delivery? (Do you give them choices?)

Figure 8.12 MS Streets and Trips or Map Point can also be used as a poor man's TMS: you can route local or long-distance shipments by simply typing in the zip codes for your orders into the route planning tool.

Figure 8.12 shows how MS Streets and Trips can be used to generate an optimized route, starting in Oklahoma City and ending in Boulder, Colorado. It may be a bit awkward to use and it isn't integrated, but it does work.

Collaboration

We'd be remiss if we didn't mention probably the most important aspect of Lean logistics: extending the small group concept (kaizen) into the supply chain. More often than not, we look for complicated answers to questions that are easily answered, only if we ask the questions to the right people in the first place. Most people and companies will go to great lengths to try to figure things out that someone else can easily tell them. For example, back in the mid 1990s, an industry initiative was started called collaborative planning, forecasting, and replenishment (CPFR).

> **Collaborative planning, forecasting, and replenishment (CPFR):** A collaboration process whereby supply chain trading partners can jointly plan key supply chain activities from production and delivery of raw materials to production and delivery of final products to end customers. Collaboration encompasses business planning, sales forecasting, and all operations required to replenish raw materials and finished goods.
>
> —*APICS Dictionary*, **12th edition**

It was a great concept—trading partners would start trading data down the supply chain, and this communication would help reduce costs, primarily by reducing pipeline inventories. Although there were pockets of success, the overall concept flopped.* Why? We simply don't trust each other, even when there is no reason to distrust each

---

* Walmart provides most, if not all, of its suppliers with detailed point-of-sale information on a fairly constant basis—we've heard as often as every fifteen minutes. This information is then used by the supplier to replenish Walmart's distribution centers (DCs) and ultimately drive production. Walmart does this to reduce supply chain costs because if its suppliers have lower costs, that results in better pricing to their customers.

other (many trust items, e.g., confidentiality, can be overcome with contracts). Toyota has found that sharing these data are beneficial in cutting costs; therefore, everyone, including the customer, benefits from collaboration. A great example of this is that Toyota has freely shared information regarding TPS, knowing full well that only a handful of companies (none in their industry) will actually implement the system fully, and since it is a system, partial implementations will only produce incremental savings and improvements. Even if a competitor did succeed in implementing its own version of TPS, Toyota would say that it is good for society and not give it another thought. Toyota is more concerned about how it can improve internally than in how its competition runs their companies.

So, what can you share to help reduce logistics costs? Refer to the inbound logistics section that references other ways to reduce costs. Each of these can be improved if more partners participate; for example, instead of sending items less than truckload, a milk run could be set-up at truckload rates. By sharing resources, costs can be reduced.

Visibility and Reliability

Visibility is often a subject of complaint by just about everyone in the supply chain, since almost everyone is dependent on someone delivering something. In this day and age, there is little excuse for this because most ERP systems have the ability to view the status of orders, especially if tied to a transportation management system. If this is not the case, most TL, LTL, and small package carriers have the ability to track items online by PRO (progressive) or other tracking number. Also, there is push technology associated with most of these carriers to automatically send e-mail updates when there is a change to shipment status.

The real issue with visibility isn't that it can't be done, but that the data usually is not updated or correct in the first place. This is often a process problem and can be fixed by using value stream mapping to identify and fix these issues. Reliability is a lesser problem because carriers have gotten better at delivering on time. However, when things do go wrong, they are often process related as well and may require a process review—again with value stream mapping or some other process review.

In this chapter we have reviewed two aspects of physical materials management in the supply chain: warehousing and logistics. More than in our previous chapters, we find that there are many overlapping techniques between traditional management of warehousing and logistics and Lean management. However, for many reasons, traditional supply chain management has been slow to adopt these techniques, such as milk runs, freight consolidation, and especially, close supply chain partnerships.

In Chapter 9 we will cover an area that has very little overlap between traditional methods and Lean methods: quality.

9
QUALITY CONTROL

In this chapter we will contrast the traditional quality control approach with the Lean approach, understand Lean quality tools such as poke yoke and jidoka, understand the details of Technical Standard 16949, and review seven basic quality tools in Lean.

Quality control can mean different things to different people. Let's consider the *APICS Dictionary*, 12th edition definition: "The process of measuring quality conformance by comparing the actual with a standard for characteristic and acting on the difference."

Under traditional quality control, inspection of goods and services (checking to make sure that what's being produced is meeting all expectations) takes place at the end of the operations process. The problem with this sort of inspection is that it doesn't work. It won't ensure quality, however you define it. Traditional quality control was originated and has been perpetuated with good intentions, but some of the methods that have been used are not very effective. Take for example ISO 9001. It is rare that you will see product quality improve as a result of implementing the ISO process. This is because the people using ISO have ignored the product by concentrating only on obtaining certification. Unfortunately, ISO makes this easy by focusing on the quality documentation process.

Sampling is another method that can be problematic, but to be fair, just about everyone, including Toyota, uses this. The context in which it is used is the key, with many organizations just tracking results on control charts and little else. In running large batches, pulling samples and measuring them seems reasonable, but depending on the process, defects can slip by undetected.

Quality control (QC) departments were created to check quality, but unfortunately, this is often after items have been made. In addition to this issue, removing the responsibility to check quality from the operators is misguided. This appears to be another division of labor that has "watered down" personal responsibility on the shop floor. It isn't that inspectors can't or shouldn't be used, but your first line of quality is the people performing the work. We could go on and on about how bad quality control can be, but to be fair, traditional quality methods have often helped improve quality, but by no means can we say that it is the best or easiest way.

Lean Quality

Lean quality is less about tools and more about getting everyone involved. Lean quality is built upon the origins of QC, but using the small group concept, with the groups made up of people that actually work in the production area—along with others for a fresh set of eyes. This small group concept is one of the foundations of Lean via kaizen. These groups can work on items other than quality, but the overall focus is continuous improvement.

Quality circles were all the rage in the 1980s, when the Toyota Production System was first being introduced into the United States. At the time, there was quite a panic within the United States, with the Japanese automakers making huge inroads into the U.S. market. In the rush to "copy" what the Japanese were doing, the main message was totally lost on most in the United States. Lean was looked at as a set of tools that could be implemented, instead of being a philosophical change to the way a company operates. Unfortunately, quality circles failed and, by and large, Lean is still looked at as a tool set.

Toyota has gone through the same quality evolution as most, but has applied its core beliefs to the concepts and techniques. After WWII, the Japanese manufacturing base was rebuilt and the Japanese became disciples of Dr. W. E. Deming and statistical quality control (SQC). To be sure, no one can dispute the wisdom of Deming, but Toyota found that SQC was simply not good enough for them. Acceptable quality levels were not good enough, nor was a defect rate of one in a million—their aim was for 100% good units (zero defects)! This level of perfection was necessary for two main reasons: The biggest was for the customer. Even one unhappy customer out of a million was too much!

The second reason was more of an internal reason. Just in time (JIT) requires perfection because any disruption in manufacturing causes JIT to come to a halt. One-piece flow requires every item to be usable, and this is a significant change from having a mountain of inventory to fall back on. Additionally, some have suggested that this is attributable to the Japanese culture, but this is only half right. It is a cultural change, but one that has every employee involved and committed to producing 100% good parts. Even so, Toyota adopted several elements of Deming's teachings. These included plan-do-check-act (Figure 9.1).

> **PDCA (plan-do-check-act):** An improvement cycle based on the scientific method of proposing a change in a process, implementing the change, measuring the results, and taking appropriate action. It also is known as the Deming Cycle or Deming Wheel after W. Edwards Deming, who introduced the concept in Japan in the 1950s.
>
> —*Lean Lexicon*, **4th edition**

Plan-do-check-act is the embodiment of the scientific method into Lean practice. The scientific method is summarized by hypothesis–experiment-evaluation. PDCA is used in many instances, such as for gathering data, when developing a new process or improving an existing process, or when implementing almost any change.

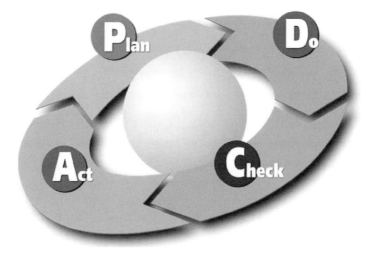

Figure 9.1 This is also known as the scientific method. It is the basis for kaizen in Lean practice.

Elements of a learning organization that mirror PDCA include:

- Identify root causes and develop countermeasures
- Initial problem perception
- Clarify the problem
- Locate area/point of cause
- Ask "why" five times; investigate root cause
- Countermeasure
- Evaluate
- Standardize

There are many tools available for problem identification and solution. The key to this process is to identify the root cause of a problem, which is where the "five whys" play an important role.

Identifying the root cause of a problem is the first step in the scientific method. A common method of achieving this currently is by using an A3 "sheet," which forces a concise summary of a problem and presents a solution on a single sheet of paper. The advantage of using A3s is that the methodology creates focus on the root cause of problems as well as telling a story of how the problem will be solved. A good A3 can be thought of as "standardized storytelling," meaning that it conveys both facts and meaning in a common format.

Countermeasure is used instead of solution. This is in recognition that the countermeasure may cause other problems that will need to be addressed in turn. Many tools from Six Sigma are appropriate for this process, especially in the problem-solving area. The DMAIC framework for problem solving, specifically with what Six Sigma really does—addressing variability—is also worth mentioning.

DMAIC stands for define, measure, analyze, improve, and control.

- Define—Scope the project. Find out or identify customer requirements.
- Measure—Quantify current performance. Locate the problem.
- Analyze—Identify and confirm root causes.
- Improve—Implement and test solutions.
- Control—Confirm the implementation. Hold the gains.

So, the shift was made from inspector-led quality to operator-led activities. This is where the people manufacturing the items are responsible for the quality. However, this was not good enough because it ignored some basic issues—quality starts at design. So, quality had to become everyone's focus, not just the operators'. This approach eventually became know as total quality management. Let's follow this progression with a bit more detail that will be helpful to understanding this topic.

Total quality management (TQM): A term coined to describe Japanese-style management approaches to quality improvement. Since then, total quality management (TQM) has taken on many meanings. Simply put, TQM is a management approach to long-term success through customer satisfaction. TQM is based on the participation of all members of an organization in improving processes, goods, services, and the culture in which they work. The methods for implementing this approach are found in teachings of such quality leaders as Philip B. Crosby, W. Edwards Deming, Armand V. Feigenbaum, Kaoru Ishikawa, J.M. Juran, and Genichi Taguchi.

—APICS Dictionary, **12th edition**

Lean and Total Quality Management—Visual Control

A great tool that is used throughout Lean is visual control, and Toyota has learned to integrate this into QC. The use of visual control was the "next" step in Toyota's quality "evolution." Visual control was accomplished by using these three methods:

- Judgment of the operator was used when appropriate. This would have covered instances of finish quality, where it would be difficult to quantify. For example, was the polished finish on the part to standard? A person could be trained to make this determination.
- Mechanical devices are the most common type of visual control. These can include measuring devices that can be used to determine if the part is to spec or not.
- Poka-yoke devices and fool-proofing are other types of devices or processes that can be used in visual control. These normally take the concept of mechanical devices a step further. For example, instead of having a gauge where you must measure the part to determine if it is good or not, you develop a gauge that is preset to the standard or passing measurement (can be a range as well). These have been in use for quite a while and are known as go/no-go gauges. These fool-proofing devices can take many forms.

Poka-Yoke	Control	Warning
• Contact	• Parking height bars	• Staff mirrors • Shop entrance bell
• Fixed value	• Predosed medication	• Trays with indentations
• Motion step	• Airline lavatory doors	• Spellcheckers • Beepers on ATMs

Figure 9.2 A few examples of the different types of poka-yoke devices.

Poka-Yoke Methods and Examples

Poka-yoke devices can do two things: they can control the activity or warn you if something is not to specification. Poka-yoke devices usually take one of three forms: contact, fixed value, or motion step. Some examples are listed in Figure 9.2.

A few other real-life examples are the poka-yokes that you can find in your car. These would usually include the gas opening fitting only the appropriate type of fuel nozzle, the gas cap attached to the car, the car keys not being able to be removed until the car is in park, and warning lights to alert the driver of problems.

The most important part of visual control is the empowerment of the workers on the line to shut down the line, if a defect is found and not immediately "fixable." How many production lines do you know of where this is encouraged? In the United States, it usually is a quick trip to the unemployment line if you ever shut the line down. The ability to shut down a process when a problem occurs is called jidoka.

Lean and Quality Control—Jidoka/Autonomation

The next step in Toyota's quality progression is what is known as jidoka or autonomation. Here is where automatic machine or line stopping functionality is built into the machines/production lines. This means that the machine or line shuts down if a part is produced out of standard.

> **Jidoka:** Providing machines and operators the ability to detect when an abnormal condition has occurred and immediately stop work. This enables operations to build in quality at each process and to separate men and machines for more efficient work. Jidoka is one of the two pillars of the Toyota Production System along with just-in-time.
>
> —*APICS Dictionary*, **12th edition**

> **Autonomation:** Automated shutdown of a line, process, or machine upon detection of an abnormality or defect.
>
> —*APICS Dictionary*, **12th edition**

Jidoka sometimes is called autonomation, meaning automation with human intelligence. This is because it gives equipment the ability to distinguish good parts from bad autonomously, without being monitored by an operator. This eliminates the need for operators to continuously watch machines and leads in turn to large productivity gains because one operator can handle several machines, often termed multiprocess handling.

—Lean Lexicon, **4th edition**

One misperception is that autonomation means robotics. Most Toyota facilities lack robotics, and typically they are only used in areas where there are safety or quality concerns. For example, most automakers use robotics in their paint rooms to eliminate the exposure to dangerous fumes. Additionally, automation can aid in quality control, if it can be done at a reasonable cost. However, full automation is usually very expensive, and therefore out of the question.

Another feature typically built in to the lines or machines is that they will shut down when the required quantities of parts are made. This keeps inventories in check by limiting what is produced. Although people may be removed from the "checking" part of the QC process within autonomation (considered the most mundane by most, including Toyota), people are still very much involved in the continuous improvement activities of the work area. This never stops.

Lean and Total Quality Control Management—Companywide

During its quality progression, Toyota came to the realization that a lot of factors affect quality on the shop floor. Here, Toyota incorporated the small group philosophy again—thinking that this is better than Feigenbaum's total quality control (TQC), where QC "specialists" are used. The important point here is that everyone in the organization, including up and down the supply chain, is expected to participate in quality control, not just one group. This goes beyond the typical sloganeering—posters and banners that proclaim this, but usually have no supporting process.

All areas in the organization are important, but product design has the biggest impact on actual product quality: Can a quality item be built again and again with zero defects? Representatives from every group in the company make sure that each part designed can meet this test: Can they make it with no defects? Can their suppliers make it with no defects? Can they assemble it with no defects? Can it be shipped around the world with no defects? And if needed, can we deliver superior service to the final product? This runs counter to the normal "throw it over the wall" behavior seen in many organizations. Each part of the process is done in a stovepipe environment, and once an area is done, it is thrown to the next group and becomes their problem. Because of this, it is typical to see the following organizations deeply involved with the quality effort: product planning, suppliers, design, manufacturing, testing, sales, purchasing, and service.

As with most of the Toyota system, companywide quality control is founded on simple logic that unfortunately is missed by many manufacturing firms. Quality at Toyota follows a logical hierarchy as well:

1. Quality in design—satisfaction of customer needs. First, you must make a product that the customer wants, but this goes deeper than just looks. Is it functional? Toyota designers sweat the details down to how many cup holders are in the vehicle and where they are located.

2. Quality during production—fewer defects reduces production cost. Next, you must be able to make the product cheaply and with few defects. This carries over from design, where quality issues can be designed into or out of the product. Making a product that is easy to build and build cheaply is the goal. Rework caused by defects only adds costs to the process—typically costs that are not anticipated.

3. Quality in customer service—high-quality aftermarket service. Finally, fewer defects make for happy customers after the sale. Also, having superior after-market service increases customer satisfaction if problems with the product develop. Again, this is nothing extraordinary, but Toyota goes to great lengths to do this better than anyone else.

TS 16949

Now, let's look at some of the specifics of how Toyota manages quality. Although internal specifics are not widely distributed, Toyota has endorsed the use of TS (Technical Standard) 16949 as an addition to the existing ISO 9001:2000 standard used by auto companies and their suppliers.

The goals of this standard:

- Continuous improvement
- Emphasis on defect prevention
- Reduction of variation and waste within the supply chain

This quality standard is a good model to work from, but you will need to develop and implement a technical specification that your company can use. As we get into the details, you will still see the importance of people built into the standard.

Key aspects of TS 16949 include:

- Focus on product and process design to meet requirements
- Process for measuring customer satisfaction
- Ability to communicate customer-specific requirements to the appropriate process(es)
- Focus on continuous improvement:
  Auditing all systems, processes, and products
  Effective analysis to drive improvement

As part of TS 16949, these key aspects focus largely on process and people. In this case, the people are your customers. Focusing on the product, customers, and continuous improvement—all support Lean philosophy. Interestingly, since this is shared by most automakers, why do you suppose that there is such a large gap in the adoption of Lean between these companies?

Top management involvement is also spelled out in the technical standard: link to the business plan with quantifiable objectives, and reporting and evaluation of the cost of quality. In these aspects, the role of top management is laid out. Although this may seem to be mundane to many top managers, an effective quality management system will not work without involvement from the top. Quality must become more than hollow promises of making the best products, to actually committing to becoming defect-free—100% quality. To be sure, 100% quality may not be necessary in all environments, but without measurable quality metrics, your quality will not improve.

A clear definition of responsibilities includes the authority to stop the line to fix a problem. An important point is giving the people on the manufacturing floor complete control, manifested in being able to shut down the line. As we previously stated, this may not seem like much, but how many companies do you know that would let the line be shut down? In a Lean factory, you never, ever pass on a quality problem downstream.

- Focus on developing people:
    Competence requirements
    Training
    Evaluating actions taken
- Motivate employees to:
    Achieve quality objectives
    Continually improve
    Create an environment to foster innovation

Again we see the importance of developing respect for people. In the APICS Lean Enterprise training, we stated that Lean culture was probably the most important part of Lean, but the one most often not done. This requires a committed management group and a lot of time, and unfortunately, managers in the United States usually aren't really committed to anything but "the numbers" and have short attention spans. Again, that is why Lean implementation at most companies is more doing Lean "things" than doing real Lean.

- Use of quality tools:
    Statistical process control
    Measurement system analysis
    Failure mode effect analysis

Maybe you thought that quality at Toyota was all touchy-feely; hopefully with this list of tools you will see that there are still statistical process control (SPC) tools in use. The point is that these just measure things; an SPC chart or failure mode effect analysis (FMEA) study has never improved quality—only people can. The key to the use of these quality tools is making sure that you measure process capability, not only of the processes in question, but also the inspection and test processes.

- Control of production process with:
  Control plans
  Work instructions

You want to make sure that your processes are stable and that your reaction plans actually contain responses to nonconforming material.

- Developing suppliers using same technical standard

These may be opportunities to use Six Sigma tools, but only to address variability. The use of Six Sigma tools as a one-size-fits-all "miracle" tool has proven to be disastrous, despite all the hot air from the "Lean Six Sigma" experts—case in point, General Electric. In fact, Toyota views Six Sigma as being a potentially divisive tool, pitting the so-called black belts against everyone else. Mainly, this is because of the statistical emphasis on problem identification in Six Sigma, and Lean people feel that this removes a degree of involvement from the shop floor. Why would you want to divide your people when you can use Lean to unite them? Fortunately enough for us, though, Lean and Six Sigma share many of the same problem-solving tools, so that we may safely present them here.

Seven Lean Quality Tools

Check sheet: A simple data-recording device. The check sheet is designed by the user to facilitate the user's interpretation of the results. Check sheets are often confused with data sheets and checklists.

—APICS Dictionary, **12th edition**

A check sheet is used to provide a structured way to collect quality-related data as a rough means for assessing a process or as an input to other analyses (Figure 9.3). It is meant to be a simple document that is used for collecting data in real time and at the location where the data are generated. There are five general types of check sheets: classification, location, frequency, measurement scale, and checklist.

Pareto chart: A graphical tool for ranking causes from most significant to least significant. It is based on Pareto's law, which was first defined with respect to quality by J.M. Juran in 1950.

—APICS Dictionary, **12th edition**

The Pareto principle states that the bulk of the costs or problems are the result of a few causes (Figure 9.4). This is also known as the 80/20 rule, which says that 80% of the problems will come from 20% of the causes. This principle is behind many different techniques and approaches, from ABC analysis of inventory to, obviously, product

SAMPLE Checklist	
Job or Machine: Secondary metal cutting	
Inspected by: John Smith	
Problem	Frequency
Cut - too long	/ /
Cut - too short	/
Surface scratches	/ / /
Burrs on edges	/ / / /

Figure 9.3   Example of a simple check sheet.

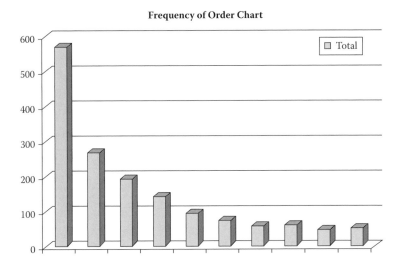

Figure 9.4   A Pareto chart of the number of orders by the number of parts for a value stream. This is an important chart to measure the mix variability of a value stream.

mix analysis and the use of Pareto diagrams for quality analysis. Overall, the Pareto diagram is used as a mechanism to focus effort on the main causes of problems.

Scatter diagram: A graphical technique to analyze the relationship between two variables. Two sets of data are plotted on a graph, with the y axis used for the variable to be predicted and the x axis used for the variable to make the prediction. The graph will show possible relationships (although two variables might appear to be related, they might not be—those who know most about the variables must make that evaluation).

—APICS Dictionary, **12th edition**

Scatter diagrams (Figure 9.5) are used to try and establish a cause-and-effect relationship between two elements, such as overtime hours worked in a week and number

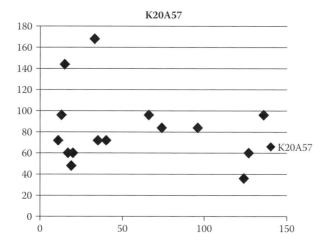

Figure 9.5   Scatter diagram with no correlation between the two variables.

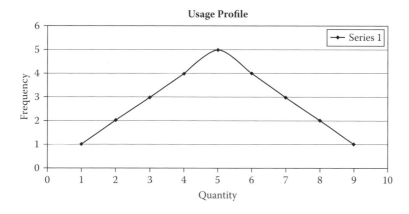

Figure 9.6   Histogram with a normal bell-shaped distribution of events around the mean.

of defects produced. It is often useful to accompany a scatter diagram with a correlation analysis to help determine the strength of the relationship of the two variables.

> **Histogram:** A graph of contiguous vertical bars representing a frequency distribution in which the groups or classes of items are marked on the x axis and the number of items in each class is indicated on the y axis. The pictorial nature of the histogram lets people see patterns that are difficult to see in a simple table of numbers.
>
> *—APICS Dictionary,* **12th edition**

A histogram (Figure 9.6) highlights the center of the data as well as the amount of variation present in the data. A wide, relatively low chart has much more variation than a high, narrow chart.

> **Control chart:** A graphic comparison of process performance data with predetermined computed control limits. The process performance data usually consist of groups of measurements selected in regular sequence of production that preserve the order. The primary

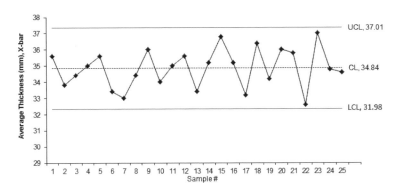

Figure 9.7   Example of a control chart, used to help separate significant performance deviations from normal, expected variation.

use of control charts is to detect assignable causes of variation in the process as opposed to random variations.

—APICS Dictionary, **12th edition**

A control chart (Figure 9.7) is a specific kind of run chart that allows significant change to be differentiated from the natural variability of the process. Even in the best designed and run operations there will be a certain amount of variation, and the temptation for most operators is to adjust the process based on seeing this variation. The power of the control chart is that it provides definitive guidelines for when an adjustment should be made. A process that is said to be "in control" will only exhibit random, expected variation, and needs no adjustments.

Cause-and-effect diagram: A tool for analyzing process dispersion. It is also referred to as the Ishikawa diagram (because Kaoru Ishikawa developed it) and the fishbone diagram (because the complete diagram resembles a fish skeleton). The diagram illustrates the main causes and subcauses leading to an effect (symptom).

—APICS Dictionary, **12th edition**

The diagram begins with a defect being listed at the far right of the main "bone" (Figure 9.8). Various possible causes are then listed in groups as branches off of the main bone. Typical branches include the four M categories—manpower, machines, materials, and methods for manufacturing—and eight P categories—product, place, price, promotion, people, process, physical evidence, and productivity—and quality, used in service industries, as well as several other groupings, such as environment and money. The branches within the groups are expanded until the root cause of the problem is reached, at which point these issues are circled and attacked by the group (Figure 9.9).

Flowcharts: The output of a flowcharting process, a chart that shows the operations, transportation, storages, delays, inspections, and so on related to a process. Flowcharts are drawn to better understand processes.

—APICS Dictionary, **12th edition**

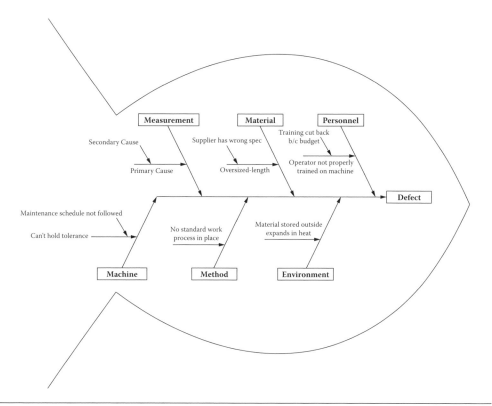

Figure 9.8   Cause-and-effect diagram, commonly known as a fishbone diagram.

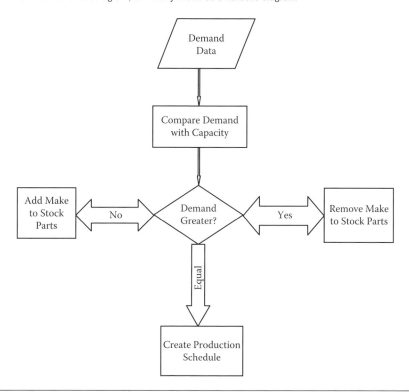

Figure 9.9   Simple flowchart to illustrate the use of a partial inventory buffer in Chapter 3.

A flowchart is important because one of the main thoughts of Lean is that operating problems generally arise from the process, not from the person. The flowchart serves an important role in helping to understand how the process was designed to be operated, and lets people evaluate the design for weaknesses and flaws.

Taken together, these tools provide a good start into understanding how in process quality practices are implemented in a Lean environment. While there are obviously many other useful tools and techniques available for specific situations, understanding the thought behind these seven tools as well as their practical application will go a long way toward helping you to contribute to continuous improvement efforts in your company, whether on the factory floor or in support areas.

In this chapter we have reviewed the details behind quality control in a Lean environment. As with the other areas that we have covered, there is an emphasis on ensuring that the process is robust and capable, the idea being that people will generally not make mistakes unless the process allows them to. This is just one example where Lean has taken a core concept (respect for people in this case) and applied it to a specific area, in this case quality control and improvement, with the result being a new approach that has strengths from the traditional approach as well as new strengths from the core value. We can find example after example of this phenomenon throughout Lean literature, which is why we have tried to emphasize that Lean is a complete operating system, and needs to be approached and adopted as such, not just as a set of loosely connected tools created to eliminate waste.

In the next chapter we will cover purchasing, which would be the starting point for many books about supply chain management. For us, though, the supply chain includes a most important link called make, so we felt it was only correct and proper to cover the elements of make before we moved on to buying materials and services. After all, if you ask most of our suppliers what their largest problem to being world class is, and they answered honestly, they would say it is us, the customers.

10
Purchasing

In this chapter we will: briefly contrast traditional purchasing objectives and approaches with Lean ones, compare unit cost approach to purchasing with "total landed cost" model, contrast suppliers as partners vs. "market driven" purchasing, and describe working with suppliers to reduce lead time, lot sizes, and cost.

Well, you have finally reached the chapter that most people associate with supply chain management: purchasing. In this book we have used a much broader definition of the supply chain, backed by many supply chain definitions, including the *APICS Dictionary* and the Supply Chain Council. The premise is that you cannot effectively manage a supply chain without being intimately familiar with not just the delivery steps between each link in the chain, but also the transformation steps within each link. That is the Lean way to approach a supply chain. Further, our approach emphasizes a generally accepted way to implement Lean in the supply chain: get your own house in order before moving into other links of the supply chain. And since we have now covered most of all of the transformation steps, we are now ready to cover the purchasing activities. But that doesn't mean we will not continue to look at the big picture first.

Developing a Systems Perspective for Purchasing

A vital first step is to develop a systems perspective. The systems perspective recognizes that if each element in the supply chain tries to optimize its own operations in isolation, everyone suffers in the long run. For instance, supply chain management requires long-term partnerships with key suppliers. Suppose management institutes a measurement system that rewards the Purchase department for obtaining products from its suppliers at low cost. No doubt, reduced material costs directly affect the profitability of the organization, but such a measurement system drives the Purchase department into an adversarial position with its suppliers, encouraging Purchase to play off potential suppliers against each other in an attempt to drive them to lower their prices. The lack of a systems perspective has now made it very difficult to establish long-term partnerships with the organization's suppliers.

—**Mandyam M. Srinivasan, "Seven Steps to Building a Lean Supply Chain,"** *Industry Week*, September 12, 2007

This excerpt neatly sums up what we feel is one of the major differences between traditional purchasing and the Lean approach to purchasing: the view of the supply chain as a group of partners rather than as a collection of companies looking to use each other to farm money.

Traditional Purchasing

In traditional purchasing, the process has followed a fairly standard purchasing cycle or model. Granted, purchasing in the traditional sense can take on many roles and responsibilities, but these are the basics.

The purchasing cycle is:

1. Recognize need
2. Specify need
3. Determine sourcing options
4. Establish pricing and terms
5. Develop and deliver PO
6. Receive and inspect
7. Approve payment
8. Expedite—optional but often necessary

Traditional purchasing has been narrowly focused on these objectives:

- Obtaining the lowest unit cost for items purchased. Many purchasing organizations have made this their most important function, but this often ignores some obvious actual costs, as well as some hidden costs that we will discuss a bit later in this chapter. Often the pursuit of lowest unit costs is driven by poorly designed metrics that reward decisions that can make the purchasing area look good, while ignoring how those decisions can impact the rest of the organization and costs. As was mentioned above, this is often known as suboptimization. And while Lean is certainly interested in lower costs, the approach of how to obtain low costs from suppliers is quite different than the traditional purchasing approach.
- Communicating specifications for purchased materials. Here the purchasing area just follows specifications set in another area, often product design or engineering. There is nothing unusual here, other than the people buying the materials may not understand what exactly they are buying. This can be an issue when the supplier needs clarification or offers alternatives.
- Supplier qualification and selection. This can run the gamut from a purchasing area "bidding" each new material purchase to just letting existing suppliers furnish new items, without testing the market. This makes the purchasing process a fairly shallow transaction-oriented relationship between the company and its suppliers. The true expertise of the supplier is often underutilized, especially during new product development.

Overall, if you were going to describe traditional purchasing, you would call it transactional.

The traditional purchasing process involved several steps—requisition, soliciting bids, purchase order, shipping advice, invoice, and payment—that have come to be increasingly regarded as unacceptably slow, expensive, and labor intensive. Each transaction generated its own paper trail, and the same process had to be followed whether the item being purchased was a box of paper clips or a new bulldozer. In this traditional model, purchasing was seen as essentially a clerical function. It was focused on getting the right quantity and quality of goods to the right place at the right time at a decent cost. The typical buyer was a shrewd negotiator whose primary responsibility was to obtain the best possible price from suppliers and ensure that minimum quality standards were met. Instead of using one supplier, the purchaser would usually take a divide-and-conquer approach to purchasing—buying small amounts from many suppliers and playing one against the other to gain price concessions. Purchasing simply was not considered to be a high-profile or career fast-track position—when surveys were taken of organizational stature, purchasing routinely rated in the lowest quartile.

—Reference for Business, Encyclopedia of Business, **2nd edition**

The above description is as concise and at the same time damning as we can conceive of what the traditional purchasing environment entails.

Lean Purchasing

Lean purchasing is the application of Lean principles within the procurement part of the supply chain to help optimize the entire supply chain.

Lean purchasing is not just an expansion of traditional transaction-oriented purchasing to enterprise-wide integration. Lean purchasing takes many of the basics of Lean that we have been discussing and applies them to the procurement function. Our focus is to show you how purchasing can have a huge impact on a company's supply chain, aside from just getting the lowest unit cost. When discussing Lean purchasing or any particular Lean process, small cross-functional groups are essential to success.

Lean purchasing is geared toward:

Reducing supplier:
- Costs
- Lead time
- Lot sizes

Reducing the supplier base
- Keeping critical items internal
- Fostering supplier relationships, making suppliers partners instead of adversaries
- Involving suppliers in new product development

In reviewing these, some procurement people/companies do some and maybe all of these. Lean concepts are all around us and are not uncommon. The importance is in the relentless, day-to-day and year-to-year application of these concepts. Unfortunately, the authors have seen many companies "go cheap" within the procurement area, either using this as a dumping ground for company misfits or just being too cheap to hire above a clerical level of talent. Given that these folks will control the bulk of your cost of goods sold (COGS), this is the one area that you can't afford to have amateurs. (This is especially true within companies that are profitable—with real purchasing/ materials professionals, you could be making even more money.)

When discussing traditional purchasing, we defined it as being largely transactional. Lean purchasing does have the "transactions," but the focus is on building the relationships. The approach of having suppliers as partners is in stark contrast to the environment where suppliers are played off of each other to obtain a lower cost. Let's take a few minutes to explore the origin of the Lean approach to suppliers as partners.

Keiretsu

Keiretsu is a set of companies with interlocking business relationships and shareholdings. They emerged in Japan after World War II as an alternative to the family-owned, government-sponsored conglomerations of companies called zaibatsu. There are basically two types of keiretsu: horizontal, mainly centered around banks, and vertical, mainly centered around a large company. Toyota is an example of a vertical keiretsu, and others would include Honda, Sony, and Hitachi. The presence of the keiretsu has been called one of the profound differences between the structure of business in Japan vs. that in the United States. For our purposes, we will explore the effect of the keiretsu on the purchasing activity in the supply chain.

> Keiretsu business groups are alliances between firms that share close buyer-supplier relationships. The issue of interlocking stocks by group affiliated companies to member companies of the group keeps ownership in friendly hands, helps prevent foreign takeovers, and aids a company's long-term survival and growth.
>
> —*BNET Business Dictionary*, **http://dictionary.bnet.com/ definition/keiretsu.html**

While there is some dispute about how coordinated the keiretsu operations really are, or indeed what constitutes a particular group, the fact is that the spirit behind this type of organization has a profound effect on the supply chain. We will see this mainly manifest itself in the attitude of companies toward their suppliers.

> There is a key difference between the way American and Japanese companies fuel the rivalry between their suppliers. U.S. manufacturers set vendors against each other and then do business with the last supplier standing. Toyota and Honda also spark competition

between vendors—especially when there is none—but only with the support of their existing suppliers.

—Jeffrey K. Liker and Thomas Y. Choi

Lean Partnership

Make sure that you are a good customer and don't expect your suppliers to cover your incompetence—besides, only a fool would think that this didn't have a real cost.

One important principle to discuss first: being Lean does not mean you expect your suppliers to hold excess inventory for you. One important issue to be discussed is the trend toward doing Lean "things." This often is misguided Lean or what is commonly known as Lame—Lean as misguidedly executed. Often, someone gets a bright idea to reduce inventory internally without changing how the company operates; this usually requires the suppliers to hold more inventory. This is not Lean and will usually result in higher costs to your suppliers and eventually to you. Simply moving costs to other links in the supply chain clearly does not make the supply chain stronger.

A good way to look at Lean purchasing is by defining expected outcomes. Liker, in *The Toyota Way*, looks at the relationship between Toyota and its suppliers and offers Principle 11 as a guideline: "Respect your extended network of partners and suppliers by challenging them and helping them improve." Here, Toyota is truly partnering with its suppliers. This is no easy partnership, as it takes years to develop the trust of Toyota, but once gained, suppliers will find that Toyota is a great partner. This does not mean that they will become "soft" at that point—far from it. Toyota is very demanding on its suppliers, but it will do as much as it can to help make the relationship as beneficial as possible for both organizations. One way to summarize the relationship would be to say: joint risks, joint rewards.

A concrete example of the effect of partnering is found in an annual study of the automotive supply chains, conducted by Planning Perspectives, Inc. of Birmingham, Michigan, quoted here from the 2004 report: "The study shows, again this year, that the US automakers' primary orientation is toward cost reduction, they have little regard for their suppliers, they communicate very poorly and they generally treat suppliers as adversaries rather than trusted partners. In all the other industries we've studied such as aerospace, electronics, and computers, no one treats their suppliers as poorly as the US automakers do," said John W. Henke, Jr., PhD, president of PPI and professor of marketing at Oakland University.

Henke then cites the following trends as a direct result of this attitude toward the supply base:

- Chrysler, Ford, and GM supplier working relations are falling behind those of Honda and Toyota at an increasing rate.
- Suppliers are shifting resources (capital and R&D expenditures, service and support) to the Japanese Big Three, while reducing these for the Domestic Big Three.
- Suppliers are increasing product quality at a greater rate for the Japanese, while merely maintaining quality levels for U.S. automakers.
- Supplier trust of Ford and General Motors has never been lower; conversely, trust for the Japanese OEMs has never been higher.
- Suppliers increasingly see the opportunity to make an acceptable return as being with the foreign domestics, not with the U.S. automakers.
- Suppliers overwhelmingly prefer working with Honda and Toyota.

In fact, according to the study, in the five key areas measured—relationship, communication, help, hindrance, and profit opportunity—the U.S. automakers are 180° opposite their Japanese counterparts (Figure 10.1).

Toyota has captured the basic idea of partnership in the supply chain as point 2 of its three principles of purchasing in North America: "Mutual benefit based on mutual trust: We believe in developing mutually beneficial, long-term relationships based on mutual trust. To foster that trust, we pursue close and wide-ranging communication with suppliers" (http://www.toyotasupplier.com/sup_guide/sup_principles.asp). According to many sources, it is very difficult to become a supplier to Toyota, but it may be even harder to "unbecome" a supplier.

In traditional purchasing, the idea is to make suppliers more competitive by pitting them against each other to win business, usually in competitive bidding processes. Toyota is also intensely interested in making its supply base more competitive over time, but the method is quite different:

> Toyota is committed to helping our suppliers increase their competitiveness in the auto-manufacturing marketplace. This commitment reinforces our policy on cultivating steady,

Criteria	Traditional Purchasing	Lean Purchasing
Protect confidential info	Little regard for supplier's proprietary information or intellectual property	High regard
Open, honest communication	Indifferent, late	High level, timely
Importance of cost vs. quality and technology	Primary focus is on cost	Seek low cost, but balanced with quality and technology
Supplier survival	Little regard	Concern for long-term success
Relationship orientation	Adversarial; focus is on OEM's short-term gain	Strategically integrate suppliers into partnership-like relations

Figure 10.1 Comparing traditional puchasing to Lean purchasing.

long-term relationships that spawn mutual benefits through mutual trust. This process takes place through two separate programs:

Annual purchasing policy: Toyota values communication and clarity of expectations with our suppliers. Toyota sets annual performance expectations for suppliers in the areas of quality, delivery, cost, and supplier diversity. These expectations are directly related to Toyota's long-term objectives. They are both supplier and product-specific.

Supplier support system: Sometimes, suppliers encounter difficulties in their efforts to meet their annual expectations. We dispatch experts to work with suppliers who ask for assistance in devising and implementing necessary improvements.

—http://www.toyotasupplier.com/sup_guide/sup_compete.asp

This challenging of suppliers to improve is one of the primary concepts of partnering. In Lean, having high, stretch objectives, dealing with partners fairly, and teaching them and assisting them to improve are considered signs of respect for the partner. Toyota expects world-class performance from its suppliers, and gives a small peak into its thought processes in this area by listing some expectations and standards that are expected of suppliers. These standards cover:

- Quality
- Cost
- Delivery
- Technological capabilities

We will organize much of the remaining chapter around these standards and expectations.

Quality

Quality is essential to customer satisfaction. Defective products lead to complaints and even recalls. We count on suppliers to pursue quality levels well above our minimum standards.

Preventing defects: Our standard practice is to trust suppliers to provide us with defect-free products. We do not ordinarily inspect the parts and materials that we source.

Built-in quality: The best way to ensure quality is to build quality into products systematically. That means designing products and processes to maximize quality.

Remember TS 16949, the Technical Standard for Quality used by Toyota, which we described in detail in Chapter 9? If not, here is the last key aspect that we covered: developing suppliers using the same technical standards. This basically means that Toyota, and Lean companies in general, expect the same quality standards and practices across all of the companies in their supply chain. TS 16949 requires suppliers to develop a quality management system that conforms to the standard, including an approval process for purchased materials (companies the supplier is buying from).

About incoming inspection as quality control, as you can note above, Toyota states that it does not generally do incoming inspection of parts. While it is common in traditional purchase environments to inspect parts, this practice shares the same faults as any other inspection: it is generally a sample and can only serve to filter defects, doing nothing to actually fix defects at the source. TS 16949 lists the following possibilities for incoming part quality assurance:

- Receipt and evaluation of statistical data provided by the supplier
- Receiving inspection or testing, i.e., sampling based on performance
- Second- or third-party audits of supplier sites when combined with records of acceptable delivered quality performance
- Part evaluation by a designated laboratory
- Any other method agreed to by your customer

If the concepts of designing for quality, quality at the source, and jidoka are followed, there should be no need for incoming inspection. This would allow a second- or third-party audit plus records of acceptable quality performance, or statistical data provided by the supplier, to satisfy this quality requirement.

Supplier Quality Audits

Quality audits are a critical piece of the relationship as well. As we have discussed, just in time (JIT) requires that only good parts be passed from one operation to another. This applies here. You have to be convinced that you will receive an expected quality level. The supplier audit should be aimed at identifying nonconformances in the manufacturing process, shipment process, engineering change process, invoicing process, and quality process at the supplier. As you would expect, the audit should be a hands-on activity, focusing on both the factory floor and support areas and financial records.

Cost

Offering high quality and excellent function at low prices increases product appeal. The conservation of material and energy that stem from cost-saving measures helps safeguard the environment.

> **Low prices through low costs:** We welcome low prices from suppliers only when we can see that they are the result of genuine cost competitiveness.

> —**Toyota, http://www.toyotasupplier.com**

Unceasing effort on behalf of cost savings: Suppliers need to strive to continuously reduce costs and to translate their reductions into lower prices.

—Toyota, http://www.toyotasupplier.com

Supplier costing is another critical area, and one that some purchasing professionals currently employ (Figure 10.2). You must understand what it costs your supplier to make the parts that it supplies to you. Some suppliers may share that data, but most of the time, you will have to build these cost models yourself. To be sure, this may not be necessary for all items, but for key items that are price sensitive, you may think that they are overpriced. Only by building the cost model will you know for certain.

This requires that the purchasing person understand as much about that item part assembly as possible. Having an understanding of what makes up the item, from the raw material used to how it is machined or processed, is essential. Once you have an understanding of these costs, you can gain a better understanding of the costs of the item and compare that to what you are paying for the item. Also remember that this does not have a profit margin or tax cost. This is why you need professional

Direct Material	Per Unit				
Unit of Measure					
x	1.27				
y	0.88				
z	0.01				
Misc.	2.33				
Packaging	1.25				
TTL COGS	5.74				
Direct Labor—Processing per Unit (with Burden)			Hour Rate	Burden %	Processor Hour
Cut	$2.69		12	40%	0.16
Process A	$5.25		15	40%	0.25
Process B	$2.46		22	40%	0.08
Process C	$5.04		20	40%	0.18
TTL labor	$15.44		17.25		0.67
Indirect Costs					
Indirect labor	17.33625	150% of TTL labor			
Indirect material	0.861	15% of COGS			
Other SG&A	2.54184	12% of direct costs			
Total costs	$46.80				

Figure 10.2 A breakdown of the cost of one part from a supplier. Understanding the supplier's costs is an important step in both price negotiation and improvement.

procurement and materials people—they have been trained in what to do and how to do it.

Armed with this data, you can work with your suppliers regarding costs, but remember, this data isn't meant to be a bat to beat them over the head with. This is meant to be a tool that you can use to negotiate with. And even more important, this will provide you with opportunities to identify waste and potentially help suppliers lower their cost. So the overriding message here needs to be that gaining cost information is not a step in gaining leverage to squeeze more money out of the supplier, but is instead meant to be another tool to promote partnership and waste identification.

Value analysis can be informal or formal:

Informal: Casual observations—"smell test"
Formal: Value stream map

Value analysis is another area that you can address with your supplier, but typically only after you have built some trust between the two organizations; in other words, you won't be able to do this with a new supplier right away. Here, you are either starting them on their Lean journey or are auditing how well they are doing. This can take the form of an informal or formal value stream analysis. An informal analysis can be done by touring the supplier facility and observing what is going on, especially keying in on the seven wastes. Most materials professionals can walk into a plant and gain a great deal of knowledge just by observing what is going on around them and maybe asking a few questions—what the authors like to call the smell test. Most of the time, just looking around can provide a rough value analysis.

The formal application is to ask for a value stream map. This may require your supplier to start their Lean journey, or it can be a point in time evaluation of how well they are coming along. You may need to supply them with some Lean resources to get them started, preferably out of your facility. This analysis may be able to help explain "excess" costs identified during the building of a cost analysis model. It wouldn't be unusual to see cost savings opportunities during a value analysis. The delicate part is to communicate this and get action.

Lean Purchasing and the "China Price"

A huge issue within traditional purchasing is the fixation with the "China price." Unfortunately, the business world is often driven by the whims of newly minted but inexperienced MBAs. These geniuses started this outsourcing craze back in the 1980s, but it really kicked in with the opening of China manufacturing in the 1990s. Their entire contention was built on looking at unit costs, and there is no doubt that unit costs for an item made in China will be cheaper than one made in the United States. Unfortunately, many companies have been misguided by these so-called experts to chase low unit costs. Adding to this was that companies were being threatened by their customers if they didn't move production overseas. This has proven to be, on the

Penn State Model

- ✔ **Purchase Price**
  - Price paid to seller
  - INCOTERMS
  - Payment terms
  - Exchange rates over time
- ✔ **Transportation and Logistics**
  - Foreign inland
  - Line haul
  - U.S. inland
  - Accessorials
  - Insurance
  - Packaging
- ✔ **Customs and Import**
  - HTUSA (tariff) rate
  - Merchandise processing
  - Harbor maintenance fee
  - Broker fee
  - Less: Duty drawback
- ✔ **Inventory Costs**
  - Cycle stock

- Safety stock
- Inventory in-transit

These costs can vary depending on the INCOTERMS in category 1 (when does ownership of the inventory change) and the way a company values its inventory.

- ✔ **Overhead and Administration**
  - Sourcing staff
  - Due diligence
  - Relationship building/travel
  - Learning curve
- ✔ **Risk and Compliance**
  - Compliance costs (technology, staff, other)
  - C-TPAT program costs
  - Cost of potential risk of supply disruption
  - Cost of potential risk of damage to reputation, health, safety, environment

Figure 10.3 Some of the most common elements that would need to be included to calculate a total landed cost for a part.

whole, not very effective. Why? It has ignored basic supply chain concepts, let alone making Lean much more difficult to achieve.

Unfortunately, these "experts" didn't understand product costing and all the elements that make up what is known as a total landed cost. Now, suddenly, after study after study has refuted their original thesis, they have coined "near sourcing" as the new end-all/be-all concept and are charging their clients hefty fees to reverse the damage that they themselves wrought. Lean companies, of course, basically stuck to their vision of building strong supply chains through close partnerships with their suppliers (see keiretsu at the beginning of this chapter). To be sure, outsourcing can be considered an option, but only if you are fully informed about all of the costs. Let's look at these costs. Figure 10.3 is an example of a landed cost model. Note that it is not a complete list, since a complete list would vary company by company. However, this should provide enough detail to get your own landed cost model started.

Of course, none of these factors takes into account the fact that you are typically greatly increasing the lead times of the products by outsourcing them, which is one of the worst things you can do from a supply chain standpoint. Remember, uncertainty increases the farther into the future you go, and forecasts become more inaccurate, so not only will you need to have more inventory in the supply chain to account for the increased lead time, but you will also need more inventory to account for the increased forecast error. This should be obvious, but was largely disregarded in the chase for lower unit cost.

And don't even get us started on traditional product costing, because there is so much to say, and happily it has already been well said. If you are interested in

Lean costing, we suggest that you read Brian Maskell and Bruce Bagalley's *Practical Lean Accounting: A Proven System for Measuring and Managing the Lean Enterprise* (Productivity Press, 2004).

Delivery

Providing customers with the products they want when they want them is an important element of providing customers satisfaction. Obviously, starting with raw material delivered on time is an important factor in delivering goods on time to the customer.

Reliable delivery: At the very least, suppliers must deliver products on schedule and in the amounts required. A Lean supplier who can only deliver on time and in the correct quantity is doing the bare minimum in the partnership, which also expects improvement and innovation.

Flexibility in production and delivery: Customer tastes change constantly. Suppliers need to be able to respond with flexibility in production and delivery (http://www.toyotasupplier.com). We used to have interesting discussions around these two points: Given a choice of one only, would you rather have a supplier who always delivers on time but can never respond to a schedule change, or one who always tries to accommodate schedule changes and occasionally misses delivery? Most of the time, the sentiment weighed on the side of the flexible supplier usually because it was felt that they showed a better commitment to the partnership and were more committed to helping satisfy the customer.

Almost everything we have discussed in the course of this book is at least partly designed to improve delivery performance to the customer. In particular, the decisions surrounding how to manage independent demand are particularly apropos to on-schedule delivery. The second point above warrants some additional discussion, we feel. As we stated in Chapter 6, the traditional approach to gaining increases in on-time delivery is to increase the safety stock of finished goods. While this will work, with some caveats as discussed in Chapter 6, there are perhaps better alternates within the Lean tool kit. In particular, a focus on quick changeover capability, common materials usage wherever possible, and cross-training of workers can provide the kind of flexibility that will respond to changes in demand that is desirable in a supply chain. It is also important to understand when to allow changes in customer demand to pass through the supply chain (preferably protecting as much of the cumulative lead time through the supply chain as possible) and when to allow this variation to be buffered according to the strategy set in the value stream. And in this context, it should be remembered that only one link in a properly run supply chain should be experiencing the full brunt of variation of end customer demand; all other links should be mostly protected from this by the leveled schedule, at least in total volume if not in mix.

In the Lean environment, our primary method of communicating the need for delivery of parts to the supplier is the pull system. In discussing JIT and the use of kanban, the idea is to extend the use of kanban into the supply base. As we have discussed in these sessions, the use of JIT, usually via kanban, should be extended in the supply chain. The full set of processes that are used internally should be shared throughout the supply base—sharing master planning information and using kanbans to control inventories between organizations. This eventually will require your suppliers to implement Lean and, you should encourage them to do so.

Improving Delivery and Flexibility by Reducing Lead Times and Lot Sizes

Reducing lead times is one of the most critical things you can do for your organization. By reducing lead time of purchased items, the purchasing department can join the rest of the company in supporting Lean. This can help contribute to the effort of making your company more flexible to ever-changing customer demands and contributes to the overall inventory reduction effort. The faster you can receive stock from suppliers, the less you (and they) have to hold.

Lot size reduction is often an easy place to start in this effort. Ask for a reduction in lot size: you may need to help the supplier understand concepts like every part every interval (EPEI) and heijunka, and it may need help with setup reduction so that the unit costs of smaller lot sizes doesn't increase, but this is still a good place to start introducing Lean to a supplier. Further, smaller delivery lot sizes may increase logistics costs, so you will need to review the Chapter 8 (logistics) to help prevent this. Also, a quick analysis of which is cheaper—holding more inventory or increasing transportation costs—is usually warranted. Just remember to use a realistic cost model to compare both costs (see examples above).

Set up blanket purchase orders (POs) with timed releases or, better yet, kanban-triggered releases.

> **Blanket purchase order:** A long-term commitment to a supplier for material against which short-term releases will be generated to satisfy requirements. Often blanket orders cover only one item with predetermined delivery dates.
>
> —*APICS Dictionary*, 12th edition

The blanket PO will eliminate the cost of having to raise a PO each time a supply is needed, which will be more often with smaller lot sizes. A blanket PO also provides more stability for the supplier, who now doesn't need to worry about whether it will receive the next order or it will go to another supplier who has outbid the first. Again, this stability is very important in making substantive, long-term improvements in the supply chain, as it allows improvement to be made in strategic areas as well as tactical areas.

For the short term, balance transportation costs—do the math. In the long term, work on eliminating waste in transportation and handling so that small lot sizes aren't more costly.

Reducing Supplier Base

Often, this is described as supplier rationalization, and is done in a manner similar to SKU rationalization. The usual purpose for doing this is to concentrate buying power with fewer suppliers. Diluting your buying power works against you in two ways. First, it reduces the amount that you spend with each supplier, giving them no incentive to reduce prices due to sales volumes. And while we don't necessarily feel that this is a good rationale for giving lower prices (the basis for this is that larger customer orders will allow larger lot sizes to be run through the plant, a decidedly un-Lean mindset), it is still the basis for negotiations for many companies. Second, it makes it more difficult to manage a great many suppliers. These facts are nothing new to the purchasing profession, but reducing suppliers is not always done, due mainly to amateurs working in the purchasing department.

How are supplier consolidations generally done? Many current purchasing professionals use their commodity codes and supplier segment analysis to perform this task. First, you need to perform a commodity analysis on your purchased items. Most ERP systems have a commodity code field in the item master. If not, your plan for every part (remember plan for every part?) should contain a commodity code that you can use. Commodity codes should represent generally the raw material or item that the supplier makes/furnishes. For example, you can have glass, metal, and wood as commodities. If this level of classification does not provide guidance on opportunities to reduce suppliers, you may need to break these general commodities into more targeted/specialized types—stained glass, molded glass, blown glass, sheet glass etc. However, only do this if the supplier base specializes this way as well: Your stained glass suppliers don't supply sheet glass. Your molded glass suppliers don't supply blown glass, etc. Again, what you want to do is to look for ways to consolidate suppliers by consolidating commodities, but use common sense. A good way to think of this process is one that was employed by a company that Bill worked for: individual parts were almost always single sourced, but there was almost always a second supplier within each commodity, so that process capability could be maintained if there was a problem with the primary supplier for the commodity. This also helps a Lean company encourage competition in the supply chain.

Keeping Critical Items Internal

One thing that a Lean (or smart) company would never do would be to outsource an item that is critical to a product or products that your company produces. In most cases, this is an item that does not have many suppliers but without it, you cannot make your product. To be sure, this is often a proprietary product and is kept internal, but with all of the amateurs eager to outsource everything, we felt that it was necessary to bring this up. For example, Toyota developed and has kept internal its hybrid drive technology. It wouldn't dream of outsourcing this to a supplier. (Although it is true that Toyota sells this technology to other automakers, it keeps the manufacturing of the key parts of the hybrid drive internal.)

Measuring Delivery Performance

Supplier Scorecard   There are many supplier scorecards, but make sure that you use at least the following metrics. They get to the core of supplier performance. To be sure, you can measure a lot of other things, but make sure that these are included.

- Delivered product's quality performance
- Customer issues caused by supplier
- Returns or complaints

The supply chain operations reference (SCOR) model is a process reference model that has been developed and endorsed by the Supply Chain Council (SCC) as the cross-industry standard diagnostic tool for supply chain management (Figure 10.4). SCOR enables users to address, improve, and communicate supply chain management practices within and between all interested parties. In 1996, the SCC was organized to create a standard set of indicators that could be compared across companies and industries, and could be captured and managed in the enterprise software applications that

Performance Attribute	Performance Attribute Definition	Level 1 Metric
Supply chain reliability	The performance of the supply chain in delivering the correct product, to the correct place, at the correct time, in the correct condition and packaging, in the correct quantity, with the correct documentation, to the correct customer	Perfect order fulfillment
Supply chain responsiveness	The speed at which a supply chain provides products to the customer	Order fulfillment cycle time
Supply chain flexibility	The agility of a supply chain in responding to marketplace changes to gain or maintain competitive advantage	Upside supply chain flexibility
		Upside supply chain adaptability
		Downside supply chain adaptability
Supply chain costs	The costs associated with operating the supply chain	Supply chain management cost
		Costs of goods sold
Supply chain asset management	The effectiveness of an organization in managing assets to support demand satisfaction; this includes the management of all assets: fixed and working capital	Cash-to-cash cycle time
		Returns on supply chain fixed assets
		Return on working capital

Figure 10.4   One portion of the SCOR model, which seeks to drive a balance in behavior by creating a mix of metrics for each aspect of the supply chain.

helped manage the physical goods and information about their movements. While we are not endorsing SCOR or SCC, we feel that companies can use the model to create their own set of balanced metrics that are relevant to their own supply chain.

Technological Capabilities

The concept here is a simple one, but it is not often considered when suppliers are selected: a company should partner with suppliers who can provide them with a competitive advantage, whether by lower costs or by providing a technological advantage to the product. Toyota uses several criteria to evaluate the technological capabilities of suppliers:

Value-add and sophistication: A big consideration in evaluating suppliers' technological capabilities is to determine their ability to offer products that are a step ahead of the competition.

Speed: The ability to translate concepts into products quickly is another important aspect.

Dramatic cost reductions: Suppliers should foster the ability to broaden the marketability of their products through dramatic reductions in cost.

Fostering supplier relationships: Involving suppliers in new product development.

The new framework for Lean purchasing moves from just buying things to becoming more integrated into the rest of the organization and how it works. Of course, this assumes that these are purchasing professionals, trained to do these things and not just put in these positions.

Design and Development

Purchasing people must work in conjunction with new product engineering. Doing this adds another resource to look for innovations in industry. Purchasing can also qualify suppliers to work with new product engineering. This means that the purchasing people must be able to determine which of their suppliers are willing and able to provide resources for new product design efforts.

Purchasing becomes a critical "player" in finding new products/suppliers that can help the company reduce costs. (Note: This may have nothing to do with SKU costs.) Finding suppliers that can furnish existing parts, at a lower total landed cost, is always good, but the focus here is really in finding new products that can help make the company more competitive. This may be a new material that is easier to manufacture or more appealing to the end customer. The key here is that purchasing must step up and become more involved by understanding company customers and processes. This moves the purchasing function from clerical to professional.

Once suppliers are found, they must be utilized. Inviting supplier engineering into your plant is a first step. They need to understand what you do and how you do it before they can help. This alters your expectations from them, from a current state where the suppliers' sales people come in and pitch the same old things, to a partnership where the supplier is expected to contribute new possibilities to the product development cycle. You have to challenge your suppliers into becoming a resource, a part of the team tasked with creating value for the end customer. This can help take some of the pressure off of your designers and engineers—make it easier for them.

> The recognition that part and process are one is the essence of what is called "simultaneous engineering." The process tacitly acknowledges the role of suppliers in the design process, but goes further—pointing out that good suppliers not only provide OEMs with parts; they provide "process knowledge," which is their real stock-in-trade. To fully demonstrate their expertise, suppliers must have early entry into the product development cycle.
>
> The best way to gain this knowledge rapidly is to work closely with suppliers from the outset. Ironically, many companies that once boasted of virtual independence are now driving hard toward "horizontal integration," becoming systems builders and assemblers, and giving their primary suppliers strawboss authority over entire subsystems. Early supplier involvement (ESI), the rallying cry of purchasing during the '80s, is evolving into continuous supplier involvement (CSI), with suppliers so thoroughly integrated into the design process that they've become literal extensions of the OEM.

—Jim Morgan, editorial director emeritus, *Purchasing*, November 12, 2001

In this chapter we have reviewed purchasing in a Lean environment. In sharp contrast to traditional purchasing, Lean purchasing emphasizes close partnership with suppliers. But what may come as a surprise in this environment is that the expectations of the supplier are extremely high, as it is expected not only to provide continuous cost reductions via its own Lean efforts in eliminating waste, but also to participate in innovations in the new product development area, helping to provide competitive advantage for the entire supply chain. It is this combination of close partnerships, mutual risk and reward, and high expectations that makes the Lean supply chain much different than traditional supply chains.

In Chapter 11, we will outline a complete, integrated system for controlling capacity and priority in a supply chain using only Lean tools and approaches. As far as we know, this is the first attempt to put this complete picture of Lean planning and control into a framework that will be familiar to supply chain professionals the world over, meaning a top-down planning and control process starting with long-range planning at the product family level and continuing through to detailed control on the shop floor.

11
LEAN SYSTEM

In the course of this book we have outlined a systematic approach to managing materials and the supply chain using Lean tools. We'd be remiss if we didn't clearly outline the specifics regarding what you need to do with your current system. As we have stated throughout the chapters, there are specific, concrete reasons for why you don't simply want to use your current enterprise resource planning (ERP) system. We need to step back and approach this holistically, rather than try to cobble a solution together using pieces that were built with a different philosophy in mind. In this chapter we will recap this approach and try to tie it all back together into a coherent system picture. We will begin with a diagram of the complete integrated system picture (Figure 11.1).

Clearly, there are areas of ERP systems that act counter to Lean philosophy, and if you continue using them, they will prevent you from achieving all of the benefits from Lean. Many industry pundits/analysts, as well as the software companies that underwrite their studies, will disagree. However, you have to consider their situation in that they simply cannot embrace Lean at the expense of their own product. Instead, we see attempts to "finagle" Lean into the current system framework by simply changing some field names and other cosmetic changes. As we have shown throughout this book, we don't feel that this approach will work to support Lean. Instead, we suggest you model a planning and control system using Lean tools. We will detail what this entails over the next several pages (Figure 11.2).

Lean wants to first create product families that can then become value streams. A product family is a set of parts that go through roughly the same processes. The idea is to create a synchronous flow in manufacturing that allows products to be produced at a uniform and linear market-driven rate—known as takt time. What this requires is that work centers be reorganized to align into a synchronous flow, with regard to the product being produced. To accomplish this, we need to determine a set of products that use the same sets of resources, so that we can potentially dedicate these resources to this set of products. The best tool so far created for this task is the X-map, or product process matrix (Figure 11.3).

Once a family has been identified, we can attempt to group the processes together to make, ideally, an assembly line, or perhaps a manufacturing cell. In some cases, however, especially where there are many items or many processes, the traditional product/process matrix sorting does not yield any readily visible product family groups. In this case, it may be necessary to go back and review whether there are any potential

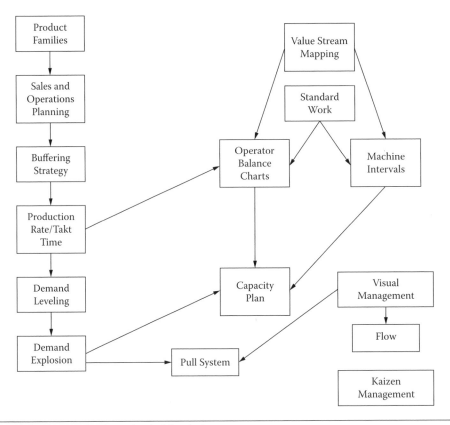

Figure 11.1   The Lean planning and control flowchart.

groupings that would dedicate some of the more significant pieces of equipment in the value stream to a product family. This approach, while less formulaic, often yields results that are acceptable and can often drive value stream improvement in the same way that the process item matrix sort can. Regardless of the method used to identify a potential family, the next step needs to be a detailed capacity analysis of the families created to see whether the work can be redistributed to the dedicated machines. If so, then we can begin to form the value stream that will not have shared resource considerations within it.

To create an X-map and then determine product families, you will need your system to be able to:

1. Create the product/process matrix. This can be done using item routings or by creating the matrix manually in a tool such as MS Excel.
2. Sort the products and processes to group the products together according to commonality of processes used. For more on how to do this, refer to the file "Sorting a High Number of Products into Product Families" from the CD accompanying the book *Creating Mixed Model Value Streams: Practical Lean Techniques for Building to Demand by Kevin Duggan* (Productivity Press, 2002) (Figure 11.4).

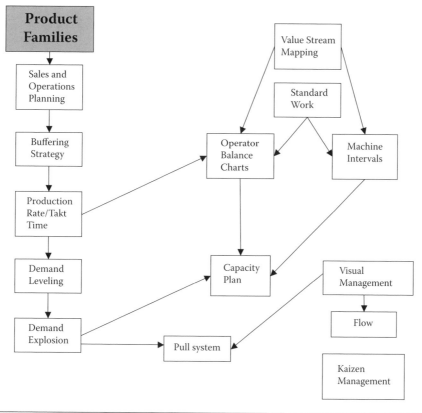

Figure 11.2 Product families.

Lean needs help in filling in the long-term planning horizon. It does this with executive sales and operations planning.

> **Executive S&OP:** That part of Sales & Operations Planning that balances demand and supply at the aggregate volume level, aligns units and dollars, and helps to establish relevant policy and strategy at both the volume and mix levels.
>
> —**Thomas F. Wallace and Robert A. Stahl,** *Sales and Operations Planning: The How to Handbook*, **3rd edition**

In the simplest view of the connection between the executive S&OP and Lean, one of the primary tasks of executive S&OP is to review the demand and set an appropriate production rate for a product family. This production rate can be taken into the Lean environment and used to calculate the takt time for the value stream.

The system to support executive S&OP should be able to handle:

1. Basic data
   a. Family data
   b. Time-phased data
   c. Planning bills of materials (BOMs) or planning hierarchies

P/N	Name	Cast	Deburr	Injection Mold	Lathe	Trim	Sand	Notch	Plate	Paint	Final Assembly	Pack	Family
MT1001	Plastic wagon, red			X		X					X	X	
MT1002	Plastic wagon, yellow			X		X					X	X	
MT1003	Plastic wagon, green			X		X					X	X	
MT1005	Plastic wagon, red				X		X	X		X	X	X	
MT1010	Plastic wagon, brown				X		X	X		X	X	X	
MT1020	Plastic wagon, green				X		X	X		X	X	X	
MT2001	Plastic sled, orange			X		X					X	X	
MT2002	Plastic sled, green			X		X					X	X	
MT2003	Plastic sled, blue			X		X					X	X	
MT3010	Wood bus				X		X	X		X	X	X	
MT1015	Wood airplane				X		X	X		X	X	X	
MT3020	Wood truck				X		X	X		X	X	X	
MT4000	Die-cast car	X	X						X	X	X	X	
MT4005	Die-cast airplane	X	X						X	X	X	X	
MT4010	Die-cast bus	X	X						X	X	X	X	
MT4020	Die-cast truck	X	X						X	X	X	X	

Figure 11.3 An X-map or product/process matrix. Can you see that plastic toys could be a product family?

    d. Calendars

    e. Commentaries

2. Fundamental S&OP calculations

    a. Make to stock

    b. Make to order

    c. Mixed or finish to order

3. Basic displays

    a. Historical data

    b. Current and future data, minimum eighteen months into the future

       i. Planned sales

       ii. Planned shipments

       iii. Customer orders

       iv. Planned supply

       v. Planned inventory

       vi. Planned backlog

    c. Various reporting alternatives, including:

       i. Ability to compare various versions of the plan

       ii. Convert inventory and backlog into "days"

       iii. Convert into various units of measure

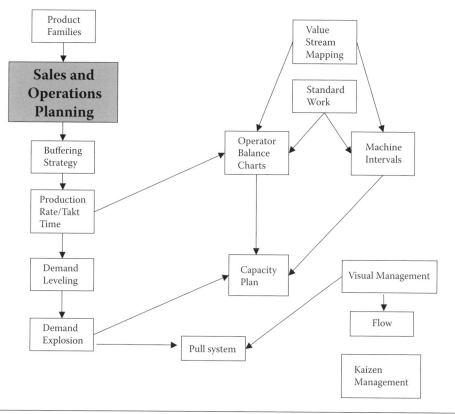

Figure 11.4 Sales and operations planning (S&OP).

        iv. Convert from S&OP families into Lean or manufacturing families

        v. Aggregate data into higher-level groupings

4. Rough-cut planning

    a. Basic data

        i. Key resources

        ii. Time-phased capacity data

        iii. Load profiles

    b. Calculations

        i. Explode S&OP plan through the load profiles to calculate requirements for each resource

        ii. Differentiate between the various drivers of resources (production, shipments, sales, etc.)

    c. Basic reporting

        i. Summary report of capacity available vs. required per time period

        ii. Pegging displays to show details of capacity data

5. Financial planning

    a. Integrate to budget and business plans

    b. Compare financials from S&OP plan to current budget and business plans

   c. Translate between various currencies

6. Performance measurements

   a. Customer service

   b. Performance vs. budget in dollars

   c. Performance vs. plan in units

—From Chris Gray, *Sales and Operations Planning Standard System*,
Trafford Publishing, 2007

Buffering strategy refers to creating a process whereby the value stream can take variable customer demand and produce to a level schedule (Figure 11.5). In the ideal situation, the production schedule will be level for both volume and mix. If this is not feasible, then it is still important to level for volume, making the schedule fit the available capacity, or to have in place a flexible capacity plan that allows the value stream to "chase" the actual demand.

Determining the proper strategy for a value stream is an inexact science. Often there are multiple possibilities for a solution, and only trial and error can decide on the best approach. However, data analysis can certainly be a big help in getting started in the right direction. To accomplish this, you must be able to extract and analyze large

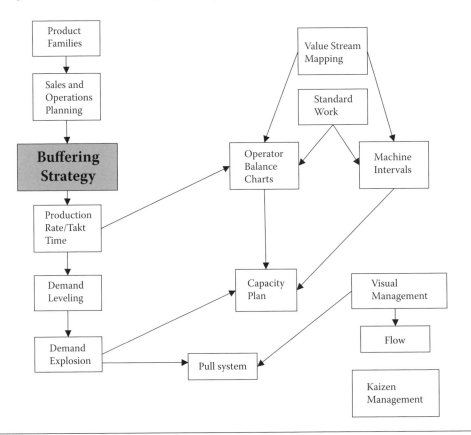

Figure 11.5   Buffering strategy.

volumes of data easily and quickly. These data will revolve mainly around sales history for the items in the value stream.

Most systems already provide such data as average usage or total yearly usage, which can be used to separate the high-volume items from the low-volume items. For our purposes, however, this is secondary to the mix variability of the items. The key question for us is: How frequently is an item ordered? Using sales history, preferably sales by day or the actual customer order file itself, determine how many times per year each item was ordered. These data should be grouped into intervals, which is the time period that will be covered by a supply order in the value stream. For each item it can then be determined how many of the total intervals contained an order for that item. Items that are ordered in most or all of the intervals are good candidates to keep as stock items, whether for leveling mix or buffering for volume. Items that appear in only a few intervals should be handled as make-to-order items. A value stream with only high-frequency items is a good candidate for mix leveling. A value stream with a mixture of items is a good candidate for a partial inventory buffer to level for volume. A value stream with mostly low-frequency items is a good candidate for buffering with backlog. See the CD from the creating mixed model value streams: Practical Lean Techniques for Building to Demand by Kevin Duggan (Productivity Press, 2002) for a demo of this analysis (Figure 11.6).

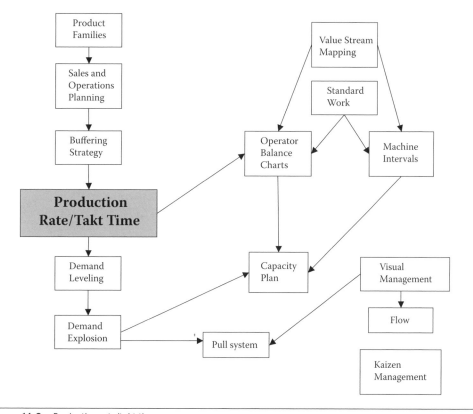

Figure 11.6 Production rate/takt time.

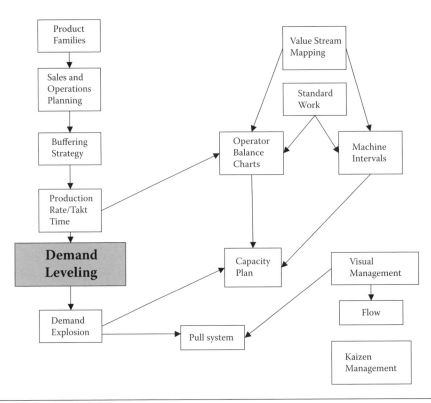

Figure 11.7   Demand leveling.

As we stated earlier in the book, the production rate from the executive sales and operations process should be used to calculate the takt time for the value stream. Takt time can then be used for setting the capacity required for all manual operations, as well as for determining pitch for measuring the value stream. The calculation of takt time is a simple one: effective working time for the value stream divided by the production amount. Note that both the effective working time and the production amount should cover the same timeframe, such as a day, a week, or a month. This timeframe should match the interval for the value stream (Figure 11.7).

Demand leveling is the execution of the buffering strategy. This involves taking actual demand and creating a production schedule that supports the strategy chosen. In Chapters 2 and 3 we described the various strategies available to create a production schedule from independent demand. These include level using either variable inventory or backlog, chase using variable capacity, or a hybrid using a combination of level and chase, also known as postponement. Each of these strategies calls for its own unique set of calculations and displays.

Chase is currently the strategy that is supported by most ERP systems. This, we believe, is because of the inventory-centric stance of ERP. The idea is that if the correct level of inventory is present, then the desired level of customer service will be attained. This relies on the items having a normal distribution of demand around the average, represented by a bell-shaped curve. Since the current trend in manufacturing is toward more customization, resulting in more low-volume, erratic demand parts than before, it is increasingly common to find items that don't have a normal distribution of demand, meaning the assumptions of this approach will not hold true. Besides that, from an execution viewpoint this is the most difficult strategy to manage, since each new set of demands could potentially require a new capacity configuration for the value stream.

The logic for the chase strategy is straightforward. The user sets a desired inventory level for each item in the finished inventory (even if it is zero), and the system does its best to create supply plans that maintain the inventory at that level. This means that if the demand is more than is expected, the supply will also be more than is expected, and capacity will need to be increased. The opposite holds true as well, of course. The fact that this happens at the item level is not a problem, since the assumption is that capacity is flexible and will be adjusted to meet the level of demand. Any capacity planning tools present are there to simply inform the value stream managers of how much capacity is required to meet the demand. There is also an assumption that either the material plan will be flexible enough to respond to these variations in demand, or some device, such as a firm time fence, will be used to prevent material plan changes from happening once the material plan is being executed.

Level is the strategy that is one of the bases of the House of Toyota. Known by the name heijunka, meaning to level for both volume and mix (although we believe it is impossible to level for mix without having leveled for volume automatically), leveling the mix is a powerful technique that helps drive the effectiveness of pull systems. Completely leveling mix usually requires buffering with a finished goods inventory of all possible items, although it is theoretically possible to level mix using backlog as a buffer. In our experience, though, the backlog would have to be very large, making the lead time so long that it is infeasible. This is because the backlog would need to cover the time span when infrequently ordered items would be ordered. Even though all items would be labeled as finished goods items, it would be entirely possible to find that many items are not in inventory at any one point in time (these items would be the ones that sold more than expected). To provide a mix-leveled schedule, the system needs to be able to take the demand over some user-specified period and parse it up into equal segments the length of an interval for the value stream. The system should also allow the user to create sequencing rules for creating the detailed schedule.

For leveling volume only, the system support needs to be quite different than for leveling mix. In this case, the system needs the capability to switch back and forth between aggregate views of demand and capacity and item level views of demand and inventory. One suggested approach for this environment is:

1. Compare demand for an interval to the capacity available for the interval.
2. If capacity and demand are equal, create the schedule in the sequence desired by the user.
3. If demand is greater than capacity, identify items in the sales mix designated as buffer items that have sufficient inventory to cover the demand and therefore

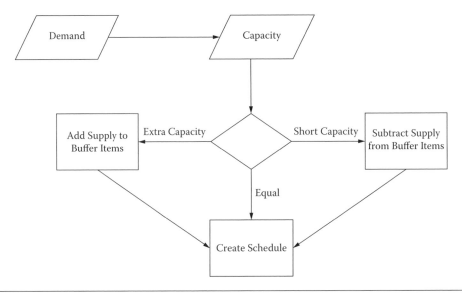

Figure 11.8   Leveling with inventory.

do not need additional supply. Allow the planner to subtract supply until supply and capacity are equal.

4. If demand is less than capacity, identify items designated as buffer items that
   are not at their maximum inventory level and allow the planner to add supply
   until supply and capacity are equal.

5. Create schedule using sequencing rules.

For leveling with backlog, the system needs to provide a real-time, aggregate available-to-promise (ATP) function for the order management people (Figure 11.8). This
available to promise is different than the traditional available to promise that is based
on the schedule for each item. This one must be done at the aggregate level, which
means that you are promising production capacity, much more than when a single
item could be built. Because we are dealing with a make-to-order environment, the
items will have no available production for the traditional ATP calculation to "find."
The date where the next capacity period satisfies the order amount needs to be shown
to the people taking the order so they can give the customer a promise date for each
line on the order. The system must also give the planner visibility of the lead time
being promised to the customers, as this is important information to use when deciding on changing capacity.

For hybrid approaches, a combination of the tools listed above can be used, that is, a
backlog tool for promising the finishing of the product to customer order and a leveling tool for the management of production up to that point (Figure 11.9).

Demand explosion is the process of taking the schedule created in the demand leveling step and multiplying quantities through the bill of materials for each item and
applying the appropriate lead time offsets in order to keep promise dates relevant. This
is also known as a gross explosion, since inventory is not netted during the process.

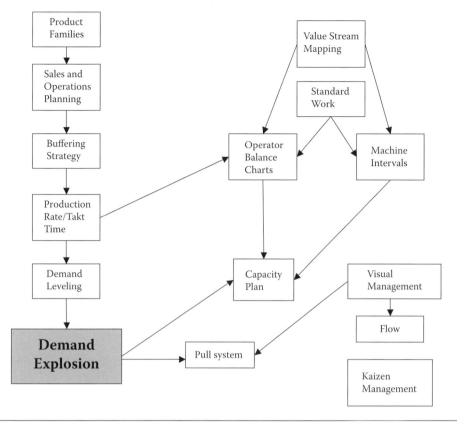

Figure 11.9 Demand explosion.

Requirements explosion: The process of calculating the demand for the components of a parent item by multiplying the parent item requirements by the component usage quantity specified in the bill of material. Syn: explosion.

—APICS Dictionary, 12th edition

The result of this explosion is the requirements by date for each item in the value stream. The requirements for each item should be grouped into intervals for each item, giving a complete picture of when each item will need to be produced or purchased. This information is then used to help calculate the capacity requirements of the value stream, provide suppliers with volume estimates for purchased parts, and provide usage figures for supermarket sizing in the value stream. This information is *not* used to create a material plan (Figure 11.10).

Value stream maps are the blueprints for Lean transformations. By comparing the current state map with the future state map, which has had the seven things that make a value stream Lean applied to it, we get a set of kaizen activities that must be accomplished to achieve the future state. The project plan is then created to implement these kaizens.

The value stream map is a paper-and-pencil representation of every process in the material and information flow, along with key data. It differs significantly from tools

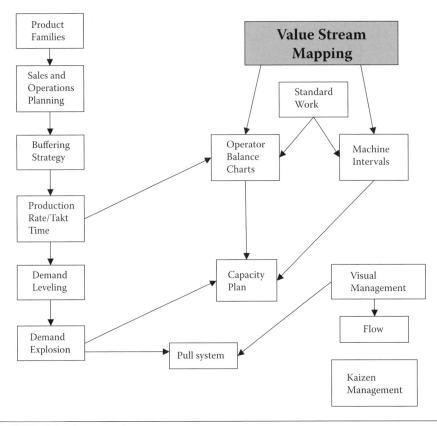

Figure 11.10   Value stream mapping.

such as process mapping or layout diagrams because it includes information flow as well as material flow.

Mapping is a critical initial step in Lean conversions because it shows you where you could apply Lean techniques, such as kaizen events, for maximum effect. Mapping helps you avoid the common mistake of cherry-picking individual Lean techniques, which creates isolated islands of improvement and limited benefits. The cycle of mapping current conditions, then quickly drawing and implementing a leaner future state, improves the overall flow of value to the customer and delivers the biggest benefits. For more on value stream mapping, see *Learning to See* by Mike Rother and John Shook (Figure 11.11).

Standard work defines the content, sequence, and timing of work to achieve an optimum process for manufacturing product. It also details the motion of the operator and the sequence of actions, and provides a routine for consistency of an operation. Standard work in Lean is not the same as the routing in ERP, although at one time they had a similar purpose. Recently, however, the routing has become the property of accounting and is primarily used to drive standard cost for items. Because of this, it often cannot be used to provide the information needed to plan and control operations on the factory floor. Standard work consists of various pieces of information and data based on three main elements: takt time, work sequence, and standard work in

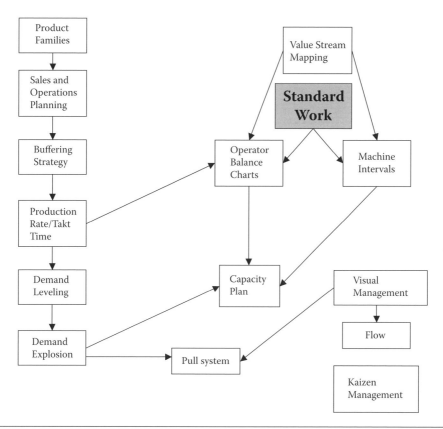

Figure 11.11   Standard work.

progress inventory (SWIP), which, taken together, describe the workings of a process. This information should include:

1. Process capacity for each machine in the process, as well as overall capacity
2. Standard work combination table, which includes detailed steps to perform the process, and the time required for each element, separating human from machine time
3. Standardized work chart, a graphical representation of the operator, the material, and the machine in relation to each other
4. A job instruction sheet showing the preferred method of performing the work

The time elements of standard work, combined with the requirements from the demand explosion, are used to determine the capacity needed in the value stream (Figure 11.12).

Operator balance charts are the result of combining takt time and standard work. The idea is to give each operator around a takt time's worth of work for each item. The result is a set of processes where each operator should have around the same amount of work, which facilitates one-piece flow between the various steps.

Creating or modifying operator balance charts is necessary each time takt time changes. This should be fairly obvious, and yet it is often ignored in practice. This

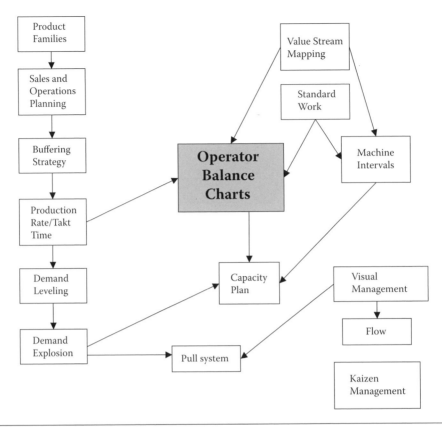

Figure 11.12   Operator balance charts.

is probably because creating operator balance charts is detailed, painstaking work, requiring knowledge of workers' capability, the workspace layout, and the machine characteristics.

An important departure from the norm that we have made in this book is the idea that only manual processes should be balanced to takt time. All processes where cycle time plus setup time is longer than takt time should use an interval as the time used to balance the operators work, since only in an interval will the operator perform all of the tasks necessary to complete all of the work in the process (Figure 11.13).

For any process where the cycle time is less than takt time but the cycle time plus the setup time is greater than takt time, we need to calculate the interval for the machine. The interval determines the lot size in Lean, based on a simple approach: we want to do as many setups as possible to keep the lot sizes as small as possible. Thus, after we subtract the cycle time and any waste from the effective working time from a machine, the rest of the time can be devoted to setups. The calculation of time remaining for setups in a timeframe divided by the total setup time for the family shows how many complete setup cycles can be achieved in the timeframe. We can convert this into how long it will take to achieve a complete setup cycle. This interval timeframe then dictates the lot size for the parts in the loop, the timeframe for operator balance charts for processes with an interval, the minimum amount of backlog (and lead time) in

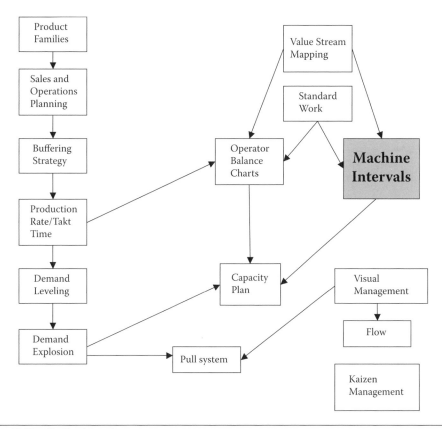

Figure 11.13 Machine intervals.

make-to-order environments, and the minimum length of the schedule for the value stream (Figure 11.14).

The capacity plan is the summary of several of the elements. From the operator balance charts we can get the total number of operators needed to do the in-cycle work (out-of-cycle work should have its own set of standard work and balance charts and should be added to the cycle work total), from the interval calculations we can determine the amount of time that the machines will need to run, and from the demand explosion we can determine the material required from each production loop. Taken together, these elements show how the value stream will operate, from the number of hours worked to the way the schedule will be created and the amount of material that will be required. This concludes the planning portion of the system, and leads us into the execution and control portions of the system, highlighted by pull systems, visual factory, and continuous improvement (Figure 11.15).

This is known as "going to the gemba," *gemba* being the Japanese word for "actual place," describing where value-added work is done. This again relies on the principle of deep understanding of the work, as going to see the problem will not mean much if you don't know what you are looking at. At Toyota everyone who is going to participate in a problem-solving activity will have seen the problem firsthand. One of the reasons that Toyota has not whole-heartedly embraced Six Sigma is

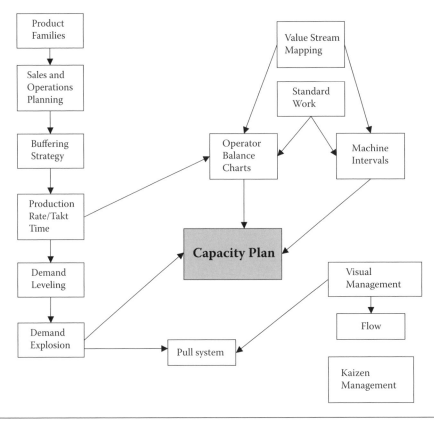

Figure 11.14 Capacity plan.

that it believes that in Six Sigma, data replaces hands-on involvement in problem identification.

Going to the gemba only works when you can understand what you are seeing. One of the objectives of visual management is to have "going and seeing" take the place of reports and data, encouraging familiarity with the work being done, which is necessary to make improvements to the work.

What should be visual?

- Location, name, and address. Location should be visible so everyone knows where they are within the value stream and the factory.
- Assigned products/stored materials. Assigned products and materials should be marked for easy delivery, and so everyone knows what should be there. This is a combination of plan for every part and 5S.
- Takt time: Takt time is the pace of production. It should be measured by pitch in the value stream.
- Layout and flow of operators, machines, and materials. This should be a combination of operator balance charts, value stream maps, and layout sketches or diagrams.
- Work distribution (operator balance charts). Work distribution should be part of the standard work for the area, and is also shown on the operator balance charts.

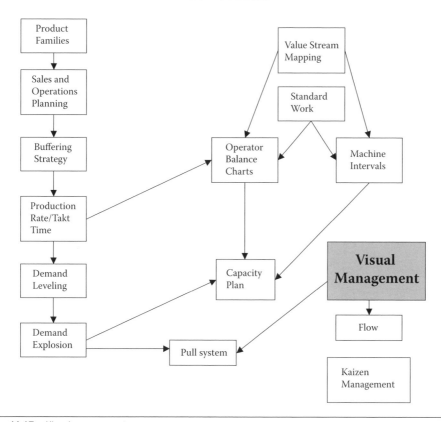

Figure 11.15 Visual management.

- Job instruction. Job instructions are part of the standard work for the area.
- Planned vs. actual output (production analysis board). The planned vs. actual output board is a way of keeping track of pitch. The key to this board is to make sure that any variances are addressed promptly through root cause analysis.

Visual factory is an important element of Lean, and while this list is not all-inclusive, it gives a good place to start to make things visual.

Again, the idea behind visual factory is to enable the people working in the value stream to have the tools at hand to make decisions and to support continuous improvement, without having to consult a computer screen in order to take some action. In place of computer reports are displays on the factory floor, such as first-in–first-out (FIFO) lanes and pitch boards, which indicate whether production is proceeding at the correct pace (pitch). This is significantly different than the approach of ERP systems, which seeks to gather detailed information from each operation and then produce a series of status reports on everything from where parts are currently located in the process to the productivity of individual workers. An overlooked issue with these reports is that they are normally obsolete soon after they are printed.

Visual factory also must support another basic tenet of Lean: go see for yourself. The idea is that to fully understand a problem, it is necessary to see the situation with your own eyes. This avoids interpretation of the condition by other people, and gives

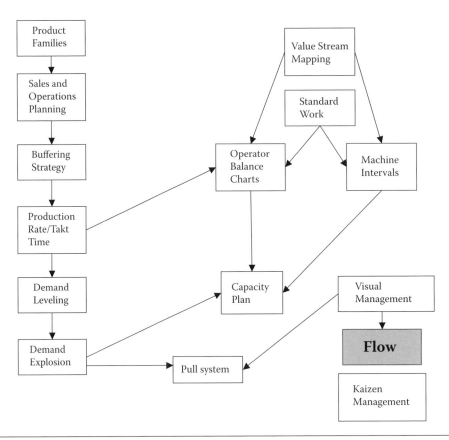

Figure 11.16   Flow.

you a chance to compare the process being performed to the standard work for that process. In Lean thinking, there is no other way to be sure that you completely understand a problem. It goes back to the idea of comparing data vs. facts: data are one step removed, an indicator; the facts are to be seen at the place of work (Figure 11.16).

Flow is critical to the Lean planning and control system, as it facilitates visual control of work on the factory floor as opposed to controlling it in the computer. Further, flow shortens lead times, which enables more of the bill of materials to be made within the customer's (market) lead time. Flow, especially FIFO flow, and shorter lead times allow levels in the bill of materials to be eliminated, as parts will no longer be kept in stock in between processing steps. This leads to a simplification of the entire control hierarchy, from fewer transactions to fewer reports and less reliance on forecasts. Because of all of these factors, the ability to create flow in the value stream has a significant impact on the configuration of the planning and control system. Basically, more flow means less waste.

To help facilitate the creation of flow during value stream design, the system needs to be able to create and maintain operator balance charts, help with FIFO lane sizing, help with re-laying out the value stream for flow, and help with combining multiple processes into one process (Figure 11.17).

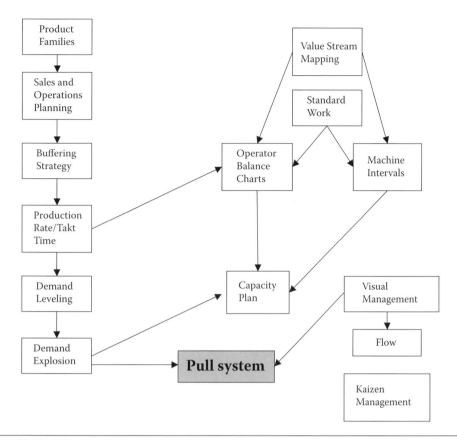

Figure 11.17   Pull system.

Pull systems are used to connect two processes that cannot be connected via flow. The basic mechanism of a pull system is to replace parts that have been used from the inventory. The usage of inventory authorizes the feeding process to make more parts. As such, they control both inventory and production.

Many ERP systems currently support pull via kanban. To the extent that they can print cards, this can be useful. Unfortunately, they often tie the kanban operation to the MRP planning system, which, as we have seen earlier, will not be effective. Because of this, it is often easier to create the kanban cards and board manually.

As we discussed in Chapter 6 (inventory management), the starting point for the size of a supermarket is, of necessity, the amount of inventory that is currently on hand when the supermarket is established. The kanban system itself then needs to provide the mechanisms to drive the inventory to the correct level and mix of products required. Supermarket sizing algorithms can help with a theoretical understanding of how a supermarket should look, but in practice the kanban signaling system must provide practical management of the supermarket (Figure 11.18).

The heart of Lean thinking is continuous improvement, embodied by kaizen. What is the point of doing kaizen? Taiichi Ohno, the founder of the Toyota Production System, said it best: "All we are doing is looking at the timeline from the moment the

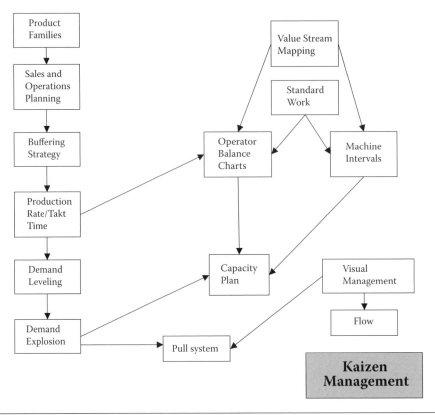

Figure 11.18   Kaizen management.

customer gives us an order to the point we collect the cash. And we are reducing that timeline by removing the non-value-added wastes."

Kaizen is a Japanese philosophy that focuses on continuous improvement. To be effective, kaizen must operate with three principles in place:

- Consider the process as well as the results (i.e., not results only) so that actions to achieve results are revealed.
- Think of the whole process and not just what is immediately in view (i.e., big picture) in order to avoid creating unintended problems elsewhere in the process.
- Conduct the kaizen in a nonjudgmental, nonblaming environment that will allow the reexamination of the assumptions that resulted in the current process.

There are two ways to use kaizens:

- Kaizen for ongoing, incremental, continuous improvements. This is often referred to as everyday kaizen.
- Kaizen event or kaizen blitz for immediate, intense, specific problem solving that occurs over a four- to five-day period.

A kaizen event or blitz is typically a focused kaizen within an area over a brief period of time (often no more than one to two days). A large number of people and resources are committed to performing major process changes. It is not unusual for entire production lines to be studied and moved during a kaizen blitz. There are a number of fundamentals that make up a successful kaizen event or blitz.

- **Speak with data:** Assumptions have no place in a kaizen blitz. Changes should only be made based on real data gained from the current state.
- **Develop a vision of the future:** Create a vision of what life will be like by the end of the week. This could be done during or prior to the event.
- **Involve everyone:** For a kaizen blitz to work, everyone has to be involved. This may mean shutting down a line or a department for the duration of the event.
- **Prepare the group:** It is essential that everyone involved is trained in how to perform a kaizen blitz. There will be times during the event when people's opinions will be examined closely; without proper preparation, people may find these times upsetting.
- **Plan for success:** Choosing the right target, especially for a kaizen blitz, is extremely critical. The event must be built for success, particularly if it is the first one. Choose something that will have a big impact on the people as well as the organization.
- **System support for kaizen should be very simple:** Choose support processes that encourage creation of everyday improvement ideas, and make these ideas easy to execute for the teams on the factory floor. For event kaizens, use of A3 forms is becoming a standard process, and needs to be supported. A way to tie the kaizen activity to recognition of the people involved in the improvement activities would also be useful.

Summary and Conclusions

In this chapter we have shown a Lean planning and control system in detail. We have described the various elements in some detail, and tried to list at least a few of the most important items requiring system support. The next question, of course, is: Where can I get one of these systems? And like it or not, we believe that the answer is: you will have to make it yourself. We are not aware of any system commercially available that supports the approach we have outlined here. This is not to say that you cannot purchase various elements from software suppliers, but merely that we know of no system that has integrated all of the elements into one unified planning and control system that supports Lean principles.

This is not all bad news. For one thing, many of the elements of this system are relatively simple and straightforward, and will require no special computer skills to create support that will be adequate to get the job done. For the more difficult elements, the knowledge of how to make any one of them work independently already exists: the challenge is in the integration of the various pieces.

Appendix 1: The Myth of the Bell-Shaped Curve: Inventory Level and Customer Service

We start with the general assumptions of finished goods inventory:

1. The more intermittent the demand, the higher the inventory level will need to be to provide a certain level of customer service.
2. We can accurately measure the variation of any item using a standard deviation calculation.
3. There is a diminishing return to higher levels of standard deviations, but in general, if I keep more inventory, I will achieve higher service.

This set of assumptions is based on the classic bell-shaped curve representing normal distribution: In this example, we have charted the order quantities vs. how many times that quantity was placed over 25 weeks. The result is a bell-shaped curve, or a normal distribution of data around the average (125 total sales over 25 weeks, or 5 per week).

Here are the order quantities for one part over 25 weeks:

1 2 2 3 3 3 4 4 4 4 5 5 5 5 5 6 6 6 6 7 7 7 8 8 9

This results in the following chart and graph:

Order quantity	1	2	3	4	5	6	7	8	9
Order frequency	1	2	3	4	5	4	3	2	1

We can then apply the following statistical method for determining inventory strategy for this part: inventory will equal average demand + (standard deviation * safety factor). In this case, average demand is 5 per week, and standard deviation is 2.04 pieces (Figure A1.1).

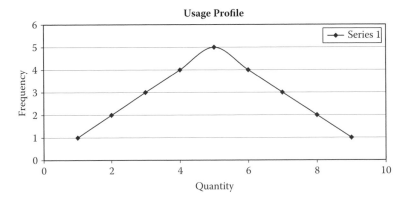

Figure A1.1   Average usage—Assumption 1.

If we want 95% on-time delivery, the safety factor should be 2, meaning that we should carry 4.08 pieces of safety stock, meaning that each week we should try to have 9 pieces in stock. In our example, this would actually have resulted in 100% on-time delivery, since we never sold more than 9 pieces in any 1 week. The statistics are:

On-time delivery: 100%
Inventory turns: 5 per week/9 pieces inventory = 1.8 weeks of inventory
52/1.8 = 28.9 turns per year

This is a pretty good performance on both counts.

Quantity	0	20	25	40
Frequency	21	1	1	2

With these data (Figure A1.2), the average usage per week is still 5, and the standard deviation is 12.25.

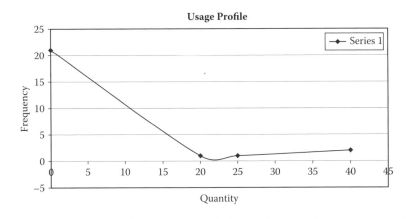

Figure A1.2   Average usage—Assumption 2.

Using the same formula as before, we should keep 30 pieces in inventory to get a 95% on-time delivery percent.

Actual results are:

50% on-time delivery
Inventory turns: 30/5 = 6 weeks inventory
52/6 = 8.67 turns per year

This is not so good compared to the bell-shaped part.

And why does this matter to us? Mainly because we have taken a very inventory-centric view when it comes to planning our value streams, for the most part. What this means, again, is that the primary objective of the planning system is to maintain the proper level of finished goods inventory, with the promise that the desired level of customer service will follow. From a Lean perspective, however, things should be approached very differently. Our first approach should be to simply ask: What would happen if we simply took what the customer ordered and tried to make it and ship it? The answers that come out of this simple question help to drive the continuous improvement effort that is central to Lean thinking. For instance, a common answer is that the customers will not wait for the entire manufacturing lead time until they receive their product. This answer should lead down two separate paths: How can we shorten our manufacturing lead time (shorten the queues!), and is there a better place to keep inventory that would be more economical and still allow us to meet the customers' lead time?

The moral of this story is the same one we have been trying to teach throughout the book: the proper technique for any circumstance depends on the conditions. We find more and more companies are blindly applying the latest, "world class" approaches without a thorough examination of whether their own circumstances are suitable for the approach.

The alternative to the above is to recognize the erratic nature of the demand for this part and, even if it is a relatively high-volume part, treat it as a make-to-order part and find another way, other than inventory of this item, to balance work into the value stream.

Appendix 2: The Bullwhip Effect

The phenomenon of volume variation amplification is very common in most material management systems and is commonly called bullwhipping the supply chain. One of the most commonly used inventory strategies, namely, keeping an inventory of a certain number of days or weeks of demand in stock, is one of the most blatant contributors of bullwhipping the supply chain. Let's take a minute to explore how this occurs.

We start the picture with the inventory of the finished goods, using an inventory policy of two weeks of future demand as the inventory level and a starting inventory of two weeks, namely, two hundred pieces (Table A2.1).

We have a small spike of demand in weeks 3, 4, and 5, but overall this doesn't look too bad, although it is important to recognize that we already have a build plan that calls for a week of production (week 3) that is higher than any sales week in the entire horizon. Let's look at the component picture, using the same inventory policy, and a starting inventory of 200 pieces (Table A2.2).

The build plan is getting a bit more erratic. Let's look at the next level of components (Table A2.3).

It's looking worse by the minute—one more level to show the ripple effect of a relatively small spike in demand (Table A2.4).

Notice the worst effect occurred as demand dropped back to the normal level: as each level tried to use up the now excess inventory, it decreased the demand for all of the lower levels, to the point where the last component level did not need to build product until week 9, when it will need to build 50 pieces, and things will return to normal in week 10, when the system again has demand at 200 per week and an inventory of 200 pieces. Until the next small spike from the end customers causes the next tidal wave down at the bottom of the supply chain.

The rule: Any inventory policy that calls for more inventory as demand increases, and conversely less inventory as demand decreases, will bullwhip the supply chain.

Table A2.1 Bullwhip Example—Starting Point

PARENT ITEM LEVEL 0	1	2	3	4	5	6	7
Demand	100	100	150	150	150	100	100
Target inventory	200	250	300	300	250	200	200
Inventory adjustment	0	50	50	0	−50	−50	0
Build required	100	150	200	150	100	50	100

Table A2.2 Bullwhip Example—Impact of a Small Demand Spike

PARENT ITEM LEVEL 0	1	2	3	4	5	6	7
Demand	100	100	150	150	150	100	100
Target inventory	200	250	300	300	250	200	200
Inventory adjustment	0	50	50	0	−50	−50	0
Build required	100	150	200	150	100	50	100
COMPONENT ITEM LEVEL 1							
Demand	100	150	200	150	100	50	100
Target inventory	250	350	350	250	150	150	
Inventory adjustment	50	100	50	−100	−100	0	
Build required	150	250	250	50	0	50	

Table A2.3 Bullwhip Example—A Demand Spike's Impact at a Component Level

PARENT ITEM LEVEL 0	1	2	3	4	5	6	7
Demand	100	100	150	150	150	100	100
Target inventory	200	250	300	300	250	200	200
Inventory adjustment	0	50	50	0	−50	−50	0
Build required	100	150	200	150	100	50	100
COMPONENT ITEM LEVEL 1							
Demand	100	150	200	150	100	50	100
Target inventory	250	350	350	250	150	150	
Inventory adjustment	50	100	50	−100	−100	0	
Build required	150	250	250	50	0	50	
COMPONENT ITEM LEVEL 2							
Demand	150	250	250	50	0	50	100
Target inventory	400	500	300	50	50	150	
Inventory adjustment	200	100	−200	−250	−50	−100	
Build required	350	350	50	−200	−50	−50	
Adjusted build (no negatives)	350	350	50	0	0	0	

Table A2.4   Bullwhip Example—How a Small Demand Spike Ripples through the Supply Chain

PARENT ITEM LEVEL 0	1	2	3	4	5	6	7
Demand	100	100	150	150	150	100	100
Target inventory	200	250	300	300	250	200	200
Inventory adjustment	0	50	50	0	−50	−50	0
Build required	100	150	200	150	100	50	100
COMPONENT ITEM LEVEL 1							
Demand	100	150	200	150	100	50	100
Target inventory	250	350	350	250	150	150	
Inventory adjustment	50	100	50	−100	−100	0	
Build required	150	250	250	50	0	50	
COMPONENT ITEM LEVEL 2							
Demand	150	250	250	50	0	50	100
Target inventory	400	500	300	50	50	150	
Inventory adjustment	200	100	−200	−250	−50	−100	
Build required	350	350	50	−200	−50	−50	
Adjusted build (no negatives)	350	350	50	0	0	0	
COMPONENT ITEM LEVEL 3							
Demand	350	350	50	0	0	0	100
Target inventory	700	400	50	0	0	100	
Inventory adjustment	500	−300	−350	−50	0	−100	
Build required	850	50	−300	−250	−250	−100	
Adjusted build (no negatives)	850	50	0	0	0	0	

Appendix 3: Lean Implementation Methodology

Lean Transformation Methodology

We have written this book to help to bridge the gap between traditional planning approaches revolving around ERP and the purely Lean approach, which has somehow evolved into trying to use no systems at all to support the manufacturing process. We feel that most manufacturing processes are too complex to respond well to anything less than a comprehensive approach to manufacturing products. Because of this, we feel that a mixture of solid education on the benchmark principles of Lean combined with a tool kit that helps solve some of the more difficult problems posed by these principles is the correct approach to transforming the value stream from its current state to its future state, and focusing on the elimination of waste during the process.

What follows is a general outline of our approach for Lean transformation.

Approach for Implementing a Production Lean Transformation

Our transformation approach was built to support the seven principles of a Lean value stream:

1. Takt time
2. Finished goods strategy
3. Flow
4. Pull
5. Interval
6. Schedule one point
7. Pitch

The general approach follows.

Executive Overview

The executive overview is an education process where we update the management team of the company on the process and the results that they should expect from the Lean transformation project. We also help them understand what roles they will play during the project and ensure that we have certain important management structures set up, such as a steering committee and contacts for when certain strategic decisions need to be made at a high level. The desired metrics should be discussed during this session as well as a review of the management tools available.

In this session, we will also discuss the necessary metrics, the levels of detail, and the frequency with which they should be monitored. The use of a Lean report card, understanding the current baselines for each value stream, and an agreed set of metrics to drive the business are key deliverables.

Lean Assessment and Data Readiness

The Lean assessment is a two-week process combining all the disciplines, manufacturing, office, and finance to prepare a projected return statement for management. This is a survey of the current state of Lean activity and thinking combined with a review of the cost structures supporting this current state. Using an industry standard guideline of what can normally be expected of a formal Lean transformation, a projected return or savings may be calculated. The initial kaizen or improvements for each area will be identified as well as a data readiness process that helps the project team understand the data required to support a formal transformation to Lean.

The following areas are covered during the assessment and readiness:

Value stream mapping: A way of organizing the Lean project to incorporate the seven principles of a Lean value stream.

Continuous improvement: Activities, usually in the form of kaizens, held on a regular basis, geared toward meeting goals of the Lean enterprise (increased productivity, higher quality, reduced inventory, reduced floor space, and reduction in lead time).

Communication and cultural awareness: Principles of Lean understood and lived.

Mistake-proofing (poka-yoke): To design parts, processes, and procedures so that mistakes cannot happen.

Operational flexibility: The ability of employees and processes to flex to meet varying customer demands. Considers cross-training capabilities and machine overlap.

Flow: Evidence of one-piece flow areas, first-in–first-out (FIFO) control, or "train schedules."

Pull systems: Managed supermarkets, kanban systems, or other usage-based replenishment strategies.

SMED/quick changeover: Single-minute change of die—being able to change over a machine or process in less than ten minutes.

Total productive maintenance (TPM): A standard work process, by which all equipment is regularly inspected, cleaned, and lubricated. The goal is to have the equipment available whenever it is needed.

Visual systems (5S) and workplace organization: A safe, clean, neat arrangement of the workplace, which provides a specific location for everything, and eliminates anything not required.

Review and document the data sources and owners: All data need to be evaluated for accuracy and completeness. Then the data need to be mapped to the Lean transformation process.

This normally begins with the plant tour, which helps with the understanding of the environment. The Lean assessment (for an example, see the APICS Lean Enterprise Training Program) is a useful tool, combined with the current state value stream map, to capture the initial or baseline state before implementation. With this information recorded, the continuous improvement metrics can be defined. This information, based on the data collected, and verified together with the other major Lean disciplines, such as 5S, work standards, employee knowledge, etc., is reflected in the Lean assessment, the Lean report card, and the data readiness report. This information combined with the office Lean assessment will provide the projected savings to Company X.

Product Family Creation

Proper definition of product families is important to achieve flow in the value stream. With the correct product family in place, machines can be dedicated to specific families, limiting the amount of shared resource management that must be put in place in the value streams.

We will use a combination of the X-map technique and group discussion to determine the product families.

Value Stream Maps—Current and Future State Maps

We typically take about a week to create current and future state value stream maps. Depending on the size of the group, we can often do more than one value stream during the week. The current state map documents the way the value stream functions today, and it usually takes about one and half days to create this map. Following the creation of the current state map, we take about a day to teach the seven principles that make the value stream Lean, and then spend the next two days designing the future state of the value stream. We spend the last day creating the implementation plan and capturing all the detail kaizens and activities necessary to go from the current state to the future state. This implementation plan then serves as the guideline for future activities in the value stream. At the end of this activity we would have both the current and future state value streams drawn.

Takt Planning Decisions

We often find that, although it seems fairly straightforward, there is quite a bit of uncertainty when it comes to determining how much volume should be produced in any particular value stream. We feel that this production rate should be a management decision governed via a process such as a sales and operations planning (S&OP) procedure, where management decides how much product to produce to satisfy a certain customer demand rate and agrees on the resulting inventory, which will then be created by this production rate. If this process is not in place, then we will attempt to come to some reasonable rate of production based on the demand currently present in the value stream.

Demand Analysis and Leveling Strategy

During this phase of the project we look at the actual customer demand and make a determination on how all the correct buffers to level the work within the value stream will be placed. We usually end up either working with a partial supermarket or maneuvering the due dates on the customer orders in a make-to-order environment, but we also can use a buffer of labor to smooth out the work within a value stream if neither of the other processes is available to us. This decision is an important one when we go to construct the heijunka process later on during the implementation.

To do this process we will need either fairly extensive sales history in the form of past bookings, or the current backlog reports, which list sales by item, hopefully in buckets no larger than daily, although weekly can be acceptable if we're going to have a fairly large interval for the value stream. This is typically an exercise that requires quite a bit of attention from the current group that plans the value stream, although again we will have several tools available to us to help with the decision-making process when it comes to how we will go about leveling demand into the value stream. This group should be prepared to discuss how the business is planned today and should be planned into the future. The rules for the demand leveling will be recorded and challenged as part of this section. This demand leveling tool is used daily by the schedulers to sequence and level the production by deciding to build, pull from a supermarket, or replenish a supermarket.

Equipment and Interval Decisions

Once we have captured the demand, we can then begin to analyze the amount of equipment needed to support the volume that must be produced in the value stream.

We typically like to see a machine loaded to between 80 and 85% of its defined capacity with just cycle time for the parts needed. If we find that we have equipment that is loaded higher than this percentage, then we may go back to the product family analysis and see if there are items that can be moved to other product families so that we have machine loads that are more reasonable. After we have the correct amount of equipment available in the value stream, we then decide on what interval the value stream can support. Interval defines the lot size for the value stream and is expressed as a period of time, or in other words, how many periods of demand I need to make at once from a single setup so that I can fit the total amount of runtime plus changeover time into the available capacity of the machine. The smaller the interval, the more flexible and efficient a value stream will be, so we will often create kaizens during this phase to reduce setup times and improve uptime percentages so that we can achieve a smaller interval. Again, the interval decision is an important one in the construction of the heijunka process.

Standard Work and Operator Balance Charts

Standard work will address the amount of labor that needs to be present in the value stream to achieve the correct volume. In most environments this is always considered to be an exercise in balancing detail work content vs. takt. In other environments, however, where machines need to be set up and the setup is done by the operator, we have found that it is easier to understand and oftentimes more accurate to balance all activities of the operator, including setup, machine maintenance, and other activities, against the time available in the interval to which the value stream will operate. By doing this we ensure that we have enough labor to accomplish all of the activities necessary in running product, and we also make sure that setup time and other elements of waste are not lost in the planning of the value stream. Otherwise, we do a fairly straightforward and traditional set of standard work activities to make sure that the operators are working in the most effective and efficient manner possible, with the least amount of waste.

Shared Resources Approach

A shared resource refers to any resource that must be used to produce parts for several different value streams. The main difficulty here is to make sure that each value stream gets a proportionate share of the resource, ensuring that all the value streams that use the resource get the products that they require. Oftentimes this is done through the use of a supermarket after the shared resource, which serves as a buffer between the value streams and the shared resource. We often like to use flow instead, however, and accompany that with a set of rules on how to cycle through the various FIFO lanes for each value stream to ensure that some product is produced for all value streams within an interval.

FIFO and Flow Creation

Where possible, we'd like to try to get one-piece flow implemented within the value stream. One-piece flow requires fairly uniform work content between all the various items being made by the value stream, high uptime and reliability on the equipment, and short setup times, or at least setup times that can fit within takt. Where one-piece flow is not possible, we typically find that FIFO flow is a very effective way to keep product moving through the value stream. This often requires some extensive work with both the schedulers and the shop floor personnel, but almost always results in significantly less work-in-process (WIP) inventory and a much simpler approach to the scheduling process, with much less expediting and chaos than in the current state.

Sizing FIFO lanes is an inexact science. At the beginning of the Lean transformation they must be able to hold all of the inventory that is waiting to be produced at each process. We then must find a mechanism to reduce them over time until they reach the target size that we have determined to be necessary to make the value stream run effectively. The thing to keep in mind, however, as with all inventory, is that any products waiting in a FIFO lane are still effectively waste, and therefore we should be actively working to try and eliminate it.

WIP Burn-Down Plan

We usually find that there is much more work in process in the current state than is desired for the future state. There are often several different ways to reduce this work in process (WIP) over time, and it is important to choose a plan that meets the overall objectives of the company both operationally and financially. Once these decisions are made, we can go ahead and set up interim operating procedures that will bridge the current processes with the future state operating procedures. The WIP burn-down plan also is excellent training on removing waste from supermarkets and FIFO lanes for future kaizen activity.

Supermarket Management

The usual guideline is: "Flow where you can, pull where you can't." We often manage to create value streams that have only one-piece flow or FIFO flow; however, we usually find that we need to put at least one or two supermarkets in place in these values streams, especially in dealing with suppliers. In some cases, a supermarket may be required to support a production loop, especially in a shared resource area. The supermarkets need to be sized correctly according to their purpose. Supermarkets also need to be able to give a clear replenishment signal to the supplying processes, and be monitored in case they need to be adjusted for mix changes or obsolescence of material.

Demand Leveling and Heijunka Creation

The heijunka, or load leveling, process is one of the most important activities in maintaining the health of a Lean value stream. The process involves taking customer demand, generally seen to be variable and erratic, and translating it into a production schedule, which for preference is smooth and level. What this means is that we have set up the value stream in the previous steps to be able to perform a certain amount of work. Our job is now to make sure that the value stream receives that amount of work so the material can move along at the correct pace and satisfy the customer demand. Another way of saying this is that we have set up the value stream generally based on the average amount of activity that we expect to see, and it is now our job to somehow provide the average amount of work of each interval to the value stream. The heijunka typically must operate in the timeframe of an interval for the value stream, and typically also has available to it some sort of a buffer, either a supermarket, labor, or the ability to change due dates on customer demand, to enable the workload to be leveled within each interval. Once the load-leveled production schedule has been created, it is then introduced to the pacemaker operation in pitch increments so that the progress of the value stream can be measured in a simple and straightforward way.

Visual Factory—5S/Visual Workplace Training

Continuous Improvement   Once the value stream has been planned in terms of how it will run and satisfy customer demand, we can then take advantage of the simplified processes by putting in visual controls and measurements to monitor how well the system is working on the factory floor. These typically consist of such things as pitch routes, which monitor flow through the FIFO lanes, sign boards for the operators to post any operating problems that need attention, principles of 5S for workplace organization, etc.

The essence of Lean is that things should be continually changing, whether the changes are improvements made to cycle time, changeover times, uptime, or other Kaizen-related activities within the value stream, or from external conditions such as changing customer demands or new product introductions or phasing out of old products. Because of this, it is important to have a robust model of how the value stream should operate, including the capability to take into account changes in any of the operating conditions that affect the value stream. This mindset of continuous improvement is one of the cornerstones of leading thinking and needs to be adopted by everyone within the organization.

Quality   During the course of creating the future state value stream we may find that there are issues with yield or scrap within the value stream. If this is the case, we may suggest that the company embark on an aggressive Six Sigma program to begin to eliminate one of the most significant causes of waste in many value streams.

Metrics   If it is often said that what gets measured is what gets improved. Because of this, we feel that having the correct measurements in place to drive behavior is very important. As part of the ongoing management of the value stream, we will suggest several key measurements to indicate the health of the value stream, as well as several indicators to monitor whether new improvements are being made to the value stream.

Appendix 4: Using Your Value Stream Map for Green Initiatives and Risk Management

Lean and green go hand and hand. Lean focuses on ways to reduce waste within an organization, and green thinking focuses on reducing wastes as well. We'll look at ways to determine where these green-related wastes enter into your business, how to measure them, and the steps you can take to eliminate them. We'll also look at sustainability issues, including product and packaging returns, as well as energy-related green issues.

Although many companies include green thinking in their value stream mapping (VSM), just as many companies don't. Normally, you would add this process to your value stream map as an associated process, but we are going to focus solely on this for illustration purposes. Additionally, we are going to call this waste stream mapping (WSM), and we will attempt to illustrate many common green-related wastes that may not be picked up during your VSM process.

These green-related wastes might include things such as:

1. Transportation-related wastes such as delivery or pickup-related trucks waiting at your facility or dock to be unloaded. In most cases the drivers will keep their engines running.
2. Packaging of parts, subassemblies that get built into your process. In many instances, these items are packaged individually, then packed into larger boxes, and perhaps packed into even larger cases.
3. Material-related wastes, such as raw materials, can be minimized in order to reduce cost and waste. This applies to the material being used, specifically:
   a. Is it the most effective material? Will steel sheet work instead of stainless steel?
   b. Are the sizes purchased conducive to reducing scrap?

Many companies have been doing this for a number of years, but it will not hurt to take another look at these efforts during waste stream mapping.

4. Utility-related wastes—water, electrical, heat, or heat-related handling that can be minimized, reduced, or eliminated. Typically, these will be directly related to some aspect of your production process, and mapping out these uses will be helpful in identifying wastes.

5. Emissions-related items are typically a result of the production process. These are typically some sort of vapor, gassing, runoff, or other type of volatiles. These are sometimes the most difficult wastes to measure because they are a by-product and typically are ventilated out into the atmosphere.

There are many ways to try to capture this information, but our answer to this is to furnish a waste stream template for you to use as an addendum to your VSM, and if you have not specifically targeted green-related wastes, the benefits of doing this should make VSM even more compelling.

The information gathered in the WSM framework can also be used to launch risk management (RM). Unfortunately, RM is another largely ignored or ill-understood part of supply chain management (SCM) and is important whether you are Lean or not. This is becoming a hot topic in SCM, and that means that there is plenty of confusion and an opportunity to make this much more complicated than it needs to be—at least to start. We have heard of many RM initiatives bogged down by custom RM systems being developed to process nonexistent data—a catastrophe waiting to happen. We hope to show you a framework that uses the WSM information to help start your risk management initiative, without relying on technology or consultants peddling technology. As with most parts of a Lean system, simple is always better.

One of the great things about VSM is that it can furnish a great deal of detail for many things. Our template simply uses an existing map and adds some templates to help both do green initiatives (with the focus on reducing resource use and lowering cost) and identify potential risk management areas.

Lean Green

In Figure A4.1, you will notice that the common VSM data box under each work center, has not been included in this example. We are not going to use any of that data, so they have been removed to simplify the process. The data box has been replaced by a resource template; we will explain this in the section below. The circle represents where we are going to concentrate our efforts. (We will add the risk management view later.)

For green Lean, we are going to concentrate on resource usage, specifically at each work center. Resources are simply all of the items that are needed at that work center, in order to process the item. Resources are materials, labor, assets, and utilities. Most

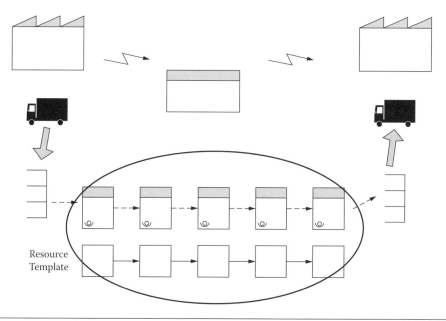

Figure A4.1   Waste stream mapping.

of this is straightforward, but space and utility use can get a bit tricky. If you have done activity-based or value stream costing, you should have a lot of this data.

All of this is put into a template format and added to the VSM.

A sample template would look like that shown in Table A4.1. The template lists the resource inputs and outputs and should capture the essence of what is done at the work center. As inputs get transformed to outputs, there should be a logical flow to resources. For example, as material gets transformed, a piece of raw material will get cut down to a

Table A4.1   Resource Template

INPUTS	OUTPUTS
TRANSPORTATION	LTL, TL, container, small package
What are materials shipped in?	
	MATERIALS
MATERIALS	Work output—size, pieces
Work material used—size, pieces	Not packaged, eaches, box case, etc.
How are they packaged?	Scrap—size, pieces
Consumable used—can be machine based	Consumables remaining (remaining life)
ID any hazmat items, etc.	By-product
	Other wastes—ID hazmat, toxins, etc.
LABOR	Does output increase size requirements, WIP, etc.?
Number, labor class, hours	
	UTILITY BY-PRODUCT
ASSETS	Heat, waste water—measure if possible
Equipment used	Other emissions—what, volume, hazard?
Work center area	
	ASSETS
UTILITIES USED	Does output increase size requirements, WIP, etc.?
Type, actual use if available	

Table A4.2   Work Center 1—Rough Cutting

INPUTS	OUTPUTS
TRANSPORTATION	Hand cart to next WC
LTL—pallet to WC1	
	MATERIALS
MATERIALS	8 each—12" × 12" × 0.2 ga metal sheets
1 each—metal sheet 3' × 4' × 0.2 ga	Pallet to shipping, metal band recycled
Package—pallet 100 pieces, metal band	4 each—6" × 12" × 0.2 ga scrap
1 each—J245 C56 saw blade	1—each J245 C56 saw blade—50% life
LABOR	ASSETS
One metal shop operator—20 min	1' × 1' of storage area used
ASSETS	UTILITY USED
J345—electrical saw	1 kwh
Work center area—8' × 8'	
WIP storage area—4' × 4'	
UTILITY USED	
Electrical—saw, lighting	

workable size at a work center, and then would be passed on to the next work center for additional transformation. However, some of the outputs will take a different path. For example, scrap might be disposed of immediately or stored for later sale. Utility output like heat may not be captured and is dissipated in the plant environment. As with most mapping exercises, you are not trying to fix anything during this mapping process, just concentrate on identifying all of the resource inputs and outputs.

An example of a completed template is shown in Table A4.2. The next step is to identify in each of the templates items that fall under one or more of the five wastes; these are highlighted above. The next step is to determine how to eliminate the waste. In the example above, changing the raw material size to 24 inches × 4 feet would eliminate the scrap. The saw blade was new and was used to cut eight blanks, leaving the blade with 50% useful life remaining. Could a better blade be found that would last longer? A quick cost analysis could be done to determine if paying more for a better saw blade would make sense. The WIP storage area could be eliminated or reduced as a result of other Lean activities. Finally, look at utility usage: is the electrical saw and lighting the most efficient way (utility-wise) of cutting the metal and lighting the area? Note: these are two different issues.

You should visually show the flow of resources, specifically materials, and scrap and other wastes and where they occur. A simple line and arrow showing scrap going to trash or a recycle bin would be sufficient.

Risk Management

So, what does green Lean/resource management have to do with risk management? If you think about it, a lot more than meets the eye. Risk management, specifically within the supply chain, is a process of identifying items within the supply chain that could cause problems. Granted, this is a pretty broad statement, so we'll try to break it down so it makes sense and can be used to actually manage risks.

As we mentioned, risk management is full of challenges, mostly because of two extremes: either nothing is done, or it is made so complicated it either can't be done or the users get caught up in the complexity. In most cases, people just really don't know what to do. So, where to begin? Again, your value stream map is a great source document for risk management. In doing this, another similar template will be used, but this time, it will be used throughout the map, not just in the work centers.

Looking at what is needed to do some basic risk management, the resource template is a good starting point. It provides some of the information needed to assess risk, but we do need to look at it in a different way. We are going to continue to look at resources, but we are going to expand this list to cover additional resources. Also, we are not concerned with output, but rather a high-level risk assessment.

Table A4.3 shows a risk management template. This risk assessment is to provide a framework to identify risk items that should be addressed. We have purposely avoided assigning probabilities, point values, etc., that often get people wrapped up in preparing the process but often failing to act—what we like to call getting ready to get ready. Risk management in this framework provides a list of items that can be prioritized and then worked on. For example, you may identify a commodity in your product that appears to be headed for a shortage position, that will make it tougher to get and more expensive. Your choice is to live with this or do something. The "do something"

Table A4.3   VSM Area—Describe

RESOURCES	RISK FACTOR
Transportation	Outbound transit supplier risk—availability, cost trends, health of transportation market
MATERIALS	
Commodity	Item/Commodity risk—market cost and availability trends
Supplier	Supplier risk—number of suppliers, market health, location of supplier(s), in/outbound transport risks, tier-related risks—suppliers and commodity
Market	Customer/market risk—dependence, health of product line, competition, price trends
Waste	Waste risks — availability of service, price of disposal, recycling and/or emissions real/potential costs. Hazardous material issues — handling and handling cost trends
Labor	Availability of skilled employees, specific skills — internal and external (suppliers, tiers) and cost of labor trends
ASSETS—EQUIPMENT AND SYSTEMS	
	Age of equipment/systems, availability of service parts and technicians. System(s) still supported?
UTILITIES/ENERGY USED	
	Cost and availability trends

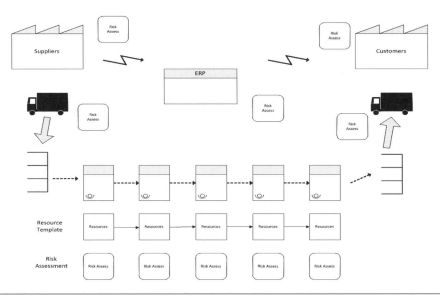

Figure A4.2   VSM with resource and risk management templates.

can be a lot of things: start forward buying to alleviate some of the shortages/price increases, or examining if you can replace that commodity with something else, or at least exploring the possibility. We hope these templates will help you to talk/fret about these topics less, and actually do something.

Both green Lean and risk management/mitigation can be done quickly and without the burden of any systems—a big chief pad will do, but it might be easier within a database or spreadsheet. To be sure, we are not attempting to try to convey all of the details involved in green or risk management; these will become apparent as you delve into the specifics. However, we don't feel that you have to have every detail "figured out" before you start; then you are just getting ready to get ready and will probably never even start. The key to this is to keep things simple (like most of what Lean tries to do) and build off of work already done—your existing value stream map (Figure A4.2).

Index